Building a Portfolio for

Early Years Care and Education S/NVQ Level 3

Mary Townsend

BOOK ONE

Units C10, C11 and C16

Illustrated by Cathy Hughes

Chapter 1

Chapter 2: C10 Promote the sensory and intellectual development of children

contents

Chapter 3: C11 Promote children's language and communication development

Element C11.1 Identify stages of children's language and communication development

Element C11.2 Provide activities, equipment and materials to extend and reinforce children's language and communication development

Element C11.3 Share books, stories and rhymes to extend children's language and communication development

Element C11.4 Provide communication opportunities to enhance and reinforce children's language and communication development

Element C11.5 Interact with children to promote their language and communication development

contents

Chapter 4: C16 Observe and assess the development and behaviour of children

All articles have been published previously in *Practical Pre-School*, except for 'Choosing books for young children' pages 128-129.

Chapter 1

Introduction

So you're about to start a National Vocational Qualification (NVQ) Level 3 in Early Years Care and Education. That's good, because it means that you will have a nationally recognised qualification which will enable you to get a job anywhere in the United Kingdom, or even further afield. Early years provision is growing rapidly in the UK, and many more qualified early years practitioners are needed.

NVQs are based on the National Occupational Standards which have been agreed by experts working in a range of settings across the early years field. They cover all the competences expected of an early years practitioner. There are three levels - Level 2 for people working under supervision, as an assistant or voluntary worker; Level 3 for people working under their own initiative as supervisors; and Level 4 for people in a managerial role, with responsibility for complex and non-routine tasks, or responsibility for quality control in a number of establishments.

'I didn't really think about why I did things before, but now I think much more about how it is going to help the children.'

NVQ candidate

This qualification will help you to gain a better understanding of children's needs - it will help you to reflect on why you do certain things with and for children. And the great thing about NVQ is that you don't have to give up work to do it, because it's based on the work you do every day. You can also work towards an NVQ as a volunteer, or combine a part-time job with voluntary work in order to gain wider experience. You may not even have to go to college at all - that will depend on how much experience you have, and whether you have done any previous training. We will talk about this in more detail later.

NVQs are not like other qualifications. Instead of doing a course at college, you gather your own evidence that you can do all of the things you need to do to keep children safe and happy, and help them to develop. A lot of your evidence will come from what you are doing with the children every day. You will put all your evidence into a folder, or portfolio.

For Level 3 there are 11 mandatory units which you have to do, and you choose three optional units to suit your own job role and interests. What you choose will depend on which kind of setting you work in, or which area of work you are most interested in. You should by now have been given a copy of your candidate handbook with full details of the units. Don't be put off by your first look through it. It looks complicated, but once you have worked through one unit, the others will seem much more clear. You don't have to start at the beginning and work through the units in a particular order. You can choose which unit you feel most confident about, and start with that.

By now, you may have had an induction at your NVQ assessment centre. The staff will have explained what NVQs are all about, and how the centre operates. Each centre operates differently, although they all use the same Early Years Standards. The centre will allocate an assessor to you, who will work with you throughout your NVQ. You will get to know your assessor really well, and work closely with her or him. She will help you to plan what sort of evidence you will need to provide. She will also visit you in your setting and observe you working with the children.

The aim of this book is to help you to gather your evidence from the things you do every day with the children, rather than having to work through set tasks and assignments which are often not appropriate to your situation. That means it will be individual and meaningful to you, which is what NVQ is all about. We will look at the different ways you can gather the evidence and give you some useful formats to use, as well as resources to help you with your planning. Throughout this book, we will be referring to your candidate handbook. This is the book which contains the Early Years National Occupational Standards, which you will have been given when you registered. You will always need that with you.

You need to bear in mind that your centre may require you to work in a particular way, and in that case you may not have the freedom to gather the evidence in the way we recommend, but you will still find the book very useful.

How do NVQs work?

NVQ Level 3 is made up of 11 mandatory units and three optional units. Each unit describes a particular area of early years work. Each unit is broken down into elements, which identify all the things you need to be able to do, to show you are competent in that area of work.

Let's take an example - Unit C10. The title of the unit is 'Promote the sensory and intellectual development of children.'

Find it in your candidate handbook. Read the list of elements at the beginning of the unit. Don't worry about all the other reading at the beginning of the unit yet. We will go back to that. These are the elements:

C10.1   Develop children's attention span and memory

C10.2   Develop children's awareness and understanding of sensory experiences

C10.3   Develop children's understanding of mathematics and science

C10.4   Develop children's imagination and creativity

Many of the activities you carry out every day with the children will provide most of the evidence you will need. If you're not sure what some of them mean, look at the 'Notes on this element' on the appropriate pages in the handbook.

> *'I understand a lot more now. I can put it into practice straight away because I'm working with the children every day.'*
>
> NVQ candidate

You will notice that each element has two main parts - performance criteria and range. The *performance criteria* (we will refer to these as PCs) are all the things you need to show you can do for that element - for example, in C10.2, the first PC states 'Planned activities provide stimulating sensory experiences appropriate to children's developmental level and the environment'.

Break that statement down. 'Planned activities provide stimulating sensory experiences ...' Think about some activities you have planned or been involved in which have

provided stimulating sensory experiences for children - an interesting display? A feely box? Water play? Playdough? Cooking? A walk? You will be able to think of many more.

The PC also states '... appropriate to children's developmental level ...' - some activities will be more suitable than others at different levels of development, and safety will be a particular issue here.

Lastly, '... and the environment'. Your environment will determine which experiences you will be able to give the children. If you are in the town, the experiences may be different to those in the country, or you may be in a setting which does not have access to safe outdoor space. You need to think about how you can make the children's experience as wide as possible within your circumstances.

Useful tip
Some performance criteria can seem very complicated. If you break them down into bits, as we have shown you, it will help to make them clearer. It will also stop you missing vital bits.

Now look at the *range*. This means all the different situations you may have to work in - for example, you need to cover all aspects of the senses. You need to think about how you will cater for children with disabilities such as hearing impairment. You also need to give children experiences both indoors and out. The range will be different for each element, but by the time you have completed all the units, you will have covered every aspect of child care and development you are likely to come across.

This does not mean that you will necessarily have done all of these things. Sometimes, you will not be able to show that you have actually carried out all of the range, but you will need to show evidence that you could do it should the need arise.

Your assessor will want to observe as many of the performance criteria and range as possible, and she will plan with you when and how she will do that. She will also plan with you how you will provide the rest of the evidence you need. We will look at the different sorts of evidence you can use later. If you need any help with ideas or activities for the element or unit you are working on, you will find some useful resources in each chapter. For example, there are resources to support sensory experiences on pages 43 - 46.

There are two other important sections in each unit which you need to be aware of. At the front of your candidate handbook you will find a section called the 'Statement of underlying principles'. They include:

◆ the welfare of the child

◆ keeping children safe

◆ working in partnership with parents/families

◆ children's learning and development

◆ equality of opportunity

◆ anti-discrimination

◆ celebrating diversity

◆ confidentiality

◆ working with other professionals

◆ the reflective practitioner

These are the principles which every early years worker must always adhere to if they are to commit themselves to giving children the best possible care and education in their early years. They have taken into account the United Nations Convention on the Rights of the Child and the Children Act 1989. You may have had them explained to you in your induction, but if not, you need to go back to the front of your candidate handbook to find a full explanation of what each one means. If you can, talk them through with your assessor. It would also be useful to discuss them with your colleagues in your work setting.

When you're gathering your evidence for each unit, you must always be aware of the underlying principles. To help you to do this, there is a grid at the beginning of each unit which shows which underlying principles, or values, you need to show evidence of in each element. (Throughout this book, we will refer to them as values, for short.)

Go back to the beginning of Unit C10 and look for the grid entitled 'Values statement' under the heading 'Principles of good practice'. Under each element it shows you which PCs refer to some aspect of the principles, or values. Try using the grid now to find the relevant element and PC, and think about how you might show that you are aware of the values. If you have any difficulty with this, go through it with your assessor.

Here's an example:
Go to the column headed **Element 4**. Look down the grid until you come to number 1. This means **performance criteria 1** in Element 4.

Look across to the left to see which value it covers. You will find **celebrating diversity**.

Now go to Element 4 in your handbook (headed C10.4) and look at PC1. It says 'Planned activities are appropriate to children's developmental levels and positively encourage children to explore a variety of roles, cultures and methods of self-expression'.

Element 4 is all about developing children's imagination and creativity, so there is lots of scope for exploring different roles and cultures. In role play, children should have the opportunity to experience play food and cooking utensils, dressing-up clothes and dolls from different cultures, and act out non-stereotypical male/female roles. In art work, they should have access to paper, paints and crayons of a range of skin colours. In music, they might use instruments and listen to music from different countries.

Remember!
Celebrating diversity is not just about celebrating festivals like Diwali or Chinese New Year. It's about integrating it into everything you do so that it becomes a natural part of life, not something strange and different.

Finally, we need to look at the **description of knowledge, understanding and skills**. You will find this at the end of each unit, after the last element. This is where you need to provide evidence that you have the knowledge and understanding to show that you know why you do the things you do with the children in your care. This section looks a bit daunting, but don't panic! You will be able to cover a lot of it through the evidence you will be collecting for each element.

This section is divided under four main headings:

◆ Development

◆ Curriculum practice

◆ Equipment, materials, environment

◆ Relationships

However, you will find when you start working with them that there is quite a lot of overlap from one section to another, and we will show you how you can cut down on the work by taking several points together. We will do this within the chapter for each unit, so don't worry about it at this stage.

Many assessment centres provide teaching sessions either in the daytime or evening, or learning packs which you can use at home, and will usually recommend some text books. Your local Early Years Development and Childcare Partnership (EYDCP) will probably also have courses you can attend. Your setting should receive information about these. If not, ring your local education authority and ask what is available. It is especially important that you attend training on First Aid and child protection carried out by experts in these fields. Although it is not a requirement for NVQ to take a recognised course in these areas, all early years practitioners should have a thorough knowledge of both.

You are not required to attend a course to gain your underpinning knowledge for NVQ, unless attendance at college is a requirement in order to gain funding. If you are an experienced practitioner, you may feel that you already have the knowledge you need, or feel confident to fill any gaps through your own reading and research. If you are less experienced, you will gain a great deal from attending these sessions, and from sharing your ideas with other candidates.

note:
This book does not aim to provide you with all of the underpinning knowledge you will need for your NVQ. It is a resource book and guide, to help you to gather your evidence for each unit.

Gathering evidence

NVQ is different to other qualifications in that, instead of taking an examination, you show that you are competent by collecting evidence of what you do in your day-to-day work with the children. The role of your assessor is to judge whether your evidence is sufficient to prove that you are competent.

Your candidate handbook has an explanation of the different sorts of evidence you can use. You will find this in the section at the beginning entitled 'The assessment process'. You may have already had the methods explained to you at your induction, but we will explain them again here.

There are two main types of evidence:

- Performance evidence - what you can do

- Knowledge evidence - what you know

At the beginning of each unit there is a description of the different ways you can collect your evidence. It's not the same for every unit, but it will always be from the following approved methods of evidence collection listed in your candidate handbook:

- Direct observation by a qualified assessor

- Questioning

- Witness testimony

- Work plans

- Inspection of the setting by a qualified assessor

- Reflective accounts

- Log books, diaries and notes

- Work products

- Case studies, assignments or projects

- Child observations

- Simulation, role play or skills rehearsals

- Skills transferable from other performance

- Past achievements

- Formal written or oral tests/extended questioning

To make it easier for you to collect the evidence, we will look at some useful formats you can use. Your assessment centre may have their own formats, so you need to check first. Evidence does **not** have to be written. If you feel worried about doing a lot of writing there are other methods you can use. For instance, you can record your evidence onto a tape recorder, or use a word processor. We have already said that your assessor will ask you oral questions. You may be able to make an arrangement with her to do extra questioning. This will depend on the amount of time she is allowed for assessment because, of course, it will be more time-consuming for her. If you feel that you may be eligible for extra support, talk to your assessor. Many centres are able to access funds to help candidates with additional needs. Some assessment centres have access to a range of specialised equipment available for people with disabilities.

Direct observation
The most important type of evidence is direct observation by a qualified assessor. You will see in the section on performance evidence in your candidate handbook that there are some PCs (performance criteria) which must be observed. Your assessor will also have to observe at least one aspect of each range category. For the rest of the range, PCs and knowledge, you will provide other types of evidence from the list above. Your assessor will write down what she observes on an **observation record** which is provided by the assessment centre. She will give you this to keep in your portfolio. An example of what it may look like is given overleaf.

Date	OBSERVATION RECORD	PCs range	Knowledge evidence
21.7.00	Sarah supervised snack time with the children - fruit and drinks. She let the children pour their own drinks, and they passed the cut-up fruit - a choice of apple, orange and banana - around the table. Sarah talked with the children and was aware of their needs, giving help where necessary. When they had finished she asked them to wash their hands in preparation for the cooking activity they were about to do, and cleaned the table with antibacterial spray.	C2.1.1,5,8 R2,3,4 C2.2.11 R2,6	C2KE2,7,11
	She helped the children to put on aprons. It was a large group but other adults were helping. Sarah showed the children the scales, and how to weigh out the ingredients for the pizza base. The children helped with the weighing, and Sarah melted the butter in the microwave. She talked about how it had changed from solid to liquid as she showed the children the difference. She put the ingredients into several bowls and the children took turns in mixing the dough.	C10.3.1,5,6 R2,3,6 M7.3.2, 3 4,5 R2,3, 6,7,8,9	C10KE8,11,16,17,21,31 M7KE2,8,10,22, 23
	Sarah then gave the children cheese to grate, or vegetables to cut up, and she and the other adults supervised them closely. There was a lot of conversation about colour, shape and so on. Once the vegetables and cheese were ready, every child had a piece of dough, which they rolled out. They really enjoyed this. Sarah placed the vegetables and cheese within easy reach of the children, and they chose what they wanted to put on their pizza. There was a brief squabble between two children, which Sarah dealt with calmly. She gave praise and encouragement throughout the activity.	C3.4.1,2,3,4, 6,7 R2,4,6 C11.2.2,4,5, 6,7 R7,9,11 C5.2.1,2,3 R1,4 C5.3.3,5, 6,7,8 R2,4,6	C3KE11,13,16 (This observation may not cover the whole of the knowledge evidence for these sections)

Signed ...Anne Other... (assessor)   ...Sarah Bright... (candidate)

Questioning

Your assessor will often ask you questions about what she has observed, to check your understanding. She will write down answers to any oral questions she asks you. She will give you these to keep in your portfolio. The question sheet may be a similar format to the one below:

Date	ORAL QUESTION RECORD	PCs range	Knowledge evidence
20.10.00	**1. Unplanned activities for creativity/imagination?** When the children are outside playing in the sand, they think of imaginative ways to use it, eg digging a hole to Australia. On climbing frame they imagined it was a train & they were going on a journey.	C10.4.2 R2,3 M7.1.7, R.6	
	2. Importance of process/end products? The important thing was that the children were being creative, artistic and using their imagination. They were not being directed, they were free to choose what they wanted to do. It's the doing that counts.	C10.4.10 R2,5	C10KE27
	3. Factors affecting memory and concentration? If they're feeling ill or tired they lose concentration. If they're going through emotional difficulties, eg parents splitting up. If they're very young.		C10KE6 M7KE5
	4. How is children's expression constrained by stereotypical roles? Some children make the assumption that the boy will be the doctor, the girl the nurse. Attitudes such as boys play football, girls skip. We need to encourage equality.	C10.4.11 M7.1.5	C10KE25 M7KE3

Signed........Anne Other...(assessor) ....Sarah Bright..(candidate)

Witness testimony

For things which your assessor is not able to observe easily, or to cover areas of the range, you can ask other people you work with to write a witness testimony. If you are a childminder you can ask parents and other professionals who visit you to write a witness testimony. You may need to explain the National Occupational Standards to them, so that what they write is relevant. You will need to have a list of people who have supplied witness testimonies in your portfolio, with a note of their job role or status. An example is given below.

Date	WITNESS TESTIMONY	PCs range	Knowledge evidence
6.11.00	The nursery has an open door policy so parents feel welcome to come to the nursery at any time. Sarah is very relaxed with the parents and encourages them to talk to her about their child's development, and any worries and concerns they may have.	C11.1.1 P2.1.1,4,5 R1,2,3 P2.3.2	C11KE8 P2KE4,6
	She also shows the parents the activities the children have been doing that day when they come to collect them, and encourages the children to talk about what they have done. Often parents just like to chat, and Sarah is always willing to listen. She upholds the nursery's policy on confidentiality at all times.	P2.3.5, 6,7,8 R1,4 C5.3.10, R3,6	C11KE12 P2KE10 C11KE31 P2KE8
	Sarah was concerned about a Chinese boy who was not speaking much at nursery. She talked to his mum, who said his English is good and he chatted away at home, and she was surprised he didn't at the nursery. Since then Sarah has encouraged him to join in with group activities and he is gradually starting to talk more.	P2.1.8,10 C11.1.5 R2,4 C11.5.6 P2.1.9 C5.1.8,10 R3	

Signed...... *V Goode* ......witness ...... *Sarah Bright* ......(candidate)

Status of witness...... Nursery Manager ......

Work plans

If you are involved in planning the routine and curriculum in your setting, you can use your plans as evidence. If you do this, you will need to write a brief explanation of how you were involved in the planning. It would be useful extra evidence to say how the plans were put into practice, and to evaluate their effectiveness - what the children gained from them, whether you would change them next time and so on.

If you are not involved in the planning, you will need to produce some evidence that you are able to plan. The activity plan on pages 28-29 will help you to do this. If you answer the questions thoroughly, this activity plan will cover much of the knowledge evidence you will need (an example of a completed activity plan is also provided, on pages 14-15, to give you an idea of what is expected).

Inspection of the setting

For some units, such as E3 which covers health and safety and planning the environment, your assessor will need to inspect your setting. She will ask you questions about how far you are responsible for these areas of work, and whether you understand the reasons for things being the way they are. She will usually record this on the direct observation and oral question records.

Reflective accounts

These are a really useful way of writing (or talking) about things you have done which your assessor was not able to observe. There is no special format, you can write on ordinary A4 paper. (Alternatively, you can put your reflective account onto audio tape.) An example of a reflective account is given below.

Perhaps something unexpected happened in the nursery, or you dealt with an accident, or a query from a parent. It could cover areas of the range. It's useful to try and identify which elements or units it will be relevant for, then you can make sure you cover the relevant details. When you write your account, try to reflect on why you dealt with it the way you did and what you learned from it. Don't forget to refer to the knowledge evidence section, and cover any relevant points. A significant feature of the NVQ is that it aims to make early years workers into reflective practitioners who are constantly reviewing the way they do things, so that they can improve

---

Reflective account of a visit to the library

Every week we take a group of children to the library in the afternoon to look at new books and choose some books for the nursery. We sometimes use the computer in the children's library as well.

C11.4.1,6 M7.1.3, 6 R5, 7

On the way there the children talk to me and to each other about different things we see. One week they saw a fire engine with its lights flashing. The children were excited to see it and this prompted a discussion about when they had seen fire engines before. Often interesting topics and memories about past events are discussed on the walk to the library. The children also develop their listening skills and safety awareness when they listen to instructions, such as how to cross the road safely.

C11.3.1,3,4,6 R1,2,3,4 C11KE14

At the library the children choose books and look at them, sometimes share books together and sometimes listen as a story is read aloud. They handle books and get used to holding them the right way round and turning the pages one at a time. They look at the pictures on the page and some children talk about what is happening in each picture. I talk to the children about what is happening in each picture. I talk to the children about how to look after books and show them where the title and author of the book is. When I read a large story book with simple words I follow the words with my finger to show the children that words carry meaning and how print differs to pictures.

C11.3.2 C11KE6,7,25,27 C5.2.7 C5.5R8 M7.1.5

About a month ago we attended a session at the library which celebrated black culture. A librarian told stories to the children which included 'Lima's Red Hot Chilli'. The children then tasted some Caribbean food including mango, honey cake and a fruit drink. The children enjoyed the morning's activities, and celebrating a different culture with young children helps to overcome discriminatory and stereotypical ideas they may have formed. It is important to show respect and value different cultures, religions, languages and dialects to increase the self-esteem of children from different cultures. In the same way books can also counteract stereotypes based on gender or disability by showing positive images of, for example, women as engineers or doctors.

Signed......Anne Other..............(assessor) .   Sarah Bright..................(candidate)

---

their practice. None of us ever stop learning, no matter how experienced we are.

Log books, diaries and notes

These can be used to record your day-to-day work with the children. You may if you wish keep a daily diary, but they can become repetitive. It's useful to have a sample of your routine, but once you have written that for perhaps a week, be more discerning about what you write.

You may find it helpful to carry a notebook around with you to record things which happen during the day. You can then write anything relevant in more detail in quiet times during the day, or when you get home. Aim to pick out significant events rather than list all the routine things you do day after day. To record these events you can use the free description format of a reflective account, or you may find the format shown on page 16 helpful because it's a bit more structured.

Work products

You can use things like:
◆ policies and procedures of your setting - you must write a short note to show either how you have been involved in preparing them or how you use them in your daily work.

◆ curriculum plans - write a note to say how you were involved in planning and carrying out the activities. Evaluate how successful they were and what the children gained from them.

◆ examples of activities you have done with the children - only if you feel they are needed to support the evidence. Don't include a lot of children's work.

◆ menus, charts, details of outings and special events - explain how you were involved in preparing these.

◆ letters to parents, children's records, child observations and anything else you feel is a relevant piece of evidence - you must get permission from your supervisor or employer, and always remove names and check that the child or adult will not be recognised from anything in the piece of evidence, in order to maintain confidentiality.

◆ photographs of yourself working with the children, with a caption saying what the activity is, and how you are involved.

Remember!
Whatever evidence you use from your workplace, do check with your employer that you can use it first.

ACTIVITY PLAN

NAME: Sarah Bright   **DATE:** 15.6.00   **ACTIVITY:** A sound game   **AGE OF CHILDREN:** 3 - 4yrs

Before the activity:
Describe the activity you are planning. Describe how it fulfils the values statements for the element or unit you are working on.
I will play high notes and low notes on the piano. The children will listen to the notes and place a teddy on a ladder - at the top if they hear a high note, at the bottom for a low note. They will take turns to play high or low notes, while the others say if it's high or low.

Why have you chosen this activity? What do you think the children will gain from it? *(Think about areas of development.)*
The game will improve children's listening skills and help develop auditory discrimination. It will help children describe different sounds, so extending their vocabulary.

Which children will be involved? Why? *(Will it be free choice? Have you targeted children who need particular help with, for instance, colour recognition?)*
A group of 6 to 8 children will play the game. The group should not be too large as the children might become restless waiting for their turn.

ACTIVITY PLAN continued

What equipment/resources/preparation do you need?
A piano, a ladder, a teddy.

What will you do during the activity? *(Language you will use, help you will give, etc.)*
I will talk about hearing, using our ears to hear all sorts of different noises and sounds. Then I will show the piano to the children and discuss the different notes, using high, low, in the middle, notes. I will try to extend the game to include loud and quiet, fast and slow. I will supervise the children and encourage them to take turns. I will encourage and praise them.

After the activity:

Did the activity go well? Why? If not, why not?
The activity went quite well, as the children enjoyed moving the teddy up and down the ladder.

Would you change it next time? If so, how and why?
I would make the game slightly longer, by using other instruments, such as a xylophone, so that the children have more 'hands on' experience.

How would you adapt the activity for older/younger children? For children with additional needs or disabilities?
For older children I would get them to play loud and quiet, fast and slow. For children with a hearing impairment I would use gongs and instruments that vibrate a lot, and get them to feel the vibration of the instruments, and do more on rhythm than high and low.

What did the children gain from the activity? Was it what you thought they would?
The children had to concentrate by listening carefully to the different sounds. It helped them to develop their auditory discrimination.

What did you learn from it?
Once children understand an idea or a game, it gives them the confidence to develop other ideas, and try other things a bit more complicated.

Evidence covered:
C10.1.1, 2, 8, R2   C10.2.2, 3, 4, R4   C11.2.1, 6, 7   C11.4.2, 7, R1, 3   C11.5.3, R1, 3, 4   M7.1.3, R1, 5, 7
M7.3.2, 3, 4, 5, R2, 3, 6, 7, 8   M7.4.1, 2, 3, 7, 8, R2, 3, 4, 5

Signed ......Sarah Bright...... (candidate)   If anyone observed you ask them to sign that this is a true record, and to comment if possible.

Signed ......A. N. Other...... Role: ......Assessor......

Comment: The children enjoyed this activity and gained a lot from it, but I agree, adding some more instruments would extend the experience for them.

CANDIDATE DIARY

NAME: Sarah Bright   **DATE:** 22.9.00   **INCIDENT:** Council's recycling lorry came to nursery to empty the newspaper container

What happened? Who was involved? *(Don't use names - number of staff/children/parents)*
The children heard the lorry at the gates of the nursery so we decided to take the children outside to watch the newspapers being collected. The children enjoyed watching the lorry pick up the container and empty the papers.

How did you react? What did you do?
I used this unplanned opportunity to talk with the children about recycling things such as paper, cans, glass bottles and so on. We talked about what happens to the papers after they have been collected, and where the lorry was going to next. Also as we watched the lorry I used language such as up, down, full, empty.

Why did you do it this way?
It was a good chance for the children to see at first hand what happens to the things we recycle at nursery, and introduce them in a very simple way to the concept of looking after the environment. It was also a good opportunity to extend their language skills.

Did it work? If not, why not?
Yes, the children were really interested.

What have you learned from it? What would you do differently next time?
(Think about the values statements)
That it's important to be flexible, and take opportunities to give children new experiences when they arise. I wouldn't do anything different next time.

Which PCs/range/knowledge does this relate to?
C11.2.4,6,7 R7,9,13,14
C11.4.1,2,3,5,6,7 R1
C10.2.2 R1,2,7,9
C10.3.2 R2,3
M7.3.7, R1,6,7,8
M7.4.4, R1

If anyone observed you ask them to sign that this is an accurate record
and to make a comment.

Witness................... V. Goode ....

Status .... Nursery Manager ....

Witness comment (if applicable)
This was a spontaneous event which proved valuable and rewarding.

Case studies, assignments or projects

This covers a range of other evidence, such as:

◆ assignments and projects set by your centre:
  • your centre may ask you at the beginning of the NVQ programme to carry out a project to cover all aspects of child development, because several of the units ask you to show your knowledge of this, and it's easier to cover it all together.

  • your centre may ask you to do an assignment for Unit C15, Child Protection, because there is very little which can be directly observed.

◆ written work to cover areas of the underpinning knowledge and range which you have not covered with other, work-based evidence, perhaps because it is outside your experience or you needed to do some reading or research.

◆ a case study of a particular child, carried out over a period of time.

Child observations

There is a whole unit dedicated to child observation, but don't wait till you get to C16 to start carrying out observations of children. You need to get into the habit of observing children, because it is an important skill. Observations help you learn a lot about child development, and individual children's needs, and they help you to plan appropriate activities for your children. They are also useful evidence for most of the units. You need to gain permission from the parents before you include observations in your portfolio. Some employers ask for parents' permission for this when their child joins the setting, so check what the position is in your setting. If you are not confident about child observation, read the chapter on C16. A helpful format for you to use when you record your observations is provided on page 18.

Simulation, role play, skills rehearsal

If you are not able to demonstrate a particular competence in your workplace - for instance, if you don't have the opportunity to bath babies or make feeds - you could be observed doing these things in a classroom situation. Or if you wanted to demonstrate your ability to handle a difficult situation with a parent which it would be inappropriate to observe, you could be observed in a role play. These are only used in exceptional circumstances.

Skills transferable from other performance

This can be used when it would be inappropriate to carry out direct observation, such as in the case of a child's disclosure of abuse. Some of the skills you would need in this situation may be observed in other work situations, such as how you support a distressed child, how you communicate or how you handle difficult situations.

Past achievements

You may have a great deal of past experience as well as other relevant qualifications when you embark on your NVQ. You will be able to draw on this as evidence for your portfolio. Your centre will normally be able to advise you on this, and may take you through a process called accreditation of prior learning (APL) or accreditation of prior achievement (APA). In order to include any evidence from the past, you will need to prove that it is your own work, and that the information is not out of date - for instance, the work needs to show an awareness of equal opportunities and anti-discriminatory practice; information related to child safety and protection must take account of the Children Act; and curriculum practice must take account of the Early Learning Goals or the National Curriculum. Evidence from the past cannot take the place of direct observation, but it can be used to cover parts of the range and knowledge evidence.

Formal written or oral tests/extended questioning

It is not usual to use tests as evidence for NVQ, because it is a qualification based on assessment of your competence in the workplace. However, there is a possibility that it may be used in the future for some aspects of assessment.

> **Remember!**
> It is absolutely vital that you keep all of your evidence together in your portfolio, with your assessment plans, and keep it in a safe place.

How do I reference and record the evidence?

Your centre will usually show you how they want the portfolio organised. It's usually best to divide the evidence unit by unit, but not essential. If you're working with several units at once, it might be better not to separate it into units, because you need to number it as you go along, so that you can record it onto the unit assessment records. Have a look at your candidate handbook with the standards in it. The format for recording your evidence varies slightly from one awarding body to another, but you will often find that for every PC, range and knowledge evidence statement you have to say what sort of evidence you have used, and what page number it's on, so that your assessor and internal verifier can check it. You need to number every piece of evidence as you do it. This is not easy to get to grips with at first, so ask your assessor to explain how she wants you to do it.

CHILD OBSERVATION

Title of observation:

Settling in

Type of observation: *(eg target child, free description, developmental check-list)*

Time sample

Aim of observation: *(Which aspect of child development/behaviour are you aiming to observe?)*

1To observe how a child copes with settling in to nursery

First name of child: *(or fictitious name)*   Sandeep   **Age:** *(yrs & mths)*   2yrs 9mths

Description of setting: *(where observation is taking place, number of staff, children, equipment available, etc.)*

Nursery playroom, 3 staff, 15 children. Morning session - registration time, play and structured activities, drinks time.

The observation: Write this on a separate piece of paper, or other format you have chosen. Write what you actually observed in detail, using present tense.

Evaluation: Comment on what you learned from the observation - link this to your aims. Evaluate what the child's needs are, and make recommendations for future planning.

Signatures: Sign your observation and ask someone who witnessed the observation to sign it if possible.

Signed .... S. Bright ....(candidate)   **Signed** ...... Anne Other ....(witness)

Observation

9.00 Sandeep is cuddling her mum and looking anxious. She is watching the other children playing but doesn't join in.

9.30 Sandeep's mum says goodbye and a member of staff sits with Sandeep. She cries for about a minute and then goes to sit with the rest of the children for register time, with the members of staff.

10.00 Sandeep is sitting at the painting table with an apron on. She is absorbed in sponge painting. She finishes her picture and gets up from the table. She watches another child washing his hands. She looks anxious again.

10.30 Snack time. Sandeep sits at the table with the other children but doesn't speak. She is offered a piece of toast but shakes her head. She drinks her orange juice.

11.00 Sandeep is playing with the play people on the carpet. She looks at another child also playing there but doesn't speak.

11.30 Sandeep's mum returns to collect her. She is sitting with the other children listening to the story but as soon as she sees her mum she runs to her smiling.

Evaluation

Sandeep was obviously quite anxious about her mum leaving her but she only cried for a very short time. She spent a lot of time watching other children but didn't speak to anyone, child or adult. She did enjoy painting and later in the morning started playing alongside another child. She will need a lot of reassurance over the next few days. Staff need to gently encourage her to join in with things, but not be too insistent. She will join in when she's ready.

Evidence covered:

C16.1.1, 2, 3, 4, 7, 8, 9, R1, 3, 6, 7, 12   C16.2.1, 2, 3, 5, R2, 4, 5   C5.1.2, 4, 5, 7, 8, R2, 5
M7.1.1, 2, R4   P2.1.1, R1, 3   P2.2.3, 6, R3, 4, 7

Personal skills review

In Chapter 2, we suggest that Unit C10, 'Implement planned activities to promote children's sensory and intellectual development', might be a good unit to start with, but that depends on your experience, the age of the children you work with and which areas you feel most confident about.

The personal skills review provided will help you to identify the areas of your work you are confident about, and areas where you need to take some action to improve your competence. Read through the summary of units and elements and use sections 1- 4 in the skills review first of all to help you to decide which unit to start with. You can photocopy and use the blank review sheet (Personal skills profile) on page 21. You will need your candidate handbook to help you.

When you have chosen a unit, do another personal skills review, this time based on the unit. You may find it easier to do this element by element at first.

◆ Go through the PCs and range for the element you are working on and fill in the appropriate boxes 1 - 5 on the review sheet.

◆ Go to the knowledge evidence section at the end of the unit and pick out the statements which are relevant to the element you are working on. Note which you need some help with in section 6 on the review sheet.

◆ Decide which activities you can arrange for your assessor to observe (box 7), and what other types of evidence you can use.

Note: As you become more confident, use this format to look at the whole unit rather than just one element.

The personal skills review will help you to be prepared for when you and your assessor plan your assessment. If you have done other units already and you feel confident to go straight into planning, you can leave this section out.

Action you may need to take
If you have identified areas you may have difficulty with you will need to discuss with your assessor what you are going to do to put these right. For instance:

Section 2 You may simply need to practise an activity until you feel more confident. Ask your assessor or colleagues for guidance if necessary. If you need ideas for activities you will find the resources in this book helpful.

Section 3 You may need to ask your employer to give you the opportunity to move to a different age group, or to allow you to do things not normally within your role. If there are serious gaps, you may need to spend some time in another setting - for instance, if you work in a creche where you never have the same children for more than an hour, or you only have children under two years old, you do need to consider getting wider experience.

Section 4 If you want to use something from the past as evidence, your assessor will have to make sure that it is sufficient, takes account of current legislation, local regulations and best practice, and that it is authentic and reliable - that is, that it's your own work. Past experience cannot take the place of direct observation.

Section 6 When you fill in this section, remember to check the knowledge evidence. We have identified the relevant knowledge evidence for each element in each of the chapters. You may need to attend some training, ask for support, or do some reading and research to improve your understanding. Your centre may offer training sessions, or learning materials and supported study.

Assessment planning
At this stage you may want to arrange a meeting with your assessor so that you can start planning your assessment. If this is your first unit, we would recommend that you plan together, but once you are confident, you can plan on your own if you wish. You will find a chapter on each of the mandatory units, either in this book or in the other two books in the series, to help you with your planning. Your centre will have an assessment plan format, but an example of what it might look like is given on page 32 (completed version, page 22).

♦ There are two ways of planning your assessment:
You can take each element separately and plan an activity which your assessor will observe and other evidence you need for that element, **or:**

♦ Plan a whole session which will cover a range of activities and provide evidence for more than one element or unit - we sometimes call this **holistic assessment.** We recommend this method because it is a more effective use of your own and the assessor's time. We will explain this more fully in the section on cross referencing below.

Start by choosing an activity for your assessor to observe which will cover as many of the PCs and the range as possible. Remember to check which PCs must be observed, and remember too that at least one aspect of each area of the range must be observed. It's a good idea to plan the activity using the activity plan format we suggested earlier in the chapter, so that you can make sure that you are well prepared, and also to show your assessor that you have a good knowledge and understanding of the element or unit.

Decide how you will provide the other evidence you need. You will find suggestions about the most appropriate types of evidence at the beginning of the unit. Don't forget to include any work plans from your normal work practice, with a note to say how you were involved in preparing and carrying them out.

Cross referencing
The NVQ process encourages working across elements and units - we call this **holistic assessment.** This means that you can use one piece of evidence in several units. Because every page of evidence is numbered, you simply cross reference to the relevant page, regardless of which unit it is in. For instance, your assessor may have observed you playing a colour matching game with a group of children, which you planned for Element 3 in C10 (we usually write this as C10.3). She will probably have noted how you encouraged children to relate to each other and take turns (C5.2) and how you encouraged and praised children (C5.3). You were probably encouraging concentration (C10.1) and developing language skills (C11.2,5). If your assessor planned to spend some extra time observing tidying up and getting ready for dinner, she would also see evidence for C5.3 - encouraging self-reliance; for E3.1 - maintaining a safe environment; and for C2.2 - contributing to children's personal hygiene. In the same way you can cross reference for areas of the range. You can also do this for any of your written evidence. Some candidates are unable to cope with this at first, and you may need to grow into it. As you become more familiar with your handbook, you will find it easier to cross reference.

You will probably find it easier to concentrate on one unit at a time, but be aware of when evidence can be cross referenced

PERSONAL SKILLS PROFILE

1. Things I feel confident I can do

2. Things I don't feel confident about doing

3. Things I don't have the opportunity to do

4. Things I have done in the past

5. Areas of the range my assessor can observe

6. Things I don't understand (check knowledge evidence)

7. Possible activities my assessor could observe

8. Other types of evidence I could provide

ASSESSMENT PLAN

Description of evidence/activity	To cover PCs/ range	To cover knowledge evidence	Date due
Cooking activity to be observed Write an activity plan for the cooking activity Reflective account of other activities carried out to develop maths, relational and physical concepts Cross reference to evidence from previous course on concepts Assignment to cover all areas of development	C10.2 R4,5 C10.3.1,3,4 5,6,7, R2 C10.3, R1-6	C10KE10,11,19,2 021,22,23 M7KE2,3,5,10, 17,20,23 C3,C5,C10,C11 KE1 and others	

Signed........Sarah Bright........(candidate)   ....A. N. Other........(assessor)

Date........23. 6.00........   **Date**........23. 6.00........

CROSS REFERENCING SHEET

Unit	
Description of evidence	**Unit/page reference**

to other units. To help you to do this, we have given you a simple format (see page 23). Put a copy at the beginning of each unit, and as you find evidence which you think will fit, list it on the sheet, with the page reference. At this stage, you don't need to worry about exactly which PCs, range or knowledge evidence it fits, as long as you know where to find it. When you start working on that unit, you can go back to the evidence and cross reference it into the appropriate place.

Knowledge evidence

Try to incorporate as much knowledge evidence as you can into your activity plan, candidate diary, reflective account, child observation or other work-based evidence. If there are still gaps in your evidence, you can write paragraphs on each relevant point. You should aim to make this short, clear and to the point, and wherever possible, use examples from your own work practice. Don't copy chunks from books, nor include photocopied pages.

Alternatively, if you feel confident that you can give an oral account of your knowledge and understanding, arrange this with your assessor, or include an audio-tape of your answers as evidence.

You may find it easier to pick out the relevant bits of knowledge evidence for each element, to ensure that you have covered all of the evidence but not repeated anything unnecessarily. You will notice in your candidate handbook that alongside each statement in the knowledge evidence there is a reference to the element it is linked to. To help you to identify it, we have included the reference numbers of the relevant statements in each of the elements in the chapters.

The resources in this book will help you with your underpinning knowledge. There are some good practical ideas, and some thought-provoking articles which will help you to reflect on your own practice and improve it. We have placed each article in the unit it is most relevant for but you will notice that many of the articles are relevant for more than one unit.

You will probably need to do further reading from study materials and recommended text books, or make arrangements to attend training sessions. Your centre will be able to advise you on this. A list of books you may find useful is given right.

Suggested reading list

Child Care and Education by T Bruce and C Meggitt (Hodder & Stoughton) 0 340 64328 5.

Children with Special Educational Needs by M Alcott (Hodder & Stoughton) 0 340 70152 8.

Babies and Young Children by Beaver, Brewster *et al* (Stanley Thornes) Book 1(2nd edition) 0 7487 3974 2; Book 2 0 7847 3975 0.

A Practical Guide to Work with Babies (2nd edition) by Dare and O'Donovan (Stanley Thornes) 0 7487 3635 2.

A Practical Guide to Child Nutrition by Dare and O'Donovan (Stanley Thornes) 0 7487 2375 7.

A Practical Guide to Caring for Children with Special Needs by Dare and O'Donovan (Stanley Thornes) 0 7487 2871 6.

A Practical Guide to Child Observation (2nd edition) by Hobart and Frankel (Stanley Thornes) 0 7487 4500 9.

Good Practice in Child Protection by Hobart and Frankel (Stanley Thornes) 0 7487 3094.

Child Protection and Early Years Work by J Lindon (Hodder & Stoughton) 0 340 70558 2.

Equal Opportunities in Practice by J Lindon (Hodder & Stoughton) 0 340 70559 0.

A Practical Guide to Equal Opportunities by H Malik (Stanley Thornes) 0 7487 3652 2.

Early Years Care and Education by Tassoni, Bulman et al (Heinemann) 435 40160 2.

Date	OBSERVATION RECORD	PCs range	Knowledge evidence

Signed..(assessor) ....(candidate)

Date	ORAL QUESTION RECORD	PCs range	Knowledge evidence

Signed...(assessor)   ....(candidate)

Date	WITNESS TESTIMONY	PCs range	Knowledge evidence

Signed...witness ....(candidate)

Status of witness...

ACTIVITY PLAN

NAME: **DATE:**   **ACTIVITY:**   **AGE OF CHILDREN:**

Before the activity:
Describe the activity you are planning. Describe how it fulfils the values statements for the element or unit you are working on.

Why have you chosen this activity? What do you think the children will gain from it? *(Think about areas of development.)*

Which children will be involved? Why? *(Will it be free choice? Have you targeted children who need particular help with, for instance, colour recognition?)*

What equipment/resources/preparation do you need?

What will you do during the activity? *(Language you will use, help you will give, etc.)*

After the activity:
Did the activity go well? Why? If not, why not?

Would you change it next time? If so, how and why?

How would you adapt the activity for older/younger children? For children with additional needs or disabilities?

What did the children gain from the activity? Was it what you thought they would?

What did you learn from it?

Signed .... (candidate) If anyone observed you ask them to sign that this is a true record, and to comment if possible.

Signed .... Role: ....

Comment:

CANDIDATE DIARY

NAME: **DATE:**   **INCIDENT:**

What happened? Who was involved? *(Don't use names - number of staff/children/parents)*

How did you react? What did you do?

Why did you do it this way?

Did it work? If not, why not?

What have you learned from it? What would you do differently next time?
(Think about the values statements)

Which PC's/range/knowledge does this relate to?

If anyone observed you ask them to sign that this is an accurate record and to make a comment.

Witness..   **Status** ....

Witness comment (if applicable)

CHILD OBSERVATION

Candidate's name	Date

Title of observation:

Type of observation: *(eg target child, free description, developmental check-list)*

Aim of observation: *(Which aspect of child development/behaviour are you aiming to observe?)*

First name of child: *(or fictitious name)*   **Age:** *(yrs & mths)*

Description of setting: *(where observation is taking place, number of staff, children, equipment available, etc.)*

The observation: Write this on a separate piece of paper, or other format you have chosen. Write what you actually observed in detail, using present tense.

Evaluation: Comment on what you learned from the observation - link this to your aims. Evaluate what the child's needs are, and make recommendations for future planning.

Signatures: Sign your observation and ask someone who witnessed the observation to sign it if possible.

Signed...(candidate)   Signed.......................................(witness)

ASSESSMENT PLAN

Description of evidence/activity	To cover PCs/ range	To cover knowledge evidence	Date due

Signed..(assessor)   ....(candidate)

Date...   Date...

Unit C10: Promote the sensory and intellectual development of children

Chapter 2

About this unit

Unit C10 includes many of the activities and experiences that you carry out with the children in your care on a daily basis without even thinking. Have a look at the notes on each element and make a list of all the activities you have carried out recently. It will probably be quite a long list! That's why we would suggest that this might be a good unit for you to start with, unless you are working with very young babies. It's just as important for babies to have stimulating activities, but with this age group there is less scope to cover the range of activities and experiences that you need to in order to show that you have a good understanding of how to promote children's sensory and intellectual development. If you have the opportunity to move around the different age groups in your setting, it would be useful to spend some time with each group so that you can get a feel for the different needs of the children at each stage of development.

For those of you working with older children in school in Years 1 and 2 the timetable may make it difficult for you to carry out all of the activities you need to. If possible, try to spend some time with another age group where there is more opportunity for free play and practical activities. If you are a childminder, you may have the advantage of working with a wide age range, but you may find it helpful to spend some time in a group setting, so that you can have experience of working with larger groups. A local childminder support network or pre-school may give you this opportunity.

Values

As in all units, the values statements place particular emphasis on the welfare of the child. This must be your prime consideration in everything you do with the children in your care. Every unit also emphasises your role as a reflective practitioner. This means that you need to constantly ask yourself questions such as: Why am I doing this? What are the children gaining from it? How could I do it better? Would something else be more appropriate? Are all of the children's needs being met?

The emphasis throughout this unit is clearly on the child's learning and development, as you will have realised as you looked through the elements. In Elements 2, 3 and 4 you also need to show how you will ensure equality of opportunity for children with special needs by adapting your activities appropriately. The articles on pages 47 - 52 give you guidance on how to support children with a visual or a hearing impairment. Element 4 emphasises how you should celebrate diversity by encouraging children to explore a variety of roles and cultures within their creative play, for instance by providing paper, crayons and paint in a range of skin tones, different cooking utensils and play food, dolls from different ethnic origins and dressing-up clothes which encourage children to try out different gender roles and discourage stereotyping. When you are planning, make sure you consider these points.

Getting started

In this unit you are aiming to show that you can help children develop:

◆ Concentration, attention and memory

◆ Awareness and understanding of sensory experiences

◆ Mathematical, physical, scientific and other concepts

◆ Imaginative and creative ideas

Now use the personal skills review we described in the introduction to identify which parts of the unit you feel most confident about, and which areas you need to work on. If you feel confident enough, you can go straight into your planning, using your assessment plan. You might find it helpful to refer back to the introduction, because we used C10 as an example to illustrate how to gather your evidence. If possible, plan with your assessor until you feel confident about doing it on your own. Although you can plan your evidence separately for each element and might find it easier at first, it's better to plan for the whole unit together and cross reference from one element to another as soon as you feel able to cope with it. You can also cross reference across units. Look at C11 alongside C10, and try to plan activities which will cover both units. The cross referencing sheet on page 23 will help you to gather evidence to which you can cross refer.

Element C10.1 Develop children's attention span and memory

Key issues

Activities which encourage children to develop their attention span are many and varied - construction, creative activities, play with natural materials (productive activities) and watching a television programme or listening to a story (receptive activities) and so on. The important thing to remember is that if the activity is appropriate to the child's stage of development, the child will be interested and concentrate for longer. The younger the children, the shorter the time they will be able to concentrate for, so with children under two, make your activities short, and work with only one or two children. They are not able to wait and take turns at this age. Some children will find it difficult to concentrate, and you will need to develop strategies for helping them. If you have children with attention deficit disorder or hyperactivity in your setting, find out from their parents what is likely to trigger it, and how they deal with it.

This element is a good example of where you can use cross referencing. For the other elements in this unit and in C11 - Promote children's language and communication development - you will be carrying out activities which will encourage children to develop their attention, so you don't need to plan a special activity.

There are particular activities you can carry out to help children to develop their memory. In your handbook, read the notes for this element about the three aspects of memory - recall, recognition and prediction - and the two types of activities - receptive and productive - and try to cover all of these in your evidence. Here are some suggestions for helping children to develop their memory:

◆ Circle time, when children have a chance to recall some news, or talk about a model they have just made, or an activity they enjoyed doing. For older children, retelling a story or talking about their most exciting experience (recall).

◆ Looking at family photographs (recognition and recall).

◆ Listening to familiar sounds and identifying what they are (recognition and recall).

◆ Planning future events as a group, encouraging the children to use their experience of past events to draw on - for example, a birthday or a seasonal activity (recall and prediction).

◆ Kim's game: put familiar items on a tray, cover it, and ask the children to tell you what was on the tray; or take an object away, remove the cover and ask the children to tell you what is missing (recall and recognition).

◆ Memory game (for older children): put mixed up pairs of cards face down on the table. The children in turn pick up two cards. If they match they keep them. If they don't they put them back (recall and recognition).

◆ I went to the shop and I bought… Sit in a circle with a group of children. Each child adds something to the list but has to remember everything that has already been bought, so the list gets longer and longer! An easy version for younger children is to let them hold their objects (recall).

Which type of evidence?

If you look at the evidence requirements for Element C10.1 you will see that your assessor needs to carry out *direct observation* of all of the performance criteria. It will be useful to include an *activity plan* which shows how you have prepared for the activity. Don't forget, you can use *work plans* and other records from your setting which show how you provide for children's learning needs.

> ### Remember!
> You need to show that you can work with children from babies to eight years old, so your evidence needs to reflect this. Try to carry out activities with different age groups if you have the opportunity.

Your assessor will need to observe at least one aspect of each category of the range. In this element there is only one category - children - with two aspects. Your assessor should be able to observe you working with children without memory and concentration difficulties (aspect 1), and possibly children with difficulties (aspect 2) if you have any in your group. If not, you can write a *reflective account* or *candidate diary* of a child you have helped in the past, or carry out a *child observation* if the opportunity arises, to fill any gaps.

For C10.1, the related *knowledge evidence* statements are 1, 5, 6, 7, 14, 16 and 18. Look through them and cover as much as you can in your activity plan, reflective account or other evidence. Your evaluations will help to show your knowledge. Then fill any gaps with a short assignment which covers the relevant points. Don't forget to use examples from your own work practice where possible. But it doesn't need to be an essay!

Element C10.2 Develop children's awareness and understanding of sensory experiences

Key issues

Children learn through their senses, so the more ways you stimulate their senses, right from birth, the better. There are many ways in which you provide sensory experiences for the children in your care. Some activities will stimulate more than one of the senses if you plan them carefully. This will be particularly important if you have children with visual or hearing impairment in your setting.

In your handbook, read the notes on this element for examples of suggested activities. Here are some of our ideas. You will find others in the articles on pages 39 - 46.

Sight

◆ Bright and attractive books, posters, displays and pictures around the setting to make it look interesting - the younger the child, the brighter and simpler the display and books should be.

◆ Interest tables - based on colour, shape, sets of similar objects, numbers …

◆ A walk - around the setting, in the street, in the park, to the shops…

◆ All sorts of art work

◆ Each other!

Hearing

◆ Listening (and moving) to all kinds of music

◆ Making music with instruments and other 'soundmakers'

◆ Recognising taped sounds or sound lotto

◆ Listening to sounds around, both inside and out, in different environments

◆ Listening to each other

Touch

◆ Feeling objects in a feely book, box or bag

◆ Using a variety of materials to make collages and models

◆ Handling animals (be careful about health and safety)

◆ Textured dominoes   ◆ Cooking

◆ Playdough, clay, sand, water and other natural materials

Smell

◆ A walk in the garden   ◆ Smelling activity

◆ Cooking   ◆ Scratch and sniff book

Taste

◆ Cooking   ◆ Meal times

◆ Tasting activity - make sure that you don't use anything that could cause an allergic reaction (definitely avoid peanuts) or be offensive to some families.

You will notice from the list that cooking probably offers more opportunity to promote sensory experiences than any other activity (except perhaps a walk.) One really worthwhile cooking experience is making bread, and this is not half as difficult as it may sound. If you get a one-rise dough, you can rise and cook the bread in one session. It's a good activity to do for several reasons:

◆ Bread is the staple diet in many countries of the world, so it's an excellent opportunity to look at different types of bread and where they come from. You can do this while the dough is rising - make it into a longer topic and in later sessions get someone to make other sorts of bread such as chappattis, pizza or pitta bread.

◆ It's a very hands-on, tactile activity. The children can mix and knead the bread with their hands, and everyone can have their own piece of dough. They can pummel and squeeze it as much as they like!

◆ The children are using several senses during the activity and also learning concepts (cross reference to C10.3) such as how things change when they are mixed together and heated, weight, capacity, size. They are using language to describe their experiences (cross reference to C11).

◆ You can grow cress, and make butter (by shaking the cream from the top of the milk) to use with your bread.

◆ Most children with a sensory impairment would be able to join in.

◆ It tastes good!

Look out for unplanned opportunities to promote children's sensory awareness. For instance, grass cutting, a bonfire, a lovely sunset, an unusual traffic sound, machinery, a bird or animal, snowfall. Don't be so involved in your planned activities that you miss unexpected opportunities - it can so easily happen!

Which type of evidence?

In this element your assessor will need to carry out *direct observation* in all but two of the PCs and one aspect of each category of the range. If she can observe more, so much the better. Use an *activity plan* to help you plan thoroughly for the activity your assessor will observe, and evaluate it, covering some of the knowledge evidence required. The range covers all of the senses, activities indoors and out, and children with and without sensory impairment. It's unlikely that you will have enough evidence for the whole range in one activity. You can supplement the direct observation with a *reflective account* or *candidate diary* of other sensory activities you have done with the children.

The related *knowledge evidence* statements for this element are 1, 3, 4, 8, 9, 16, 17, 18, 28. You will notice that some of these are also relevant to C10.1, C10.3 and C10.4. Where they overlap, you can write one piece of work to cover all elements.

Element C10.3 Develop children's understanding of mathematics and science

Key issues

The most important thing to remember when you are planning for this element is that the best way to help children develop concepts is through play and practical activities and experiences.

Pre-school children should not be doing worksheets. They learn by doing, not by trying to write things down. Children take a long time to develop concepts - they gradually develop an understanding through trying things over and over again. Some concepts are more difficult to grasp than others. One example of this is time, because it's so abstract. Some children will have particular difficulty grasping concepts. For these children, you will need to take things more slowly, and think of imaginative ways to present activities to develop concepts they are struggling with. For instance, if they are having difficulty recognising colours, get involved in the activities they enjoy, and reinforce a colour as you play with them, taking care not to make it become tedious.

Spend a little time watching children play. Write a list of all the concepts you can see developing. The notes on this element will remind you which concepts to look for. Let's take one activity - children using wooden bricks, cars and small play people. They have built a garage, have rows of cars in it, and play people are mending the cars. What concepts have they been learning?

◆ Size, space and shape - which shape bricks are best for building with, what size they need to make everything fit together, how much space they need for the cars

◆ Colour and sorting - sorting cars into different colours, bricks into different sizes and shapes, play people into different roles

◆ Number - counting number of red/blue/yellow cars, number altogether, adding some and taking some away as they are mended

◆ Language of relational concepts - more/less, inside/outside, bigger/smaller, under/over

◆ Forces - they may have made a ramp to roll cars down

◆ How things work - talk from past experience of perhaps accompanying parents to the garage to get the car repaired

You will probably be able to think of other concepts to add to the list.

A useful idea

Start collecting all sorts of interesting objects to make into an interest box. Have a rummage at home first, and always think before you throw anything away. Look in second-hand shops and jumble sales, or when you're out for a walk. Remember to look for things which reflect different cultures as well. Take care that the objects are safe for children to handle. The possibilities are endless, but here are a few ideas:

stones	artefacts from different countries
souvenirs	shells
tin lids	old clocks
tree bark	boxes
balls	wooden spoons
wheels	pot pourri

Children will love handling the objects, and will find their own ways of playing with them, but you can also lead them into exploring properties and sorting in different ways - metal, plastic, wood, things with holes, things which roll .....

There are also many opportunities during your normal daily routine to help children develop concepts:

◆ Getting dressed/undressed - colour, size, counting (How many buttons?), sequence (What do you put on first?)

- Walking to the nursery/shops/park - shapes in the environment, different sorts of vehicles, trees, flowers, animals, people.

- Laying the table for dinner - matching one to one - a knife, fork and spoon in every place, counting.

In the articles later in the chapter you will find a wide range of ideas for helping children to develop mathematical and scientific concepts. They will help you with your knowledge evidence, too.

Which type of evidence?

In this element your assessor will need to carry out **direct observation** for all but two of the PCs and for one aspect of each category of the range. Although there are only six range aspects, this element in reality covers a huge range of concepts, as you will see from the notes on the element:

- all the physical concepts such as weight, shape and colour, and scientific concepts such as life, growth, heat, light, change of state

- relational concepts like inside/outside, near/far, same/different

- the concept of time such as morning, yesterday, after ..., time of day

- all of the concepts related to number such as sorting, counting, matching, addition

It would be impossible to cover this element adequately with one activity, so we suggest that you choose more than one activity to be observed by your assessor. Perhaps you can plan a whole session where you are supervising a range of appropriate activities, with the help of your colleagues. Or, if that sounds too daunting, use some of these suggestions. Plan with your assessor which activity will be observed, but also plan another activity using an **activity plan** which you can carry out as part of your normal routine, and ask a colleague to sign that you did it competently. Write or give your assessor orally a **reflective account** of some of the activities you have carried out which fulfil the range, and evaluate what the children gained from them.

If you are keeping a **diary**, check for relevant entries, and reference them to the PCs, range or knowledge evidence. Check for any relevant **work products** you can use as evidence, such as curriculum plans, games you have made, accounts of outings and walks, or photographs of displays and activities. Carry out **child observations** which identify different levels of children's understanding of concepts. If you have any children with difficulty in grasping basic concepts, include them in your observation, to cover aspect 2 of the range.

Remember!
You don't need to do all of these things - choose which are best for you. When you think you have enough evidence, check with your assessor.

The related **knowledge evidence** statements for this element are 1, 2, 3, 10, 11, 19, 20, 21, 22 and 23. Read through them and try to include the information you need in your other evidence.

Also, read the sections on Mathematical Development and Knowledge and Understanding of the World in the Early Learning Goals, and in the Curriculum Guidance for the Foundation Stage. Your setting may have a copy of these, or you can obtain both from the Qualifications and Curriculum Authority (QCA). You need to be aware, too, of the National Curriculum for maths and science at Key Stage 1, and the numeracy strategy currently in use in schools. If you work in a school you will have access to these. If not, try your local library.

Element C10.4 Develop children's imagination and creativity

Key issues

Free play gives children a rich scope for creative and imaginative play, so give them time and opportunity to explore materials freely. If you restrict children's choice of activities too much, you limit their opportunity to be creative. For instance, if you don't allow them to mix play people with wooden blocks, they miss out on valuable opportunities to develop their imaginative play. You need to store materials where they are easily accessible, and teach children how to get things out and put them away properly.

Children are never too young to enjoy using art materials. As soon as babies can manage to make a mark with a pencil or crayon on a piece of paper, let them do it. Sit them at a table with some finger paints and let them enjoy the feel of it. You'll have to supervise them closely to stop them eating it! Think about your art work with the older children. Do you have a range of materials accessible so that they have the opportunity to explore and experiment with the materials? Getting 20 children to make identical Christmas cards, or fill in templates with bits of material for a display, or colour in shapes on a piece of paper is not allowing them to develop creativity. Read the articles on pages 90 - 98 to give you ideas for developing drawing and other creative skills.

This element in particular offers children the opportunity to experience a variety of cultures and roles. Make sure that you provide the right equipment and environment for them to be able to take full advantage of this. Here are some suggestions:

Role play:

○ dolls of different genders and cultural origins

○ play food, utensils and dressing-up clothes which reflect different cultures and non-stereotypical gender roles (like male nurse uniforms)

○ small play people from a range of cultural backgrounds and those with disabilities

Dance and drama:

○ Dance associated with different cultural groups

○ Drama which explores different roles

◆ Festivals

Creative art:

○ Give children access to paper, crayons and paints of different skin tones

○ Observational drawings/paintings of each other

○ Use artefacts from different cultures for observational drawing

Music:

◆ Percussion instruments from a range of cultures

◆ Listen to all kinds of music

◆ Invite musicians in from the local community groups

Which type of evidence?

Your assessor will need to *observe* all but two of the performance criteria, and at least one aspect of each range section. Your assessor may want to see more than one activity in this section, because it covers a wide range of activities.

If she does only observe one activity, you could plan, carry out and evaluate another one on an *activity plan* and ask your supervisor or colleague to sign that you have carried it out competently. You can also write a *reflective account* of other activities you have done in your setting, or reference appropriate activities you have recorded in your *diary,* if you have chosen to write one.

The *knowledge evidence* for this element is covered in statements 1, 3, 12, 13, 15, 24, 25, 26, 27, 29, 30, 31, 32. You may have already covered some of it in the evidence you have provided for the other elements, so don't forget to check. Try to cover as much as you can in your activity plans, reflective accounts and other evidence.

Once you have completed this unit, you will probably also have quite a lot of evidence for other units. If you haven't already done so, have a look at C11 - Promote children's language and communication development - and see how much of your evidence from C10 can be used. There will probably be some evidence for parts of C5 - Promote children's social and emotional development - and for C3.4 - Develop children's fine motor skills - and possibly for other units, too. Your assessor may have already been pointing this out to you. When the unit is complete, you will need to fill in the unit assessment records. Your centre will probably have explained how you should do this, but if not, ask your assessor to help you, because it is important that you complete the records as you complete each unit. If you have identified evidence for other units, fill in those records too, so that you don't provide any unnecessary additional evidence.

The next section is the resource section. We have already referred to some of the articles, but there are others you will find useful. You will also find a book list on page 24 which will be useful for further research, to ensure that you have the underpinning knowledge you need to complete the units.

Remember!

Festivals are a good way of introducing different cultural practices to children, particularly in relation to dance, music and drama, but don't fall into the trap of 'doing' Diwali or Chinese New Year and thinking you've done all you need to do. You need to constantly be looking for ways to help children to respect and value individual differences, in terms of gender, ability or disability, and culture, in everyday activities and situations. That means that, as well as providing the right environment and activities, you need to provide a good role model for the children, and challenge any stereotypical or discriminatory remarks or actions that you see.

It is important to concentrate on the skills of language and listening. It has long been recognised that the awareness of others, imagination, and intellect grow and develop through speaking and listening

Developing listening skills

Listening, speaking, reading and writing are fundamentally important activities in young children's learning . . . but, the modes of language claim special attention' Her Majesty's Inspectorate, *Aspects of Primary Education, The Education of Children Under Five,* HMSO 1989

Early pioneers in child development such as Piaget and Vygotsky placed great emphasis on the acquisition of language and listening skills as a means to success. In the early years the main focus should be on:

❑ Memory, listening, and attention skills

❑ Appropriate group behaviour

❑ Conceptual understanding

❑ Phonological and motor skills

Making time to develop a range of linguistic activities with groups of children is rewarding. However, begin slowly and with small groups until the children get used to it. You need to create an atmosphere that will encourage them to listen carefully and join in. You can do this by:

❑ Providing a quiet, comfortable area. Think about how you might organise for quiet times.

❑ Sit in a circle so that everyone can see each other's faces.

❑ Keep eye contact as much as possible.

❑ Children will learn only gradually to take on the role of audience and listen quietly, so be patient.

❑ If you have children with English as a second language, assess whether you need to give them additional support so that they can benefit fully from these activities.

❑ Settled groups of children who work together often, will help to create security and allow the children to progress.

❑ Most of all HAVE FUN!

Attention

Attention is the foundation upon which everything is based.

❑ To begin an activity ask the children to shake their hands up high, shake them low, to this side, to that side, and so on, until you have all eyes looking and faces attentive. Do the actions with them.

❑ If you have register time, take out the blue register and say to the children 'I am going to look in my green register to see who is here.' Wait for a response. Our children love this type of mistake and are always quick with their responses - 'It's not green, it's blue!' The teacher adds, 'That's what I said, I'm looking in my pink register.' This always provokes lots of laughter and ends with me saying how silly I am.

❑ Sit in a circle at the end of an activity. The children have to catch your eye and you should wink at them before they can leave the group.

Listening games

❑ Stop and go games. Play the music and ask the children to stop when the music stops.

❑ Use a drum as a beat. Walk slowly to a slow beat, run to a fast beat, skip to a repeat beat, and so on.

❑ If you have instruments and accompaniment, ask the children to stop playing when the music stops. Start when the music starts.

❑ Introduce riddles. 'I am a fruit. I have a skin, which you must peel, I grow on a tree, I am yellow' and so on. Keep giving clues until they guess correctly. (It helps to then show what you have been describing. The game can continue by asking the children to think of other descriptive words for the object not yet discussed.)

❑ Act out nursery rhymes. Sing the rhymes as a group. Ask for volunteers to be the characters. They must perform the actions as the rhyme is sung.

Memory games

❑ Place a pile of clothes on the floor and ask the child to put on a number of items - 'Jane, please put on one sock and a cardigan'. Increase the number of items as the children demonstrate success.

❑ Kim's game - put a selection of items on a tray. Look for a few moments and then cover. Ask the children one by one if they can remember an item. As they are successful, place the item into view.

❑ Spot that tune - hum or play the first few bars of a song or rhyme. Ask the children if they can recall which one it is.

There are many more activities that will help to develop these skills. The adults involved in the group have a responsibility throughout the day to make each activity come alive by showing enthusiasm. Don't miss the opportunity to encourage interaction - when singing songs, do the actions with the children in a dramatic way. This will help the children. Remember, you are the role model.

Vicky Hislop

The five senses are excellent starting points for activities with young children. Lesley Button suggests some ways to develop a child's sense of touch

Exploring **texture**

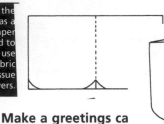

Developing a child's sense of touch helps with their understanding of the world around us. It is an important part of hand control - do you handle objects roughly or use a more sensitive touch? Part of our understanding of safety relies on touch - is something too hot or too cold, too sharp or too slippery? It is only by encouraging and developing this sense that children can develop and build up their own knowledge of their surroundings.

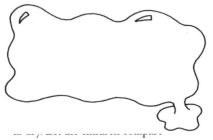

the feel of both, the dry sand trickling between their fingers, and the mouldability of wet. Add more water to the wet sand so they may experience a very sloppy mix.

Vary the temperature of water in the water tray, comparing cold and warm. For all these experiences, where practical, let them use their feet too.

Use clay, Plasticine or playdough and encourage children to really feel the material, to stroke, bang, squeeze and mould. Try adding extra water to all these materials. Observe and feel what happens to each.

You can cut all these materials to provide a smooth hard surface. Add pieces to one surface, in coils or strips, to provide a raised bumpy texture or press objects in to leave an indented texture.

Fill a large container with dry sand, sawdust or similar and hide objects inside so that children may feel for the hidden treasure. Or try being really messy and hide small objects in semi-set jelly - you can make this by adding slightly more water than the

I would suggest that the rubbing is done as a separate activity on paper and then cut and glued to the card. You can use either assorted fabric scraps or crumpled tissue for the flowers.

instructions recommend.

Developing language

It is important during all these experiences that you encourage children to express and describe their feelings. You may be able to add a whole list of words which do not appear in the dictionary!

As children develop their language concerning the textures they feel there are many activities in which they can be involved either individually or as groups.

Make a large feely bag. Show the children five or six objects of different textures - a fir cone, a pebble, piece of playdough, and so on. Let them feel them first and then put them in the bag. Can they pick out named objects without looking at them? If one child holds one of the objects and describes what it feels like, can the others guess what it is?

You can make a large Humpty Dumpty collage using different texture materials for the bricks on the wall. Feel each brick and describe how it feels. You can develop this by making texture flash cards. Let each child choose a card. Tell them what the word says. If you place either Velcro or double-sided adhesive tape on the back they can place it on the brick which best matches the description.

Use glue to write letters or names on card, sprinkle with dry sand and allow to dry. Can the children identify by touch only? This can lead on to talking about people who cannot see. How do they read?

fold to the front.

Make a greetings ca

Combine materials of diffe textures to make a card which is both simple and effective. It combines rubbing and collage.

Make feely books. Collect pieces of bubble wrap, corrugated card and velvet and stick one to each page. How many different words can they think of to describe the texture on each page? You can also use textures for sorting activities or shape identifying - the circle is rough, the triangle soft.

Creative collages

Collage allows children to be creative with materials of different textures - it also encourages the use of scissors and the development of hand control. Use a good adhesive. There is nothing worse than completing a work of art only to find that when the glue dries out it hasn't been strong enough to stick. Use sand, sawdust, woodshavings, broken egg-shells as well as material scraps. You can dye sand or pasta shapes to give both colour and texture. Cook the pasta in water, add food colouring and then allow to dry or soak the sand in food colouring and water. Store both materials in jars for future use.

Textured materials can also be used for rubbings. Practise using the side of wax crayons to create rubbings on a variety of objects - shopping baskets, tree bark, brick-work. Which textures give the best results?

Lesley Button

Creative Development

Autumn is a time for all the senses and Rhona Whiteford's seasonal art work is in the context of the whole seasonal experience. All great art is based on personal experience and emotion!

Inspirations for **autumn**

There's something exciting about that first chill in the air that heralds autumn. The season of mists and mellow fruitfulness comes with leaves to kick or crumble in your hands, new musty smells, and the sound of leaves rustling as they're blown across the pavement.

I like to do this activity as a record of autumn experiences, then the conversation round the art table is so much more meaningful. To make autumn lollipops, you need to go out with the children and collect leaves, dry grasses, nuts and seeds, roots and twigs.

Using all the senses

Go outdoors and actually feel autumn with the children! You could take a walk round the woods, the park or simply round the block. Most importantly, help them identify their experiences using all the senses. Listen to the sound of leaves, the bird song and the wind. Children with hearing impairment may enjoy feeling the scamper of blown leaves across the hand or the creak of a tree's movement through its trunk. Smell the damp leaves, the mud and late flowers like chrysanthemum.

Look all around at the trees, the movement of clouds, the colour of the sky, the soil or at a tiny insect scurrying down a crack in the path. Feel those crisp, dry leaves and the supple slippery evergreens and encourage the children to spot the differences. Look for varieties of shape or form (but watch out for thorns). The big 'no, no' when outdoors is taste, as many fruits and fungi are

dangerous. However, you can always bring in autumn fruits such as apples, blackberries, pomegranates or plums to taste on another day back at base.

Temperature is a meaningful experience so discuss the clothes the children have on and the reasons why they may be warm or waterproof. Help them remember what type of clothes they wore when the weather was hot. This helps develop a sense of time as the previous autumn may not be part of their memory.

What is the point?

Apart from enjoyment and adventure 'experience walks' are great opportunities to broaden language, not only enlarging vocabulary but also the social aspect of developing conversation with other children and non-family adults. It builds confidence, gives more experience of appropriate group

behaviour and broadens the mind if handled well.

It's a great chance to develop observational skills in a new environment, but many young children need to have things at distance pointed out to them. Look for the top of a tree, the roof of a tall building, the clouds (but never the sun, which can damage eyes). Stand under the biggest tree you can and look up its trunk into the canopy. What colour are the leaves now? Peer very closely at the bark near your face. Ask the children to try and describe what they can see and help identify it for them. 'This is the tree trunk and its skin is bark.' Being quietly enthusiastic yourself helps their attention and listening skills too.

You can show them textures, shapes, colours, different sizes and forms of trees, plants and leaves and use the appropriate vocabulary, like 'huge', 'tiny', 'rough', 'smooth'. I always aim to guide each child to one special discovery. Joseph may 'find' a huge tree with crumbly bark, Laura may 'find' a red leaf, and so on. Help the children recall these finds back at base. To add to mathematical experience look at shape and size and count some of the things you collect. You can begin to sort and classify, finding thin leaves or smooth seeds. You'll need to collect things for your lollipops so take a plastic bag and encourage environmentally friendly collection of things which are no longer growing,

Ask the children what they feel. Do they like what they see? What is their favourite thing? Later when you get back, ask again. What did they dislike? Don't be afraid to express your own feelings, but as the guiding adult make it clear this is your opinion and it's alright for the children to have a different one.

How to make the lollipop

Make one of these yourself to show the children and so you can plan practicalities.

You'll need 30cm circles of card or stiff paper in bright autumn colours, sheets of similarly coloured activity paper about A3 size, PVA glue or Copydex, white paper on which to write children's names, felt pens.

Prepare more circles than you need so that children can choose. Stick a strip of white paper on the back for the name and keep a felt pen in your pocket so that you can write the name as the child selects the circle. Let those who can (or want to try to) write their own name.

Now is the time to take that trip down memory lane and talk about the walk and see what they can remember. Show them what they are going to make then let them handle the finds which you can put in a wide, flat tray. Put them on the paper to see what they look like. Show the children how to make a face or a simple figure with the leaves or just a pleasing pattern. Some may come up with their own ideas like a single big leaf to represent a tree, a cloud or simply lots of leaves on the ground. There's no telling what has left an impression and the arrangement doesn't have to represent something they saw as many will be happy to explore the moment and will be satisfied with several strands of old roots just because they like them.

Try to restrict the amount of finds each one uses so that the paper is not overloaded or

too full for the child to remember the layout, then bring on the glue! You will need a spreader or brush for each child and I like two to share a pot effectively. Try to keep their arrangement as it is and show them how to lift up one item at a time to put a blob of glue in the place and then replace the item in position. In the case of narrow things, gently drop them onto the glue and try to avoid patting them down with inevitable stickiness. Now let them dry thoroughly on a flat surface before adding the handle, which is best done by an adult, but do let them watch and help. For groups who only have a short session and need things to dry quickly, try to afford Copydex but do use it under strict supervision as it can spoil clothes.

When dry, turn over to fix the handle on the reverse. Roll up the A3 paper, as shown, and secure the end with glue or sticky tape then cut across each end to neaten it off. Using two or three more strips of sticky tape, fix the handle as shown and let all the lollipops walk home with their new owners, who will hopefully be a little more wise about autumn.

Rhona Whiteford

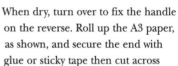

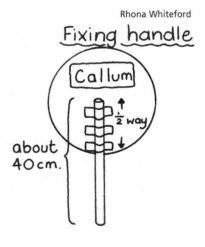

Fixing handle

Callum

½ way

about 40cm.

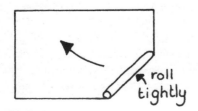

roll tightly

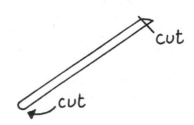

cut

cut

A familiar smell can bring back memories in a flash. Although most of us use our sense of smell instinctively it can be helpful for children if their skills are developed at an early age

Refining the sense of smell

When I tell parents that we have been doing exercises to develop their children's sense of smell they look rather surprised. 'But they can already smell, you don't need to teach it' they say. For the majority of children this is true, but their sense of smell is unrefined and when you ask a child 'What does a flower smell like?' they are more likely to say nice than very sweet.

The exercises described here are designed to refine the sense of sm but they also introduce children t some personal and social skills - learning how to use a tissue to bl their nose, and thinking of smells which make them feel happy or s: They form part of the whole Montesso. education programme and would be used over a period of two to three weeks, sometimes even longer. They can be adapted to any setting by including them in bo summer activities. The ideas could also be used on your inte table and changed on a weekly fortnightly basis.

The exercises progress from usin basic introductory scents to thos that the children have to think about. In the first exercise (Introducing smells), you are just trying to widen the child's vocabulary. In the second exercise (Match the herbs), you want the children to match pairs of smells and then later even grade them according to strength or aroma. They still have something (ie, the herbs) to match up by sight. Exercise three (Guessing game) is more abstract - the skill is down to discerning the smell.

A good introduction to these activities is to help the child to define the tastes of sweet, salty, bitter and sour. This is easily accomplished. Give each child a teaspoon. Have ready prepared in dropper bottles

samples of sugar syrup, brine, lemon and vinegar solution. Place one drop of a solution onto the child's teaspoon, let the child have a taste and then help them describe the taste. Does it taste like dinner? Does it taste like pudding or sweets? Is the taste sweet, salty or sour? The vocabulary used can then be extended to the sense of smell. Does a

flower smell salty? No. Does a flower smell sweet? Yes. Provide a piece of kitchen towel for the children to wipe their spoon between tasting. You may also need to have a jug of water and glasses at the ready just in case a child really does not like the taste, and if they wish to clear their mouth before each taste.

The simple vocabulary such as sweet, salty or sour introduces smelling words such as sweet and flowery, or lemony and fresh, or salty or savoury like dinner. Talk about words that they associate with smell. Children often have quite interesting words and one can

easily steer the more 'earthy' children away from the lavatorial descriptions!

For children who are at a stage where written words are beginning to have meaning word cards can be written to match up with particular pictures which represent smells. A picture of a flower garden could perhaps have word cards saying 'grassy', 'flowery', 'sweet' or 'happy'. Similarly a picture of a bar of soap might prompt word cards such as 'flowery', 'sweet', warm', 'bath-time' or 'soft'.

Once the child can use simple nd appropriate vocabulary in elation to taste and smell the ess of refining these senses can egin.

Introducing smells

Make a collection of clear soaps, lavender sachets, pot pourri, scented wers and growing herbs with romatic leaves. Talk about the different smells and where the children might nd these things. It's a good opportunity k about the smell of rain or the aroma newly cut grass. Talk about more familiar smells such as favourite foods or bath-time smells. This activity could be themed, such as food smells, or even sub-divided into fruit or vegetable smells.

> **Caution:** There are dangers associated with 'sniffing' certain substances so you must always emphasise that this is something which is NEVER to be done without an adult present or without an adult's permission. It would also be wise to check with parents about any allergies which children may have as some children may react to certain smells.

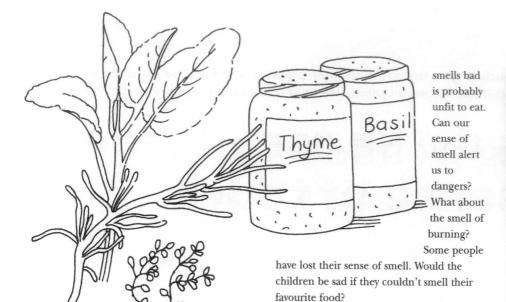

Match the herbs

Collect two identical sets of herbs and spices in jars (the ones with the plastic guards on top are the best). Encourage the child to blow their nose gently before starting (good social skill!). See if they can match up the pairs of herbs and spices by scent alone. Start with two sets of distinctive smells (mint and rosemary) and then increase the number of pairs as children become more skilful. Encourage them to describe the smell to aid their matching skill.

Guessing game

Collect small sterile jars (herb jars are ideal) and put into each a pad of cotton wool which has been soaked in a different liquid such as coffee, lemon, vinegar, perfume and almond essence. Be careful what you use and remember that some children may have an allergic reaction. Encourage them to describe the smell at first, and then see if they can guess what it is. This could be themed, such as indoor and outdoor smells, or food smells.

Note: You could use a blindfold with the later exercises, but be careful as some children find a blindfold too frightening or challenging. For others, however, it adds to the fun.

The importance of smell

Once the children are more aware of their sense of smell, you might talk about the importance of smell. If something smells unpleasant we don't want to eat it. Food that smells bad is probably unfit to eat. Can our sense of smell alert us to dangers? What about the smell of burning? Some people have lost their sense of smell. Would the children be sad if they couldn't smell their favourite food?

Take it further

You can try and develop your work with smells further. In music and drama encourage the children to 'be' smells. Get them to think about how they think a sweet smell would move. What about a bad smell? What is a bad smell like? Is it a bad egg or a smelly drain? Would they need to hold their nose? What about a nice smell? How would they sniff it?

All these activities aid the refinement of the sense of smell and increase the child's vocabulary. This of course leads to further enrichment in their lives as they begin to be aware of and to appreciate the smells around them.

Sarah Brooke-Taylor and Lynne Cashmore

All children use their sense of touch to give them information, pleasure and fun. The activities suggested here will not only help them do this, but will also help to make hands more controlled and skilful, says Keeva Austin

Developing a child's
sense of touch

Fingers are like feelers giving a child information which they learn to interpret through experience. Through their fingers and hands children begin to learn important concepts - they learn the difference between hot/cold, heavy/light, big/little, hard/soft, rough/smooth and the same/different.

Developing an awareness of texture encourages fingers and hands to become more sensitive, making manipulative skills (for example, feeding, dressing, pencil control) and physical skills, in particular the ability to hold and use tools, much easier.

For many three- and four-year-olds hand functioning will have developed enough to allow them to attempt the majority of activities we offer. What we are aiming to do is refine their sense of touch by giving them the opportunities to practise continually and improve the quality of their tactile skills, allowing them to handle appropriate tools,

objects, construction and malleable materials safely and with increased control.

Children need to go through the stage of tactile exploration before progressing to more formal fine motor skills, including writing and drawing. The activities suggested here progress from allowing the children time for free exploration through to more challenging experiences.

They can be used as part of a topic on the senses or as part of a short-term planning programme fulfilling Early Learning Goals in Physical Development.

A good introduction to these activities is to read the poem 'This is the Hand . . .' by Michael Rosen (from *A Very First Poetry Book* - Open University Press). This will encourage the children to think of all the different ways we use our sense of touch. Ask the children to draw one example and make into a group book entitled 'Touch'.

Then use a feely box to introduce a selection of textures. Place a selection of objects with different textures in the box, invite the children to be blindfolded and ask them to remove one object. Can they describe its texture? Its shape? This is a good activity to encourage not only the sense of touch but sight and descriptive language too. Turn the activity round and make it more difficult by asking the children to find a 'soft' texture or a 'rough' texture.

Invite the children to bring in other textures from home and display them on the interest table.

Once the children have been introduced to their sense of touch the process of refining it can begin.

Introducing tactile exploration (some ideas for messy play!)

Messy activities develop tactile exploration. These activities will also encourage the children's knowledge and understanding of the world by enabling them to make new discoveries, stimulate their curiosity, and give them the opportunity to learn about the properties of the materials provided. The sheer sensual enjoyment of messy play is something few children will resist. These activities should be offered purely for free exploration.

❑ **Salt drawings/finger painting**
Salt drawings are a good introduction to finger-painting and encourage the same large finger movements but with less mess. Use a tray and pour the salt into the tray. Once the children have used their hands to explore, fine funnels and containers can be introduced

Finger painting can be made using a choice of recipe.

Recipe 1 - Make wallpaper glue according to its instructions. Add dry powder paint and mix well.

Recipe 2 - Using equal quantities of flour and powder paint, mix well before adding water a little at a time until the mixture is smooth and thick.

Pour either recipe into a used washing-up liquid bottle for storage. The children can then squirt out the amount required on to a clean surface and make patterns of their choice. At a later stage laying a piece of paper over their patterns and carefully peeling back can make prints. Alternatively, try adding sand to the initial recipe to create a different texture

❑ Flour-paste paintings

This activity provides the children with a more fluid finger movement. It can be very messy! Give the children each a small amount of flour; gradually allow them to add water to it a little at a time, perhaps by using a watering can. Using their hands they mix the flour and water together until they reach the right consistency. Coloured paint can be added to the mixture if required.

❑ Cornflour slime

This is the perfect medium for drawing early writing shapes and squiggles. It also allows the child to push their fingers/hands around, creating a track, which will stay before flowing back into liquid form. Provide the children with some cornflour and slowly add water, encouraging the children to mix the two using their hands.

❑ Dry pulses, pasta and grains

Fill a dry tray with an assortment of pulses (not red kidney beans which are poisonous before cooking). Add a selection of funnels, containers and scoops and let the children play! Try using only lentils which pour just like water.

Extending sand play

The first response to sand is a sensuous one, with children taking pleasure in the tactile experience. However, it also allows children to create and destroy in a safe and acceptable way.

Sand reacts differently when dry, damp or saturated with water and children need the opportunity to explore all three states. Initial free play should focus on encouraging hand exploration, touching, patting, holding, pouring and pushing the sand. If damp, the children can mould it as they wish, filling up containers or smoothing it down. As practitioners we can then extend the child's exploration by organising the equipment.

Have the equipment clearly separated and labelled. Allow only one selection at a time to avoid the sand tray becoming over full. Here are some ideas:

Pouring items: Squeezy bottles, sand wheels, teapots, watering cans, sieves, flour shakers, colanders, flower pots.
Once they have fully explored the items extend their experiences. Compare the use of dry/wet sand - which is the best for pouring and why? Does pouring in more sand make the sand wheel spin faster or slower? Pour sand onto a metal tray and move it around - how does it move? Encourage the children to make paper cones. Can they vary the amount of sand being poured through by altering the size of the hole in the cone?

❑ Comparing sizes (Collection of spoons, spades, scoops, cooking utensils and selection of containers).

Let the children experiment to see which scoop makes the largest hole in the sand. How many scoops to fill a bucket? Does the number alter depending on which scoop is used? Encourage them to work out which container holds the most sand. Do they know which is the smallest/largest scoop? How do they know?

❑ Making patterns (Sand combs, rakes, sticks, fir cones, potato mashers, chopsticks, Lego bricks).

Once the children have made their own patterns, ask them to choose two utensils and create an alternating pattern. Later, transfer the pattern to paper. Using only chopsticks or lolly sticks, encourage them to create early writing patterns, horizontal/vertical lines and circles, drawing a man, drawing crosses.

Exploring textures

These activities are designed to encourage the children to discriminate between textures and to start using appropriate language associated with textures. They require a little more planning and preparation than some of the earlier ideas.

❑ Sorting by texture

Give the children a wider selection of textured materials including natural materials (shells, pebbles, fir cones, and leaves) and ask them to sort the materials into sets according to how they feel (soft, rough, smooth). Encourage them to explain why certain materials are in certain sets.
Encourage them to use the materials to design their own 'feely' badge.

Extend the activity further and ask them to choose just two textures and make a 'feely' caterpillar by alternating the two textures and thereby recognising and recreating patterns.

❑ Feely bingo/dominoes

This is played like ordinary bingo or lotto, but instead of pictures being used the cards have different textures. Use textures such as sandpaper, lino tiles, buttons, feathers and pasta shapes. Begin by letting

the children use their vision to complete each puzzle; at a later stage invite the children to be blindfolded and try and complete it using only their sense of touch.
For the more able child encourage them to make their own bingo boards.
Alternatively, use tactile dominoes. Begin with quite large dominoes where the children use their whole hand to feel before making much smaller dominoes where the children can only use their fingertips to explore the textures.

Taking it further

There are few play activities which do not involve hand function of some kind, and so ideas to take this topic further are endless! They may include making a word bank of 'feely' words, which can be displayed alongside the textured materials brought from home.

Perhaps textured books can be made in small groups. Each group is given a texture, for example 'rough', and the children have to find or draw objects which are rough.

Why not take the children on a walk to see some of the textures found in the natural environment?

Move the project on and do a survey on the clothes the children are wearing and the materials they are made from. Are certain clothes always made from certain textures?

Keeva Austin

If you've never had to cater for visually impaired children in your setting and are unsure how you would cope, you'll find this background information useful. Keeva Austin answers some commonly asked questions

Meeting the needs of the **visually impaired** child

The Code of Practice on the identification and assessment of special educational needs came into effect on 1 September 1994. It was issued in response to the 1993 Education Act. The code includes the principle that, wherever possible (and subject to parental views) children with special educational needs should be educated in mainstream schools. This includes the education of the under-fives and so we can expect to see visually impaired children in our early years settings.

What do we mean by visual impairment?

Visual impairment (VI) refers to those children who have difficulties in seeing which call for the use of special educational methods and adaptations to materials and who need to use specialist aids and equipment for learning. (For example, the use of low vision aids - magnifying glasses, CCTV, large print and Braille.) The term covers those children who are blind or partially sighted - but not children who wear glasses. For common eye conditions such as myopia (short-sightedness), hypermetropia (long-sightedness) or astigmatism (where the eye focuses unevenly and objects are seen as blurred and distorted) then a child's vision will be corrected through wearing glasses.

Children with a VI, though, are not a heterogenous group. The children will have a range of personalities, interests and abilities as well as a range of types and degree of VI, from relatively slight loss through more severe degrees of loss to total blindness. For example, a child may experience one or more of the following:

❑ Have only light perception
❑ Have a blurred view of the world
❑ Have only central vision and no peripheral vision (tunnel vision)

❑ No central vision and therefore difficulty with colour and fine detail
❑ Pain and distress caused by bright lights

Approximately 1 in 2,000 children is visually impaired. Yet children with total blindness form less than 20 per cent of the total population of children with a VI. The other 80 per cent may be registered blind but will have some useful vision. While this remaining vision may not always be very helpful to an elderly person, it has enormous significance for children who may benefit from training in interpreting the incomplete or imperfect images they see. Whatever the level of VI the child should *always* be encouraged to use their vision. Little vision does not deteriorate with use.

Specialist advisors or peripatetic teachers will support most VI children who are educated in our early years settings alongside their sighted peers. It will be the responsibility of this teacher to ensure the staff feel confident in working with the child by providing practical support and advice. Parents, too, should be involved in the education of their child and can offer valuable advice on the child's specific VI, the level of their sight, what tasks present difficulties and the possible implications for learning

Symptoms to look out for

Many of you will not have a child with a VI in your setting at the moment. However, in the course of your work you may be concerned about a particular child. What then are the possible symptoms of a VI, which may require further assessment? The list below is not exhaustive and a child may not display all the symptoms. Similarly, a child may have some of the symptoms but investigations

show that they are not caused by a VI. If in doubt, observe the child over a period of time and doing a variety

of tasks. Discussion with the parents should then be the first step before contacting the local education authority's advisory service for VI.

Head position
❑ Child moves head rather than eyes when concentrating on visual tasks
❑ Frequent nodding of head when concentrating on visual tasks
❑ Head tilts in what appears to be an uncomfortable position

Eye position
❑ Frowning or squinting when looking at pictures/books
❑ Aversion to bright lights
❑ Eyelids are drooping or swollen
❑ Unusual eye movements, including a rapid involuntary movement (nystagmus)

- Excessive blinking/rubbing of eyes
- Crossed eyes
- Closing or covering one eye when playing or working

Movement
- When walking, displays an unusual, very short or very long length of stride
- Poor posture
- Clumsy movements, particularly prone to bumping into objects at side or at feet
- Fear of heights
- Poor balance

Behaviour
- Not answering questions unless asked by name
- Short attention span in visual tasks
- Fumbling over fine hand-eye co-ordination tasks
- Reluctance to join in outdoor activities

Effects of a VI on development
During infancy the sighted child accomplishes vast progress. They move from being egocentric to interacting sociably with peers and adults. Their language moves from babble to well constructed sentences. Their motor development moves from them having little control to that of a two-year-old who has relatively good gross motor control and is developing fine motor control. A sighted physically able child in the first few years of life seems to learn without effort - vision plays a vital role, providing a continuous, rich, consistent, precise and reliable source of information to help the child orientate to and identify objects and people.

A visual impairment imposes many restrictions on a child's ability to learn since the majority of our learning is visually based. The effects of a VI may be seen in three ways:

1. Experiences will be limited in range and variety - a child who does not see or sees incompletely will have a reduced ability to learn by imitation; a child who doesn't observe an activity won't attempt it for himself.

2. Movement may be curtailed - if there is an inability to see their surroundings, the child will be less motivated to reach out or crawl. For security the child may tend to stay in one place, thereby restricting their range of movements.

3. Control of their environment and self in relation to the environment is restricted. There may be a delay in bonding between mother and child due to a lack of eye contact and whereas a sighted child may smile in order to be picked up and cuddled this is lacking in a VI child. Understanding body awareness and knowing where they are in space is also hindered.

A child's play requirements will depend very much on their level of vision and visual defect. Unlike a sighted child who can use their eyes to observe their environment, a VI child will need the environment to come to them. It isn't true that the VI child will have better hearing or tactile skills and so staff must help them use these senses and make sense of a bewildering world.

How you can support the child
The five points listed here are not exhaustive but provide a useful starting point for appropriately meeting the child's needs

within the early years environment. The benefits of such a framework should in fact meet the needs of all children and not just the VI child, helping them all to make the transition between home and pre-school, between the familiar to the unfamiliar and between dependence to independence.

Partnership with parents
Going to nursery, a childminder, or pre-school may be the first time the child has left the familiarity of home for any length of time without their parents. You must recognise that parents know their child better than you do. The visual functioning of many VI children may vary during the day and according to their general health - it is very demanding to use impaired vision. Therefore ask the parents:

- About visual impairment.

- What is their level of sight?

- When does the child become tired?

- What tasks do they enjoy/find difficult?

- Do they wear glasses - if yes, do they also have a tinted pair?

Explain your routine carefully to parents and expect them to ask you questions. They will need this information to prepare their child.

The learning environment
Visual environment:
The lighting and decor within the setting can both hinder or help learning. Lighting does not mean bright lights - some eye conditions require lower than normal

lighting levels. Blinds/curtains may be needed to prevent hard shadow and glare. Think about the child's seating position at circle time. Do not sit/stand in front of a window - the light may cause discomfort for the child and your facial expressions will be lost.

Consider contrast between floors-walls-skirting boards, between doors and door handles (perhaps paint handles black so they are easily located). Display boards should be bright and clear and used to break up large expanses of wall. The use of colour and contrast may also enhance safety - place a dark rug on a light carpet to alert the child to the location of a piece of furniture. Provide contrasting table mats and cups to reduce spillage.

Sound environment:
All VI children will need to use information from what they hear rather more than sighted children. The sound environment should provide information to help a child understand what is happening around them and to help with orientation. Special sound clues could be introduced:

❑ Chime bells on the door so a child knows when someone is coming in/out.

❑ A whistle to signify tidy-up time.

❑ Goodbye song at the end of the nursery session.

As a VI child does not automatically hear better they will need to be encouraged to listen (for example, through turn taking games/sound lotto games).

Tactile environment:
The layout and organisation of the room is important. It needs to be familiar to the VI child. More than one visit prior to starting will be necessary. Actively introduce the child to the environment, telling them where they are by using landmarks. For example, talk about the rough mat by the door, the change

in surface from concrete to grass when you are nearing the slide. Spend these visits, too, observing the child to see how they cope in differing situations and to observe their exploratory techniques. Remember, a sighted child can continually gaze around and will gradually absorb his new surroundings, the VI child can't.

Once the child has joined you, don't initially expect too much from them. If they are reluctant to move around then provide a

'safe corner', where they are allowed the time to explore and discover just a small space. Once they are more confident they can be encouraged to explore the wider environment.

The early years setting should be organised into defined areas: creative corner, building area and so on. Materials relating to each area should be clearly labelled and the VI child should be given plenty of opportunity to explore and handle the objects. Keep the layout the same so they can build up a visual memory of the room and develop independence.

Presentation of tasks
This is a key issue for all children. When introducing new activities/tasks always start by using established routines and then do

something new. The child must be actively introduced to environment information, for example:

❑ Activity areas - does the child know where they are?

❑ Circle time - has the child been sat in the best place to maximise visual input? Have they been shown how to do the action/finger rhymes?

❑ Art activities wherever possible have a finished product so they know what is expected.

❑ Snack-time - have you explained where the biscuits are kept and the milk is poured from a jug?

For close work (jigsaws, writing, threading) there should be a clear visual or physical edge to the work area so the child can easily locate the things they are using.

Where possible, toys/resources should be bold, bright and contrasting (remember - BBC). For totally blind children sound provides the only motivation to reach out and explore so sound making toys or ones with movable parts are essential. Toys may need to be anchored within easy reach until the child has learned to search for and find them. Encourage all VI children to use both their hands, telling them what they are touching and how toys work. In this way they will begin to understand what objects are, what they do and what they feel like.

Experiences
Children with a VI need access to first-hand experiences wherever possible. Best (1992 p74) says:

'They should not have to rely solely on descriptions given by other people of situations they cannot see clearly. These descriptions will not be as full or meaningful as first-hand experiences, will place additional demands on the child's memory . . . and may remove some of the active involvement in learning through experiences'.

Only later in life will the VI child be able to connect the miniatures in their mind with their full-size counterparts and so it is important that they handle and talk about as many manageable real things as possible. For example:

speak, they are able to communicate using a number of ways. They acknowledge our presence, express preferences with a smile or a frown and understand our displeasure when we frown or can interpret our blank stares when we don't understand what they are trying to say! These non-verbal signals are completely/partly absent with a VI child who is dependent on verbal communication and physical contact. Staff will need to adopt the following strategies:

❑ Provide a running commentary on the world (but don't talk non-stop!)

A sighted physically able child in the first few years of life seems to learn without effort - vision plays a vital role, providing a continuous, rich, consistent, precise and reliable source of information to help the child orientate to and identify objects and people.

A visual impairment imposes many restrictions on a child's ability to learn since the majority of our learning is visually based.

❑ Before setting up a laundry in the home corner, visit a real laundry.

❑ Initially use real cups and saucers in the home corner alongside the play ones to help with association.

❑ Use a variety of natural objects wherever possible.

❑ Good quality photographs are better than cartoon pictures and do not distort a child's perception of objects.

❑ Think about nursery songs - does the child know what a pail is? ('Jack and Jill') Or what a spout is? ('Incy Wincy Spider').

Communication

Language is an important means for getting acquainted and sharing experiences with any child. Before the sighted child begins to

Identify objects, describe movement, for example 'I'm lifting you into the air'.

❑ Use relevant situational language: 'We're going into the kitchen to get the drinks tray'. In this way the child will begin to connect experiences with the words that describe them.

❑ At the start of new activities explain what is happening - don't assume the child will have picked up on visual clues.

❑ Always start a sentence with the child's name so the child knows you are talking to them.

❑ Always tell the child when you are approaching/leaving.

Keeva Austin

Meeting the needs of the visually impaired child

Do you know what is meant by nerve deafness? Is glue ear a type of deafness and how common is it? Find out about the various kinds of hearing impairment, the treatment that might be offered and the support available for deaf children and their parents

Helping children **who are deaf**

Thousands of children in the UK are either hard of hearing, partially deaf or have a severe or profound hearing loss. Temporary deafness, as can be caused by glue ear, can affect 80 per cent of children during some stage in their childhood. So it is helpful for staff in early years settings to have some knowledge of the various kinds of hearing impairment and how staff might be able to support deaf children and their parents.

There are three different types of deafness:
❏ **Conductive deafness** is the most common. Basically it means that sounds cannot pass through the middle ear to the cochlea and auditory nerve. This is often caused by blockages such as wax in the ear canal or fluid in the middle ear.

❏ **Sensori-neural deafness**, or nerve deafness as it is sometimes called, usually means that the cochlea is not processing the sound effectively. Often the cause of sensori-neural deafness is not known. Deafness can be caused by an infectious disease such as

rubella, mumps, measles, or meningitis. A child may be deaf because of a shortage of oxygen in the bloodstream at birth or some other birth trauma. It is also known that premature babies are more at risk of having a hearing loss.

❏ **Mixed deafness** is where a child has both types of deafness, in other words, a mixture of conductive and nerve deafness.

What is glue ear?

Glue ear is one of the most common childhood illnesses, affecting four in five of children at some time during their childhood. It is a build-up of mucus or fluid within the middle ear, often associated with colds and coughs. In adults and older children any fluid produced by the cells lining the middle ear usually drains away through the Eustachian tube, which runs from the middle ear to the back of the throat. This tube is not fully formed in young children and may not work very well.

Temporary hearing loss

Ear infections are common in young children. Glue ear can be present with an ear infection, but not always. Reduced hearing can make understanding conversation difficult and can lead to a change in a child's behaviour as they become frustrated and less responsive, preferring to play alone.

Difficulty in hearing can cause a delay in a child's speech development. A child with this type of temporary hearing loss would still be able to hear many sounds and would generally be aware of sounds around the home. However, speech is made up of sounds with different pitches and different loudness levels that can become difficult to hear with background noise. Young children at an early stage in their language development, if affected by a hearing loss, will have difficulty hearing all the different speech sounds and this will affect their understanding of speech and the way they speak.

Treatment for glue ear

Many children may have a bout of glue ear following a cold, which can clear without any treatment. For some children a minor operation may be needed to drain the fluid from the middle ear. It involves inserting a ventilation tube called a grommet. This is a common treatment for glue ear and improves the hearing whilst the grommet is in place.

Grommets generally remain in place for six to nine months before falling out of the ear-drum into the ear canal and eventually out of the ear. The ear-drum pushes the grommet out as it seals the hole created. It is an effective treatment for many children, but does not prevent the fluid from being produced in the ear. For some children the fluid continues to be produced in the middle ear and as a result they may go on to have two, three, or more sets of grommets.

Advice for parents

Parents concerned about their child's hearing should contact their GP and/or health visitor and ask for a hearing assessment. The GP can examine the child for any signs of glue ear. Some health centres can provide a hearing assessment. The GP may prescribe

---

The ear
We need our ears for two things: hearing and balance.

Hearing involves the ear, part of the nervous system and part of the brain. All three elements must work together for you to be able to receive sound and convert it into messages for the brain to understand.

As sound waves travel through the ear they pass through the ear canal and are amplified by the middle ear so the sound continues into the inner ear. The inner ear consists of the cochlea, which is a snail shaped structure, and the auditory nerve which transmits electrical signals to the brain.

Balance involves the inner ear. There are three tubes filled with fluid (semi-circular canals) which work like spirit levels sending messages to the brain when we lean over or move around.

antibiotics if there is evidence of infection. If the condition does not improve parents can request a referral to the Ear, Nose and Throat (ENT) clinic at their local hospital.

Hearing aids
There are many different types of hearing aids, some of which can transmit sounds to the ear in different ways. All hearing aids have a common purpose - to amplify sound. They come in various shapes and types and may be worn on the body, behind the ear or in the ear. Some hearing aids, such as cochlear implants, have parts that are surgically implanted into the ear.

Communication and language
Deaf children need to develop fluent language skills at a rate relevant to their age in order to achieve their potential and understand and influence the world around them.

Language acquisition is a complex process. Successful language development depends heavily, almost critically, on the additional factors of early diagnosis; the fitting of suitable hearing aids; commitment from the family, and access to information, advice and support.

British sign language (BSL) is a visual language using gestures of hands and the rest of the body including the face. It is an independent language with structure and grammar different from that of spoken language. It can be used in education as part of a bilingual approach whereby a child learns two languages, BSL and English.

Total communication is the use of hearing aids and oral language in addition to sign language.

Routine health service checks for children

❑ Hearing screening tests are carried out for most babies at seven to eight months old by health visitors.

❑ Developmental checks which may also include a hearing assessment are done at two and three years old .

❑ Hearing tests are performed for most children on entry to the first year at infants school and when they reach the first year of junior school.

Teachers of the deaf
Very soon after a child has been diagnosed with a permanent hearing loss, the family are contacted by a peripatetic teacher, sometimes called a teacher of the deaf or hearing impaired. Their role will be to support a child's development of language and communication skills with the use of hearing aids. If it is appropriate, they will support a child within a mainstream setting. (If parents want advice on choosing the right educational setting for their child, the National Deaf Children's Society has regional representatives and education advisers who can help.)

The pre-school period is a critical time for the acquisition of language. There is a constant need for repetition of speech sounds to all babies and young children, to give them adequate experience of speech and the ability to associate speech with meaning.

What can you do to help?
❑ Try to get a child's attention before you start speaking, and make sure they can see your face clearly to make lip-reading easier.

❑ Speak clearly without shouting or exaggerating your lip pattern as this appears unnatural and makes speech more difficult to understand. Also it can appear to a child that you are angry, and for some deaf children the increased volume of sound can be painful.

❑ Check background noise is kept to a minimum. This is important with hearing aid users as they find it difficult to cut out background noise. If the noise is too great they will have to rely solely on lip-reading, gestures and body language.

❑ When communicating with a deaf child make sure they can see you. A deaf child needs to be able to see your face to understand and participate in conversation. Children with even a mild hearing loss will not hear all of what you are saying and will need to be able to see your face clearly so they can lip-read.

❑ In large group sessions it can help if a child is seated nearer to the adult to make listening easier for them. This is also important for children who are using hearing aids.

❑ Make sure that your face is covered as little as possible and that you don't sit or stand with your back facing light coming through a window as this will create a shadow.

Technology in the classroom
Equipment such as 'sound field technology', which includes a microphone headset for teachers and several loudspeakers set around the classroom or hall, has proved to be a good way of improving acoustic conditions in this environment for all children.

Radio aids are used to help make listening in the classroom easier for children using hearing aids. The teacher's voice is transferred by a microphone and transmitter and picked up by a child's radio aid system. A child using a radio aid can still hear sounds and voices in the classroom, but the teacher's voice is much clearer.

The National Deaf Children's Society loans out radio aids and some environmental aids for up to three months for children to try out at home. If you would like more details of this service, or any aspect of technology, please contact Richard Vaughan and Noel Gordon, NDCS Technology Service.

Annette Wellington, Health Advisor (Audiology),
The National Deaf Children's Society.

The National Deaf Children's Society exists to enable deaf children and young people to make the most of their skills and abilities.
The society has a national information and advice helpline for parents and professionals.
Helpline number: 0207 250 0123 Mon to Fri 10am to 5pm email: helpline@ndcs.org.uk
It also has publications such as *Understanding Deafness* and *Hearing Aids - A Guide*. You can contact them at: 15 Dufferin Street, London EC1Y 8UR Tel: 0207 490 8656 email: ndcs@ndcs.org.uk

Making children aware of the different textures of materials plays an important role in their learning of science. You can help them to explore materials in a fun way with simple games and experiments, as described by Gay Wilson

Exploring and investigating materials

Young children explore and work with materials all the time, in nearly everything they do. They find out that some things bend and some stretch, that different materials are hard, shiny, rough or smooth. Your job is to help children focus on the properties of the materials they are working or playing with and to develop their thinking and language by helping them to verbalise their ideas.

Same and different

You'll find it useful to have collections of objects and materials which fall into the following categories:

❏ rough and smooth
❏ rigid and flexible (bendy and not bendy at this stage)
❏ stretchy and not stretchy
❏ shiny and not shiny
❏ transparent and opaque (see-through and not see-through)

Get the children to compare the materials, noting their similarities and differences, and to sort objects in as many ways as they can, using all the appropriate senses. Ask them to tell you what is the same about some of the things in their set, and what is different.

Encourage the children to explore the materials using all the appropriate senses and to tell you about them. How many different ways can they sort them? At first, allow them to use their own criteria and tell you what they are. Then ask the children to sort them using the criteria above.

Always use the correct language, such as 'transparent' and 'opaque' but add a definition every time - 'that means see-through and not see-through'. It is quite acceptable for young children to say 'see-through' and 'not see-through' at this stage.

Some, of course, may remember the correct terminology at once. Others will take a long time to do so.

Make collections of objects made from common materials, both natural and made, such as plastic, wood, metal, stone, ceramic, glass, card, and so on. Ask the children:

❏ Do you know what these things are?
❏ Do you know what each one is made from?
❏ Can you sort them into sets?

Guessing games

Find out which materials disappear in water (dissolve) and which don't. Try sugar, salt, rice, marbles and gravel. You can have fun as well as learn a lot of science through this activity. Use clear plastic glasses and plastic spoons. Get the children to guess (predict) first which things will disappear and which won't.

Language development is a vital part of science learning. Put an object into a feely bag. Ask the children how many words they can think of to describe their object. Is it hard, smooth, rough, soft, squashy? Can they try and describe what is in their bag so well that their friend can guess what it is?

Sand and water

When working with materials such as sand and water, put wet sand, dry sand and water out at the same time. When the children have played with, and experienced, the materials, focus their attention on their properties. How do they behave? What does water feel like? What happens to the water wheel when you pour water on it? Can you catch water in a sieve? Is there any similarity between wet sand and dry sand? What is different? Will the wet sand turn the water wheel like the water and dry sand do? Why not? Which sand is best for making sand pies? Why?

Gay Wilson

Keeva Austin looks at how important it is to make use of made as well as natural or living materials. They are familiar resources to use with the children and with a little forethought are readily available

Making the most of made materials

Giving the children regular access to a range of materials develops their capacity for problem-solving and lateral thinking. It develops their ability to use tools (scissors, glue, pencils) appropriately. Junk play allows important practice in handling and controlling small things. Mathematical understanding begins with sorting and matching shapes and colours and comparing size and texture.

What's the difference?

Before introducing made materials to the children it is a good idea to make sure that they understand the difference between natural and made materials.

Using a selection of natural materials from your resource bank along with a selection of made materials, for example glass, tin, paper, ceramic, silver and plastic, begin in small groups to name the materials. Where do they come from? Where were they found? If a made material, how was it made and by whom?

Give the children time to explore each material and then expand their exploration and together begin to talk about the materials. You may have to help the children verbalise their thoughts - do they understand what is the difference between a living or natural material and a made material? Can they 'identify some features of living things, objects ... they observe'?

Involve parents by encouraging them to send in one natural and one made resource. Try to include a range of items and artefacts from different cultural backgrounds. Display the two sets by sorting and classifying the materials. Can the children sort them into two sets? Can they explain why certain materials are placed in a particular set? Take

photos of the sets, so the children can play a sorting game independently after this group work. Once displayed, have a selection of books relating to each set.

Design a simple sheet with two columns, one headed 'Natural materials' and the other 'Made materials'. Encourage the children to use it around the setting or to take it home and find some materials which would fit into the two sets. Can they draw and label their examples? Once completed, discuss their work in a group - does everyone agree with where they have each placed certain materials?

The scope for using made materials is endless, so I have chosen three examples to look at in detail. The activities that follow each example will encourage the children's knowledge and understanding of the world by enabling them to make new discoveries, stimulate their curiosity and give them the opportunity to learn about the properties of the materials provided.

Paper and cardboard

Paper and cardboard are a good introduction to made materials not only because they are readily available but because they are familiar to the children and easy to work with. Children should not see paper just for painting or drawing on; they need to be encouraged to talk about the types of paper and their uses. Some examples include: wallpaper, gift paper, paper money, sandpaper, toilet paper, greaseproof paper and rice paper.

These are all examples of paper but how does each one differ and why? (Think about the differences of colour, thickness, absorbency and texture.) Can the children tell you? Develop their curiosity and

experiment with the types of paper - what happens if we put toilet paper in water? Why does it do this? Which examples of paper do not disintegrate when wet and why?

Can they recognise the patterns and sequence of patterns on wallpaper or giftwrap? As a creative activity encourage them to design and print their own wallpaper.

Encourage the children to think about printed paper and make a collection showing the range of printed material - newspapers, invitations, letters, comics, books, postcards, birthday cards. What happens if the paper used to print/write on is too thin?

Looking at birthday cards or postcards is a good way of introducing cardboard. Why do they need to be thicker than the paper a letter is written on? Help the children to realise that cardboard is made up of layers of thick paper.

Children are surrounded by cardboard objects at home so encourage them to bring some examples in. Collect lots

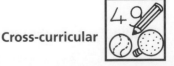

of cardboard boxes (cereal boxes and other food boxes, sweet boxes, egg boxes, toy boxes), compare their thickness and sort accordingly. Discuss what came in each box - why couldn't the box have been made of paper? Explore how boxes are able to be stored easily one on top of the other. What happens if the boxes are of irregular sizes? Once collected the boxes can be used for building with, putting things in or cut up and stuck together.

Paper and cardboard are also useful materials for introducing children to different types of adhesive. Give them the freedom to stick paper and cardboard together using paper or PVA glue. Let them use sticky tape and masking tape to join the materials together. Through experience and discussion the children will learn which kind of adhesive works best in particular situations.

Textiles

For example: lace, ribbon, velvet, cotton, hessian, viscose, plastic, knitted fabric, tweed.

Explore and discuss a range of fabrics with the children. Some are thicker and stronger, some are stretchy or have printed patterns or pictures on the fabric. Woven fabric like hessian or cotton frays. Talk about the clothes the children are wearing. Feel the items and discuss the similarities and differences. Discuss warm/cold day clothes, clothes for wet/dry days or clothes from different cultures. Why are some clothes made out of particular materials?

Experiment and explore the drying times for a selection of fabrics. Have samples the same size, wash them in water and then hang them up to dry. The children can record the results on a simple table - which fabric is the quickest to dry and which takes the longest? Can they explain why?

Metals

For example: gold, silver, iron, brass, tin, aluminium.

It may be nice but impractical to have a display of silver or gold items! You could, however, ask the children together with a parent or older sibling to make a list of all the gold/silver items they can find at home. Tin and aluminium materials are more accessible. Ask the children to bring from home a selection of food tins, foil cake cases or pie dishes and aluminium cans. Why do we keep food in tins? Sort the tins according to size or weight. Are the biggest tins the heaviest? Why not? Can they use the tins to build with (be careful they don't drop them on a toe!) The aluminium dishes can be used to make tinfoil pictures - particularly effective if black paper is used.

Take the opportunity to introduce the concept of magnetism. By providing strong magnets and a selection of materials the children can discover which items are attracted to the magnets and which are not. In this fun way they can begin to sort the objects into two sets.

Using made materials is a good way of introducing the importance of recycling. Do the children know what happens to all the paper, cartons and cans once they have been used? Discuss materials that can be saved and used again and help the children to start collecting recyclable materials. Do the children know where their local recycling bank is? How many children visit the bank with their parents? (At this point made materials can be expanded to include other examples such as glass, plastics and other discarded materials.) The children could create and build a bin in which to put their empty drinks cans.

Children are fascinated by things that work and the way they work. Don't forget that a whole range of made resources come in the form of mechanical or construction materials, for example, clocks, typewriters and radios. Given a range of equipment and appropriate adult intervention, children can begin to explore simple mechanisms. Give them the chance to dismantle some of them, such as an old radio. Continue their interest by providing Lego or Meccano - can they create their own radio?

Keeva Austin

Using objects with children can be a great way to make history come alive, but we can't just expect young children to be able to make sense of them

Old and **new**

What is old, what is new? One of the confusions that often arises when young children look at historical objects is caused by different meanings of the words old and new. Whilst we may use old to mean historical (referring to how long ago it was made and used), children may already know that the same word means broken, tatty or worn.

It is important to challenge this idea early on and clear up any confusion before you ever visit a museum for example. Lots of museums have objects that would be interesting to young children but of course many of them have been lovingly restored and look 'shiny and new'. Children visiting a museum could believe they are seeing new objects rather than understanding that these things were used in the past.

Early Learning Goals

The Early Learning Goals and even Key Stage 1 of the National Curriculum are quite vague on what young children should 'learn' in history, and rightly so. The Early Learning Goal relating to history in the Knowledge and Understanding of the World section simply says: 'find out about past and present events in their own lives and in those of their families and other people they know'.

Early years history is not about particular periods, but rather about developing a sense of time and the skills to make sense of the past. Being able to look at objects and judge whether they are modern or historical is an important historical skill and marks the beginning of being able to understand the past through artefacts.

Cleaning a copper kettle
Why not try this activity to start children thinking about the age of objects, rather than their state of wear.

You will need: a plastic jug electric kettle, a dirty copper kettle, soft cloths, copper cleaner.

If you can't get a real copper kettle, replicas were fashionable as ornaments some years ago and can often be picked up in junk shops and at car boot sales.

Begin by talking with children about the two kettles. Which is old and which is new? Ask children to tell you why they think that.

Talk about how dirty the copper kettle is looking and ask children to help you clean it. If you are using a chemical cleaner make sure you apply the chemicals and just ask children to polish to kettle with soft cloths once it has been wiped off.

Look again at the kettles. Do any children change their minds about which is the newest now that the copper kettle is gleaming?

Explain to children that there is a way that you can look at things and decide whether they were made a long time ago or not. Ask them to think about their own kettle at home. Which of the two kettles looks most like theirs? Talk with them about the shape, design (how it looks) and the materials their kettles are made of. If they can't remember, why not ask them to draw a picture of both kettles and take them home to compare to theirs. Remind them not to touch their kettle without a grown-up there as it could be hot.

If some children have metal, more rounded kettles, help them to recognise the similarities with the jug kettle like the fact that it has a plug and lead. Explain to children that things that use electricity are usually more modern than things that do the same job mechanically. This of course isn't always true, but it is a useful starting point.

History detectives

Now that they've got the idea why not give them a whole range of historical objects with their modern equivalents and get children to decide which is the modern one by looking for similarities to their own experience.

Try coins, teddies, irons (flat and steam), stamps, plastic and wooden hoops, hot water bottles (stone and rubber), clothing or anything else you can find from junk shops or borrow from parents and grandparents. Try to find things that most children will have the modern version of at home.

Try to find a local museum that has household objects in their collection. Museums that have room sets showing the objects in a context are often popular with children. Why not take children on a visit to find the historical versions of their own everyday gadgets. You could take photos of children's modern appliances for them to take to the museum and take photos at the museum of the historical objects to make a display back in your group.

The past in pictures

If you have a camera load a black and white film and help children take photos When the pictures are developed let them compare them to some black and white photos from their family collection. Try to choose photos that are in good condition so the only way children can tell the age of the photos is to look at what the picture is of. Remember

you don't need Victorian pictures. Pictures of the children's parents as children will be old enough.

Muddle up all the photos and see if the children can sort out the photos of the olden days from the modern photos.

Jo Graham

My first pet – Summer 1970

Summer holidays – August 1999

Promoting environmental awareness

Piaget (1896-1980) referred to this inquisitive stage (0-2 years) as the 'sensory-motor' stage of child development. Maria Montessori (1860-1931) observed how young children learned through their senses and how they loved to explore natural materials such as sand, water, soil and clay. She recorded how they marvelled at the changing seasons or the cycle of plant or animal life. She endorsed a 'child-centred' holistic approach. Which simply means that parents or carers should be sensitive not only to the needs of the child for food, warmth and shelter but be responsive to the needs of the whole child.

Friedrich Froebel (1782-1852) believed that young children flourish in kindergartens which provide outdoor activities that nurture the young child's exploratory drive to make sense of their environment.

Current early years practitioners such as Chris Athey, Tina Bruce, Cathy Nutbrown and Janet Moyles all advocate the importance of the child's interest and active participation if they are to successfully assimilate and accommodate learning.

Young children are greatly influenced by their parents, significant adults and other children. If we are to have a positive and successful influence while promoting environmental awareness among young children we have to provide good role models for the children to mimic.

Every parent or carer can learn to optimise every learning opportunity the young child presents, whether walking through a park or visiting a local garden centre - it may take you twice as long to reach your destination or to buy your winter pansies but think of the possible learning outcomes.

Remember that learning for the young child is exciting, spontaneous, generally ego-centric (self-centred) and that their concentration span is limited. Think how more exciting and memorable an outing to the park or garden centre would be for children if you tried to see how many different creepy crawlies (minibeasts) or leaves you could find. Or if you took a cassette recorder with you to record the birds singing or the ducks quacking.

Talking about the planet

Promoting environmental awareness among young children should be fun-filled and educational while laying down the foundations of early citizenship and responsibility for our planet. Young children love the mysteries of outer space, astronauts and stories of friendly aliens. This is a good platform from which to introduce the concepts of conservation, global warming, recycling, acid rain, deforestation, and sustainability.

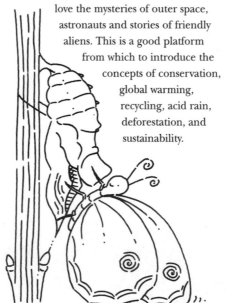

Our role is not to frighten the children with tales of gloom and despair of the Earth's dwindling natural resources but to encourage them to cultivate an appreciation of the wonder and beauty of our world while promoting the significance and importance of their contribution (even at this tender age).

Books and resources

To help children to understand the life-cycle use Eric Carle's book *The Very Hungry Caterpillar.* This not only helps children to understand metamorphosis and develop aesthetic appreciation for the beauty and magic of nature, but also incorporates values which young children may feel unable to talk about freely. They may not have the life experience or language to enable them to speak their thoughts.

Children often struggle with the conflicting notions of greed against need. They can have a problem with sharing their sweets or toys or feel insignificant, colourless, or as tiny as a caterpillar while everyone else appears to be as beautiful or popular as the colourful butterfly.

Insect Lore Europe provide butterfly kits which enable you and your child to watch the complete life-cycle, from caterpillar to butterfly.

Other books you could share with children which help promote environmental awareness are *How Green Are You?* by David Bellamy and *Why do Tigers have Stripes?* by Grolier books. These stories help highlight the plight of the whale from the effects of pollution and over fishing, and the need for clever camouflage for animals if they are to survive in the wild.

Picture and story books let children trek safely through steamy hot jungles or explore arctic regions in search of polar bears in the warmth and security of their home or early years setting.

By talking with children and using open-ended questions after you have read them appropriate stories you can enhance and broaden their understanding of environmental issues.

You could stimulate thought and encourage conversations by asking, for example, 'What do you think would happen if...?' Is it fair that some children don't have enough to eat in Africa or Peru? Or, is it right to cut down all the trees if the squirrels and monkeys have nowhere to live or hide if they get cold or frightened? You can help explain the universal need for the promotion of environmental awareness among both adults and children, and challenge any negative attitudes to their individual contribution towards a sustainable life-style.

Whatever material resource you choose to use to help promote environmental awareness there is always a golden rule - remain sensitive to the stage of development of your children. You do not want to swamp, stifle or strangle any natural line of enquiry your children may be following. Be honest in your answers and exercise what you preach. Do not be afraid to say that you don't know why penguins are birds yet they don't fly, or why tomatoes were once called love-apples.

Go to the library together and find out, or visit the zoo or local market garden.

At the supermarket

Show children the labels on selected tins of tuna in the supermarket which are dolphin friendly and explain what that means. (If you don't know, go together to a member of staff and ask.)

Recycle

Recycle your old newspapers, glass bottles, used postage stamps, and offer outgrown clothes or unwanted toys to charity shops, hospices or to missionary societies. Explain to the children how this will help other children.

By collecting and sorting aluminium and steel drinks cans you can incorporate early experiences in science by giving children a large magnet to experiment and discover which of the cans attract the magnet. (Steel

Schools programme

There is an ECO schools programme which promotes environmental awareness among children. They offer support, expertise and recognition for environmental work among children by inspecting and monitoring the group's efforts in the education of environmental issues.

When successful the group is awarded the prestigious and much sought after ECO flag which they can celebrate and proudly fly outside their setting. This shows their commitment to and promotion of environmental awareness among young children. The group needs to re-apply for the ECO award every two years and show that they are not resting on their laurels. When our pre-school playgroup obtained their ECO flag in June 1998 we were the first pre-school playgroup in Europe to achieve the ECO status. When a group has achieved their ECO flag three times they can become life members.

Contact for ECO schools is: Sue Rigby, ECO Schools Co-ordinator, Tidy Britain Group, Elizabeth House, The Pier, Wigan WN3 4EX
Web site: www.feee.org

cans attract magnets and aluminum cans don't).

Most local authorities and councils have recycling points. If you don't know where they are make a few telephone calls. If the recycling points are not convenient perhaps you could make arrangements with a group of parents, students or other settings to take turns in visiting the sites or plan a joint outing.

Responsibility

Once you embrace the promotion of environmental awareness among pre-school children your own life-style, sense of citizenship and responsibility to universal and global issues will change. You will become aware of the need to recycle, conserve energy and purchase environmentally friendly products.

Jacqueline Coulter

Anecdote

We were enjoying physical exercise with our keep-fit cassette when we came to a standstill as a group of children peered at a frightened wood louse on the floor.

We stopped the music, rescued the wood louse and found a suitable container so we could view it safely and in more detail with our magnifying glasses. We took it into the playgroup and then decided it might be hungry. We thought about what it might like to eat. The children decided it would like grass, flowers and worms. Then we got some of our reference books and the children decided that it liked to eat damp, old, rotten, smelly wood. This caused a great sense of disgust with some but fuelled the imagination of others! We agreed we'd go outside to gather some food for our wood louse. The children needed no encouragement to gather armfulls of much needed supplies for our wood louse.

I had explained that we would only gather tree bark or twigs off the ground because we didn't want to damage any of the nearby trees. However, one enthusiastic four-year-old boy asked 'Should we cut down a tree?'

Physics in the pre-school? It might sound daunting but if you have toys with wheels, ride-on toys and playdough you're doing it anyway - you just need to draw children's attention to what is happening. Carole Creary and Gay Wilson explain

Finding out about forces

Forces play a huge part in our lives. We can't see them but we can certainly see their effects and we would definitely know if they weren't there! Walking relies on the friction between our feet and the ground. Without gravity we would float off into space. We wouldn't be able to make footprints in the snow!

What do children need to know?

An understanding of forces demands abstract thinking and we are not suggesting that young children are going to learn and understand all about forces but they can experience and begin to describe what is happening when forces are acting. They can begin to think about cause and effect; for example 'If I want that trolley to move, I've got to push it'. 'If I drop my ball, it will fall to the floor'. 'I'm only having fun on this swing because someone is pushing it'.

Children will do these things without necessarily thinking about them. We need to draw their attention to what is happening and help them develop the language to describe it. They do not need to name different forces but they do need words such as pull, push, twist, fast, slow and stop. Be careful not to use words such as pressure and power when talking about forces to avoid misconceptions and confusion later on as these mean something very different scientifically.

Forces can start something moving, speed it up, slow it down, stop it, change its direction or change its shape but all of these can be described in the simple terms of push, pull or twist. (A twist is really just a combination of a push and a pull).

What experiences should you offer?

As children are playing, ask questions to make them think about what they are doing and what is happening as a result of their

actions. Any activity that involves movement must involve forces.

Bikes and scooters

How do you make your bike or scooter move? Think about pushing down on the

pedals or against the ground, turning the handlebars, putting on the brakes.

Playdough

What do you do to change the shape of your dough? Pull it or push it; roll it (a push and a pull) to make a long sausage; roll it with a rolling pin to make a pancake.

Getting dressed

Where do you push or pull when you are getting dressed? Pull on socks and trousers; pull up a zip; pull your jumper over your head and push your feet into your shoes.

Think about activities that the children are going to be involved in. Can you identify the forces they will be using? What questions will you ask to draw their attention to what they are doing and make them think about it? PE gives lots of opportunities. Children pushing up from the floor to jump, hop, skip, and so on. Rolling and throwing a ball or using a bat to change its direction are other examples of pushes.

Some forces are not so easily identified but most still come into the categories of push or pull. Earth's gravity is a pull towards the centre of the Earth. Floating is a combination of gravity pulling down and the water pushing upwards (upthrust). An object sinks when the pull of gravity overcomes the upthrust. Young children will, of course, not be expected to know or understand this but it is important that you give them the opportunity to verbalise their ideas about why these things happen. Ask the children what they think is happening and, more importantly, why? Their answers may well not be correct but will give you a good idea of the level of their thinking. You can then extend their thinking through further discussion. Good questioning and lots of talking are the key!

Carole Creary and Gay Wilson

Background information

Forces can:

❏ **start something moving**
  a push, a pull or gravity

❏ **make a moving thing go faster**
  increasing the push or pull

❏ **make a moving thing change direction**
  hit a ball with a bat

❏ **make a moving thing slow down**
  put the brakes on

❏ **make a moving thing stop**
  catch the ball

❏ **temporarily change the shape of an object**
  roll out the dough

❏ **permanently change the shape of an object**
  crush the garlic!

Water play is a routine activity and can be overlooked - just putting out a water tray and waiting for it all to happen won't work! Vicky Hislop explains how to make your water corner provide really positive learning experiences for your group

Organising **water play**

Just putting out a water tray and waiting for it all to happen without you will not work! You must have a plan for the activity and be prepared to make the most of the questions you will be asked as you would with many table-top activities. Plan ahead and decide what skills or information you are aiming to share with the children at each session and aim to deliver it. Linking in with previous discussions or ongoing themes makes sense.

How you talk to the children during any activity is crucial. Use new words, test understanding of new words and repeat them several times. Don't be afraid to try quite difficult concepts such as 'waterproof' or 'saturated' - the exposure to new vocabulary is always positive. Be prepared to 'go with the flow' (no pun intended!) when playing in water; you can come back to your plans if needs be. You have the advantage that water is not a new concept to any child. They will all have something to say about bath-time and washing seems to hold great fascination for young children. The washing machine may well be out of bounds but is nonetheless of great interest!

Introduce variety

Start by looking at the equipment you use. Children enjoy the jugs and colanders but there is more to be had from the activity by offering more varied equipment. Don't be tempted to overcrowd the tray, though; too much equipment can ruin a good idea - keep it simple.

❑ Colour the water with food colouring.
❑ Scent the water with essential oil of lemon, lavender or peppermint.
❑ Add bubbles, colour the bubbles.
❑ Use toys - dolls, doll's clothes, play people, cars, construction kits, marble run games, and so on.

❑ Add natural objects - cones, stones, wood, sand, pebbles.
❑ Experiment with junk - yoghurt pots, cardboard tubes (for a short time!)
❑ Change the temperature - add ice cubes, freeze whole trays of water then pour on warm water.
❑ Use sponge rollers and paint the outside walls.
❑ Thicken with cornflour - a thick mix is a fascinating play medium. You don't need to heat it up, just mix it in. Experiment with consistency. Pour the mixed cornflour and water into a shallow tray and let it run through your fingers and hands. A packet of cornflour, some water and a tea tray are all that is required.

When you have your new idea plan the group size carefully - most water trays do not work well for more than two or three children. With this small number you can be really involved, leading discussions and pointing out new ideas and interesting happenings. Note changes to the items you have added, suggest different ways of experimenting, link one discovery with another when appropriate and encourage the children to express their thoughts and findings as they explore. Troubled children often find the therapeutic effect of warm water, absorbing toys and close adult attention a good time to chat - be sensitive to this and make the most of the opportunity.

When you are planning your water play remember to check which children have skin problems. Scented or coloured water would play havoc with eczema sufferers. Rubber gloves are an option but finding ones small enough is a challenge. Mildly sensitive skin might survive a short session if smeared with Vaseline first - always check with the parents beforehand.

To make general sessions easier to manage you could collect equipment together and group it into subject trays for easy access. Having trays labelled would remind you what the objective of each session was.

❑ A 'floating' tray might contain: plastic tubs, boats, fish made from wood or

plastic, corks, empty film cases, bottle tops, sticks and straws.

❑ A 'pouring' tray could have: jugs, cans, tubing, plastic bottles (Body Shop empties are great), funnels and tea sets.

❑ A 'wash day/washing-up' tray would need: towels, flannels, soap, pegs, line, sponges, plastic dishes, tea set, plastic cutlery and drainer.

Water in the natural environment

Don't forget natural water when you are thinking about the children's learning. Who didn't enjoy jumping in puddles? Rain, condensation, taps, drips, drains, pipes, puddles, streams, rivers, sea, lakes,

Water stories

Mr Archimedes' Bath by Pamela Allen (Picture Puffin)

The Turtle and the Island by Barbara Ker Wilson (Frances Lincoln)

The Owl and The Pussy Cat by Edward Lear (Walker Books)

Harry by the Sea by Gene Zion (Red Fox Books)

Alfie's Feet by Shirley Hughes (Picture Puffin)

An Evening at Alfie's by Shirley Hughes (Red Fox Books)

Bumpa Rumpus and the Rainy Day by Joanne Reay, Adriano Gon (Picture Mammoth Books)

Action songs and rhymes

Get in the Bath - Play along songs (Faber music)

Water in Bottles - This Little Puffin (Puffin Books). (This reinforces the message that water always takes the shape of what it is in.) *This Little Puffin* also has many rhymes about the sea and water. A good resource.

Drips and drops - experimenting with water and paint

Using eye droppers (available cheaply from chemists) drop drips of marbling paint on to the surface of water in a shallow tray. Stir the water a little, very carefully and slowly, then briefly lay a piece of paper on top of the water. The pattern you made with the marbling paint will have transferred on to the paper.

This activity helps you to explore patterns and change, sound, colours, form and space. You can begin to look at two- and three-dimensional concepts and you can concentrate on the slow and careful movements required!

hose and sprinkler - they all represent natural water and offer a wealth of activity ideas. For example:

❑ Find a puddle, draw around it in chalk and come back later to it to see if it is bigger or smaller.

❑ An outdoor game of musical puddles is great fun.

❑ Puddle jumping (in wellies of course) is a joy on its own.

❑ Measure the rain in a rain measure and discuss where rain comes from.

❑ Make an aquarium - plastic or wooden fish work just as well as real ones, require less food and offer more play opportunities!

❑ Umbrellas lead you on to discussing waterproof, shelter, shapes, weather.

❑ Pond dipping for those with access to such a resource is a lovely way to spend time - scooping out insects such as water boatmen (remember to put them back), looking at weeds.

❑ Salt and fresh water is interesting to compare - salt water will make children instantly sick, never allow them to swallow it.

❑ Snow and ice are a perennially interesting topic - frozen water is as interesting as liquid.

❑ Floods and droughts are good topics to tackle in the water tray and work well as part of a larger nursery theme.

Outdoor play

Outdoor equipment to play in water with is good to have, but don't be too restricted by it. Some super outdoor systems with pumps, water-wheels, pulleys, pipes and streams is available and if your group can afford such an item then great! If you can't, you can improvise with drainpipes, buckets and troughs and enjoy it just as much. Don't forget the paddling pool in summer - on a hot day there is nothing better.

So, it is good to plan for the water tray. There are many interesting things you can do. As with most things, though, you must aim for a balance between offering stimulating opportunities and allowing the children simply to play. Warm water is intensely therapeutic, relaxing and liberating - don't forget to enjoy it!

Vicky Hislop

Scents and additives

These are available from The Body Shop, why not try orange too!
Use mild washing-up liquid for bubbles or hypoallergenic bath liquid.

Ursula Daniels talks you through some simple experiments which will introduce your children to an important scientific concept and help them become familiar with skills such as observing, questioning, predicting and recording

Floating and sinking

Many early years settings have a water tray always available, others can only use water outside - which can be a problem on cold winter days. Even if the children are not able to play freely with water inside, a bucket or a washing-up bowl could be used in a supervised activity provided that the floor is well protected. Check whether another area, such as the entrance, has a floor surface that is less likely to be damaged.

Whilst it is important that children are encouraged to observe, they do need to experiment for themselves in order to build up concepts. So if water can only be used outside during the summer, they need the maximum amount of free play with water during that time. In the winter, it may be possible for them to observe adults carrying out same investigations outside - that would at least avoid cold, wet sleeves.

the children to record their predictions through drawings. See if they can explain why they think that particular objects will sink or float.

whether an object floats is not related to size. Large, apparently heavy objects, such as ships, can float.

Following up

After the basic testing of objects, there are many more investigations that will develop the children's understanding. Objects can float in different positions in the water. Which objects remained on the surface? Which floated just below? Try floating an ice cube in water. If an object contains air, it is lighter than when it contains water. Float a plastic bottle, then fill it with water in stages. Each time, put the lid on and watch what happens when you put it in the water. Float a plastic box on the surface, then fill it with water and replace the lid. Now try it in the water. What do the children think will happen? Where does it float in relation to the surface of the water?

Float a dry sponge on the surface. Push it under the water and squeeze it. Watch the air bubbles come out. Try floating it again.

Objects of the same shape can either float or sink. Test a number of spheres - marble, ball bearing, golf ball, plastic ball, orange, onion, stone.

Objects sink at different speeds. Try to find some objects that sink more slowly than others. Compare a flat piece of paper with one that is screwed into a tight ball.

Water resists pressure. Push a piece of polystyrene or other large object that floats into the water - what do they feel?

Ursula Daniels

Talking

Think about things that float on water:
❏ in the bath: a plastic boat, a sponge
❏ in a swimming pool: arm bands, people
❏ in the sea: boats, yachts, an iceberg, seaweed
❏ in a pond: leaves, frogspawn, a duck
❏ in a puddle: a crisp bag

Predicting

Gather together a collection of objects: paper, stone, shell, polystyrene, dry sponge, marble, wood, fabric, metal object, fruit and vegetables.

Which do the children think will sink? Which will float? Sort them into two sets. Get

Observing

Test each object. Remind the children of what they thought would happen and observe what does happen. As you do this, sort the objects into new sets - those that you know float and those that you know sink.

Recording

Draw sets of objects that float and objects that sink. Let each child do a drawing of one object of their choice. Write on it what happened: 'The marble sank'. Put them together on a wall display or make 'Our book about floating and sinking '.

What will they learn?

Children will see that small, heavy objects tend to sink and that large, light objects tend to float. They need to know that

Vocabulary
float
sink
heavy
light
surface
above
below
deep
shallow

Melting and freezing are within most young children's experience, whether it be ice lollies, ice cream, icy mornings, or melting chocolate for a cake topping. Gay Wilson and Carole Creary explain the science behind some popular nursery activities

Freezing **and** melting

These activities, which focus on how substances behave in various conditions, are in fact an early, fun start to chemistry! But what is happening scientifically?

The science

Freezing and melting are physical changes to materials which can be reversed. The materials can be made to change from a solid to a liquid and vice versa, over and over again. The change happens with the application of heat or cold. Ice melts when the environment which it is in is warmer than freezing, for example taking it out of the freezer into room temperature, putting it into a drink, or in the case of ice lollies, sucking it in a hot little mouth! Put back in the freezer, water or ice will re-freeze and this can be done as often as you like. (But beware! Don't eat anything which has been thawed and re-frozen.) Chocolate melts with the application of heat but then it can be left to solidify again.

A good way of helping children to understand that ice is frozen water and that when it melts it becomes water again is to make some coloured ice cubes. Allow them to melt into a bowl or clear plastic container of plain water so that the children can watch

closely and see what is happening. Use food colouring, making the colour quite strong so that as the ice melts it can be seen clearly. Talk about what is happening using words like 'water', 'cold', 'warm', 'mix', 'freeze' and 'melt'. When the ice has melted and mixed with the water you could take some of the resulting mixture and make more ice cubes.

Making lollies

Children love ice lollies, rain or shine, hot or cold. Lolly-making kits can be bought, but an ice-making tray and fruit syrups or squashes are just as good. Buy lolly sticks or plastic stirrers or save and carefully wash the sticks from commercial lollies. Let the children experiment until they get the strength of flavour and colour they like best.

Why not let the children try making home-made ice pops in ice cube bags? (You can buy the bags in any supermarket.) Pour your flavouring into the bag, filling at least the first row of pockets. Put in the water, tie the bag, give it a little shake and put it in the ice compartment of the fridge or freezer. The children can then feel the difference between the frozen and unfrozen ice pops. Ask them to tell you what they feel - but don't let them squeeze the unfrozen bags too hard unless you want a flood!

When the ice pops are frozen, put different coloured pieces into a plastic cup for the

> **When children work with food, hygiene rules apply!**
> ❑ Wash hands
> ❑ Wear clean aprons

children. They love to put a whole piece into their mouth and suck on it.

When their mouth gets too cold, they can spit the piece back into the cup - if you can stand the slurping noises! Put the same number and range of colours into a cup and leave them to stand. Why do the pieces they suck melt and get smaller more quickly than those left in the cup?

Unlike ice, chocolate will not usually melt at room temperature - it needs the application of heat. A good way for the children to find this out is to put a square of chocolate into each of two bowls, preferably transparent. Leave one bowl standing and place the other into another bowl of hot water (not dangerously hot!). Get the children to watch closely and describe what is happening. Compare the square of chocolate in the bowl of hot water with the one left aside. Use appropriate language such as 'melt', 'heat', 'solid' and 'liquid'.

If you don't want to waste the chocolate used for your science investigations, melt some more and make rice krispie or cornflake cakes. Put some cakes into the refrigerator to set. Do those in the cold set more quickly than those left out?

Rice krispie/cornflake cakes

Stir enough rice krispies or cornflakes into the chocolate to coat them. A few sultanas added to the mixture makes an interesting variation. Divide the mixture into cake cases. Allow to set.
Have fun! What about a party?

Gay Wilson and Carole Creary

At Bridgwater Forest School in Somerset the curriculum on offer is based entirely outside all year round - whatever the weather. Sue Kennett, a nursery nurse there, shares some of their activities

Looking at minibeasts

In all early years settings, we are continually developing children's awareness of the world around them, their environment, people and features of the natural world. Looking at differences, similarities, patterns and change are a vital part of this emerging knowledge.

The aim of this particular activity is to give the children an awareness of minibeasts and what they are. Each child will have the opportunity to make a small pitfall trap, thus giving them a sense of achievement and confidence.

They will work as part of a team and individually which will promote co-operation and support towards their peers. They will gain an insight into the huge variety of minibeasts which there are and they will be gaining valuable environmental knowledge whilst also having fun.

the minibeasts and talk to the children about how you could make traps for them.

Dig a small hole in the ground just deeper than a small margarine tub and lay the tub in the ground, making sure the edges do not stick up. Then find some small stones and put one stone at each corner. Place some leaves and earth in the tub for the creatures to shelter in and a piece of wood on top to stop the rain getting in. You could use some small scraps such as apple, lettuce, cheese or tomato to attract the minibeasts. The following day, use magnifiers to find out about the minibeasts. With the help of simple books, you could attempt to identify the various minibeasts you have found. Encourage the children to look at features such as:

Key learning objectives
- ❏ to compare, sort and count
- ❏ to promote awareness of size, shape, length and number
- ❏ to look at similarities, differences, patterns and change
- ❏ to work as part of a group and individually and be able to concentrate in their learning
- ❏ to talk about their observations and question to gain information
- ❏ to handle appropriate tools and equipment with care
- ❏ to use a widening range of materials, tools and resources

Step by step
This is an activity which would need to take place over several days, to allow time for the minibeasts to collect in the pit. Adult supervision is needed to make sure that the

children are not exposed to any dangers regarding the minibeasts.

Start the activity by explaining to the children what minibeasts are and some characteristics about them:

- ❏ Minibeasts are small creatures like woodlice, spiders and snails.
- ❏ Many of them we do not notice because they are so tiny and well hidden, others we might find ugly and frightening.
- ❏ Three out of every four animals in the world is a minibeast and some of them are helpful to us in important ways. Others can be harmful or even dangerous.
- ❏ Minibeasts are invertebrates - they have no backbone.
- ❏ Many are insects, which have a miraculous way of changing their shape and form - up to four times in their life.

Then go on to explain how you plan to view

- ❏ Have they got wings?
- ❏ Is the head large or small?
- ❏ Does it have eyes?
- ❏ Does it have antennae or feelers?
- ❏ How many legs does it have?
- ❏ What colour and shape is the body?
- ❏ Where does it live - in long grass, in short grass, under stones, in trees, on plants, in water, in dead wood?

This activity could be followed up in the setting. For example, you could look at butterflies and moths, water minibeasts, make a wormery, explore woodlice, draw pictures of the minibeasts, and so on.

Sue Kennett

Please note: always release animals back to their habitat afterwards and make sure children understand why they should do this.

Most settings have animals to care for at some time - even if it's only a few minibeasts or tadpoles. Most of you plant seeds and watch them grow. Carole Creary explains how to make these common activities more scientific in line with the requirements of the ELGs

Identifying features of living things

Caring for a pet offers many learning opportunities for young children. Helping with the daily routine of cleaning and feeding can help them appreciate that all animals need care and that, like us, they need food, water and somewhere to live.

Similarities and differences

Most young children will not appreciate that humans, too, are animals. Encourage them to look for the similarities and differences between other animals and us. They are usually quite good at noticing differences but may need help in identifying similarities.

All animals need to eat, but do we eat the same things? If you have a supermarket nearby, go and see just how many different kinds of animal food are on sale there. Which food does your cat or dog eat? Make a pictogram of labels to find out which is the most popular pet food for the children's pets.

Do all animals drink? What do they drink? How do they drink? Watch a cat lapping its milk or the guinea pig sucking at its water bottle. Can you find out how an elephant drinks? (Use a video or CD Rom.) How is this the same as or different from the way we drink?

Let the children use a magnifier to look at their arms and legs and see all the hairs there. Can they find pictures of other furry animals? Why do animals have fur? If any children keep pets such as rats, mice or gerbils, they may have noticed that their babies don't have fur when they are first born. How else do babies differ from their parents? Can they match mums and babies? What do tadpoles or caterpillars grow into?

Frogs and snails

Watching tadpoles gradually turn into frogs never ceases to fascinate. You may take frogspawn from a garden pond but it is illegal to buy it, sell it, or take it from the wild. Keep it in a shallow tank in a cool spot and out of direct sunlight. Put a rock in the water so that the developing frogs can crawl out. A little pond weed or watercress will provide food but when the tadpoles start to develop legs, give them a little fish food to provide the extra protein they need. Make sure that the frogs are returned to a suitable place as soon as they are ready.

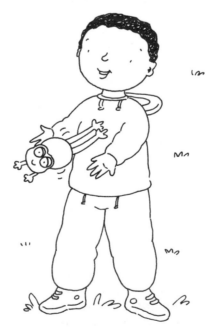

Snails are great fun to watch and feel as they crawl across your hand! They may be kept inside for a short time. Place a little damp compost in the bottom of a plastic fish tank together with a few large stones or small rocks. A jam-jar lid makes a simple water dish and a few leaves or vegetable peelings will provide food. Put only a little in each day and remove the old food to keep it clean

and sweet. Make sure that you have a cover on the tank since slugs and snails are real escape artists!

Planting seeds

Growing a plant from seed is a satisfying experience and quite wonderful if you have never done it before. Encourage children to look for similarities and differences. Choose seeds with care. Some of the most spectacular are the most poisonous.

Use a magnifier to look carefully at seeds. Are they all the same? How are they different? What do you think they will grow into? How could you find out? Make a collection of seeds that we eat - nuts, wheat, popcorn. Use this to reinforce the message about never eating seeds or berries unless told that it is safe to do so. Look for the seeds inside plums, pears and apples.

If space is a problem, use empty 35mm film canisters as plant pots. Punch a hole in the bottom with a nail for drainage and keep them together in an empty, shallow ice-cream tub. Transplant the new seedlings as they get too big for the pots. This gives an opportunity to look at the roots and see how they have grown. Although the plants need light in order to produce healthy growth, avoid putting them in direct sunlight on a window sill where they may fry during the day and freeze overnight. Seeds such as French marigold germinate quite quickly and will produce small bushy plants that can be carried home. If started off early enough you may even get some to produce seed before the summer holidays.

Carole Creary

Gay Wilkinson examines Mathematical Development. She emphasises the importance of building on children's previous experiences and suggests how the Early Learning Goals might translate into good early years practice

Mathematical
Development

Mathematics, like language and literacy, is part of the everyday world. By the age of five young children have already built up a rich experience of mathematical ideas through exploring and investigating their environment with all their senses.

As very young babies they explored the shapes and space immediately around them, reaching out to touch objects and people near to them. As they began to move around, rolling, crawling and eventually walking, they were able to extend this exploration so that they could interact within different and more complex spaces with a greater variety of objects and materials.

They have picked up and experienced how different shapes feel - the smooth roundness of a ball, the combination of corners, edges and the flat surfaces of a brick. They have tried to put objects together - building a tower with bricks - and have begun to experience how shapes might or might not fit together.

They have arranged and rearranged objects around them and begun to develop an understanding of pattern and the relationships between objects. They will have become aware of the important part that number plays in everyday life as they learn the number of their house, see and recognise numbers on buses, see and count candles on their birthday cakes, see posters using number symbols in shop windows and accompany parents and/or carers when they go shopping. They will have begun to develop a sense of time as they experience everyday routines and recognise recurring weekly, annual and seasonal patterns - days of the week, special days such as their birthday, Christmas, Diwali.

Each child joins their early years setting with their own unique experiences, and different abilities and variations in their knowledge and understanding of language to describe their thinking about aspects of mathematics. It is your role - and that of the adults working alongside the children in your setting - to recognise this learning and use it as the starting point for a programme of activities

When planning how you intend to foster children's continued mathematical development it is important to consider how their early learning has occurred. Much of it will have developed informally in everyday, real-life situations which have been meaningful and interesting; they have been part of the child's continuing process of making sense of his/her world. In organising and planning the mathematical programme it is essential that your environment builds on this early learning and uses those contexts which have already fostered children's interest in exploring mathematical ideas. In this way young children will not only become increasingly mathematically competent but, more importantly, will feel confident and positive that they can succeed as they encounter the challenges that new learning will bring.

Contexts for learning

How does your environment provide recognisable contexts and practical activities which will help young children to use and apply what they have already learned about shape, space, weight, capacity, length, size and number and develop new skills and knowledge?

❑ Does your home corner have dolls of different sizes with clothing in matched sizes?

❑ Are there complete sets of crockery and cutlery so that children can match items for a number of place settings at the table?

❑ Are they allowed to have real liquid in the teapot to pour into the cups?

❑ Can they make real sandwiches to match the number of children playing or have snack-time fruit or biscuits and share them out as they enact a mealtime?

❑ Are they able to reorganise the furniture within the space and make decisions about fit to meet the needs of their play? Might they be involved in redecorating and refurbishing the home corner - papering the walls or making new curtains?

❑ When it's time to clear up are they expected to help by ordering and putting everything away in its proper place?

The well-resourced early years environment contains a rich variety of activities and opportunities which will have the potential to stimulate young children's mathematical development. It is your role to recognise the particular mathematical potential of activities and resources and to structure them so that learning does take place.

Shape, space and measures

Children need to be helped to extend their early experiences of shape and pattern and develop a mathematical language which will help them to talk about their ideas and understanding. Activities such as building and making patterns with two-dimensional bricks or tiles of different shapes provide an opportunity to introduce the different names of the shapes and to talk about their similarities and differences.

Construction play with hollow wooden blocks or large plastic shapes offers the chance to handle and move three-dimensional shapes, learn their names and begin to understand and compare their properties as they build.

Painting, printing, modelling and collage further develop their understanding of shape, space and pattern. All of these experiences need to be freely available each day within your environment so that children can make mathematical choices within their play.

Throughout all of these practical activities the children will need the sensitive and knowledgeable intervention and participation of the adults: providing the names of plane and solid shapes - square, circle, cube, sphere; using the language of position - before, next to, under, beside, in front of, top, bottom, edge, corner, opposite; encouraging them to talk about their thinking, drawing attention to specific features and asking questions which encourage new thinking.

Learning through play

Young children have a genuine interest in play with natural materials. They love to dig and fill containers with sand or soil, adding water to change the way these materials feel and behave; play outside in the garden or inside in the sand tray is always absorbing. They enjoy water play, pouring, filling and emptying using a variety of resources. They enjoy play at the woodwork bench as they consider how to join pieces of wood together with nails of the right length. As they play they begin to encounter ideas about weight, length, size, density, volume and capacity and make comparisons and judgements. Building horizontally or vertically with blocks or interlocking cubes they will often try to

make something 'taller' or 'longer' than themselves and will concentrate for long periods in order to achieve their goal.

Cookery provides further opportunities to understand and make comparisons between the quantity, size and weight of different materials - how does 50 grammes of sugar compare in size to the same weight of butter and flour? Through purposeful and enjoyable activities such as these children will begin to learn the comparative language of measures - full, empty; heavy, light; thick, thin; long, short; tall, small, nearly as, wide, narrow - and begin to make more accurate judgements and refine their understanding.

In all their mathematical experiences, exploring shape, space and measures, young children will automatically become involved in using number to help organise their thinking. Indeed before they start nursery many children have already learned some of the number names and use counting as part of their play.

Number and calculation

It is important to remember that in the real world of the home and family they will have experienced number being used purposefully, as part of everyday experiences, by the adults around them. How many tins of cat food do we need? How many rolls of wallpaper to paper the kitchen? How many litres of petrol to fill the car? What quantity of material to make the new curtains? Their experience of number is that it is used to help describe concrete experiences where getting the right quantity is important to everyone. It is essential, therefore, to provide and organise a wide variety of practical activities in the early years environment which children recognise as purposeful. Through their involvement in these activities children will be supported to demonstrate what they already know and new learning opportunities can be planned which will

help them acquire new knowledge, learn new vocabulary and practice new skills.

Young children naturally enjoy sorting, ordering and matching materials and objects as part of their play and this will lead them into making counts. In play with the dolls' house, farm, zoo and garage they will sort and classify furniture, model animals and toy cars in a variety of ways - by colour, size, type or kind. They will collect natural objects found outside and arrange them into sets. Play with beads and making necklaces leads them into creating repeating sequences of colour and/or shape. As they arrange, re-arrange and order all these resources they will use

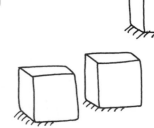

number names to help describe their activity, make predictions about how many objects they have got and check their guesses by counting.

In all of their activities - sand and water play, role play, small world play, construction, drawing and painting and designing and making - the adults should be observing children's behaviour in order to promote concepts of number and its associated language - add, minus, take away, more than, less than, the same as, equal to, least, pair, middle, several, enough, first, second, third and one, two, three, and so on.

Planned activities

In addition to these experiences you need to provide specific structured activities which promote understanding and use of number concepts. Daily opportunities to hear and participate in number rhymes, songs and stories will develop children's understanding of number value and invariance. You might consider developing your own anthology of number rhymes which are particularly liked by the children and which offer variety. (*The Practical Pre-School Number Pack* features a selection of popular number rhymes on large colour posters.) This will save you having to look up rhymes in a variety of books and ensure that you offer the children a wide range of rhymes rather than always using the same few.

Equally, when acting out a number rhyme, the children should be encouraged to undertake simple mental computational tasks as part of the activity — How many more will we need to add to make five? If we take two away how many will we have left? How many all together? Similar activities can be undertaken when they are grouped together for other events, such as preparing to go home. Simple co-operative games which promote counting can be taught and, with the support of adults, played with much enjoyment, for example ludo, snakes and ladders, and various other dice games. As children demonstrate an interest in mark making to describe what they have been doing they should be encouraged to record their mathematical discoveries, including representation of number value, with their own symbols or by tallying. As they demonstrate awareness of conventional written number forms they will need to be helped to form these correctly. As they become competent mathematical language users they should be introduced to those mathematical symbols which represent words such as minus and add.

In order to provide appropriately differentiated experiences for children which recognise their different levels of mathematical knowledge and understanding you will need to develop a sound picture of what they can do. You will need to observe them in all aspects of your provision, both as they engage in spontaneous play and as they take part in the more structured activities you provide, and record their mathematical behaviour (See assessment sheet provided.) These observational notes should be used to make an assessment of what they know and this should then be used, in discussion with your nursery team, to plan and provide new learning opportunities which will extend their mathematical competencies.

Gay Wilkinson

Sorting provides the foundation for many basic mathematical skills and children need as many opportunities as possible to practise it. Naomi Compton shares some ideas

Sorting skills

Sorting is the first step towards logical thinking in several areas of the curriculum. It involves looking at similarities and differences and has strong links with number patterns and can lead to practical addition and subtraction.

We all need to sort to organise our everyday lives - whether it's sorting out the food for a meal, the children who haven't yet had a turn, or the jigsaws into the appropriate boxes. When working with children it is important not only to teach the concept and skill of sorting but, as far as possible, to use the correct vocabulary. This means talking about the set of Lego goes in this box and the set of Mobilo goes in the other box. It also includes talking about positives and negatives, for example, 'This can go on our red table because it is red, that can't because it is not red', as opposed to 'This can't because it is green', which may confuse children in their more advanced sorting at a later stage.

By colour
Take a large sheet of paper and draw a line down the centre. Write the heading 'red' on one side and 'not red' on the other. Ask the children to find objects from around the room and place them in the correct category. This can also be done using coloured hoops.

By size and colour
This can be extended by using two sizes of coloured bricks.

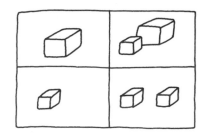

This is known as a Caroll diagram. The possibilities of sorting in this way are endless.

By colour in the playground
Ask all the children to stand at one side of the playground. They chant 'Farmer, farmer, may we cross your golden field'? The 'farmer' who is standing in the middle of the playground then replies 'Only if you're wearing yellow'. The children have to sort themselves into yellow or not yellow. If they are wearing something yellow, then they are allowed to cross the field to the other side of the playground. This continues and can be extended to include categories such as stripes, hair length, shoe fastenings and so on.

By position
The children move around and then stop when you blow a whistle. All those in front of the slide, on top of the climbing frame, and so on stay in the game, the rest are out.

By quantity
❏ Ask the children to put six marbles in each bag.
❏ Everyone needs ten cards to start the game.
❏ There are four segments of orange for each child today. This can also introduce the notion of left-overs. For example, ask one child to share out ten pieces of apple fairly to three children - there will be enough for three pieces each and one left over.
❏ Put five cars in this box. Numerals can be introduced as an extension activity - write numbers on cardboard boxes and ask the children to sort (count) marbles into the right boxes.

By size and number
The story of 'Goldilocks and the Three Bears' is a wonderful way to introduce sorting by size and number. It is even better if you have the appropriate props - a big

bear, medium bear and little bear, a big bowl, chair, bed, and so on. The items can then be sorted according to type - 'Find a set of chairs', or number - 'How many beds in the set?', or size - 'Make a set of all the small things'.

By colour and quantity
For example, with counters: three red, two blue, six yellow. This may be extended by introducing two sized counters: three big red, two small blue. This gives you the basis for practical addition. How many counters in these two sets?

Other skills
Sorting involves comparing or matching. Some children will need a lot of experience matching using just two identical objects before they go on to sorting.
Sorting leads on to many other skills. For example, once children can sort by size, they will quickly grasp the ability to order by size.

Naomi Compton

Children love using 100 squares. They look quite advanced for very young children because to our adult eye we expect to see them used with much older children and yet young children love looking for and finding number patterns. For example, all the numbers containing a 2. They soon find that they go in a straight line, horizontally and vertically. This pattern is the same for any numeral. They do not have to know what 32 actually means in terms of quantity because in this instance they are sorting according to a numeral and not an amount.

Many children are able to count to ten by the time they start school, but how many understand the meaning behind the figures? In pre-school groups we are able to provide practical activities and make use of everyday situations to encourage children to discover this for themselves. Jean Evans give some ideas

Fun with counting

How well do you help the children in your group develop their knowledge of number and counting? Why not carry out a simple survey and use it as a starting point for improving this aspect of your maths?

Start with your setting. Make a list of all the numbers there are around for the children to see. Do you have a number frieze? What about charts and books with numbers? Can you see numbers in some of the creative work displayed? Are equipment and areas labelled with numbers to help the organisation of routines? Do you record and display the results of investigations using picture and block graphs?

Next, list activities which you know involve counting, sorting, matching and ordering, including counting games. Think about how you organise them. Make a list of rhymes and stories you use regularly. Do you chant them rote fashion or do you involve props and actions?

Finally, gather the items on your lists together and consider how you might develop each one.

Creative techniques

Children will enjoy adding to the numbers in the nursery by painting numerals, making wax resist numerals (painting over numbers written with a wax crayon or candle), creating card numerals covered in scrap materials, rolling out and baking dough numerals to produce a mobile and feeling sandpaper numerals. Use various creative techniques to add the appropriate number of objects to your number displays.

Help children to realise how many places there are in each nursery area using numbers and symbols, for example a sign showing two paintbrushes means that two people can paint at the easel, four buckets means four can play in the sand.

Tidy small sand and water equipment into numbered seed trays. Draw round plastic people or vehicles on a piece of card the size of the base of the tray and add the correct number so that the children can match and count the objects. Store the trays on a low table or shelf.

Use templates in other areas. Make place settings by drawing around plates and cutlery and making cardboard templates to stick in place on the home area table. Cover with clear sticky backed plastic. Make sure that you have the correct number of items to fit on the templates and encourage children to count them as they set the table.

Review your routines

Develop the counting opportunities you have. Do you use everyday routines and count drinks, biscuits, candles, bulbs planted and leaves on plants? Do you sometimes put objects in lines and talk about which is the first in the line and which the last?

Look at your list of counting games. Do you always play the same ones? Try varying them

daily and making some of your own. A simple spinner can be made with a hexagonal piece of card and a pencil. Number the card 1-6, or 1-3 twice for younger children. Use this to decide the required number of moves on a board game, to select a number of objects from a box, or to count beats on a drum. Giant board games can be played outdoors with chalk circles or carpet squares as stepping stones and a large sponge dice. Numbered plastic bottle skittles are easy to make and can be counted as they fall. Finally, revise your list of rhymes and stories, adding suggestions for props and actions to make them come alive.

You will find that completing a check-list together will focus your attention on just how much experience with counting and numbers you are giving your children. You can then develop your provision further so that you can say with confidence 'Our children count with understanding!'

Jean Evans

Well-planned play and associated number activities offer children the chance to develop confidence with numbers, alongside building knowledge and understanding of a wide range of associated mathematical language. Sue Fisher shares some ideas

Number recognition games

Children need to be provided with a range of enjoyable opportunities for counting, recognising numbers and understanding their position. Remember that competence is not measured by a child's ability to write numbers as this often lags behind their mental calculation skills.

Fun with food

Cut up an apple or divide a satsuma into segments. Offer a piece to a child, then ask how many are left. Eat half, then ask 'How many was that?', 'How many are left?'. This activity also provides a good basic introduction to fractions.

Count and thread sweets on to liquorice bootlaces, then eat the results! This activity can be developed to provide opportunities for copying a pattern or following a sequence.

To understand about numbers, children need to develop conservation skills - recognising that a number is the same, however it is presented. Five is always five, however shown. Smarties, beads or other small items are ideal for this purpose.

Number lines

A variety of number lines can be made, for example handprints, snakes, teddy bears, footprints. You can then mix numbers up for children to re-order, take one number away for a child to guess. Older children might enjoy attempting to guess a chosen number (Is it less than four? More than two?).

Another idea that works well is to make a street with the children (see above). They can decorate collage houses and display them with door numbers added. Ask: 'Which number is next door to . . . ?', 'At the end of the street?', 'Which numbers are odd/even?' As an extension of this activity,

children can help to address cards and envelopes, post them into a home-made post box, which can then be emptied and sorted. A link with social knowledge of higher numbers is possible here through discussing children's own house numbers.

Collections and treasure hunts

You can use collections of objects to develop counting skills. A variety of items such as shells, acorns and buttons can be sorted by size, shape and type and counted to see which group contains the most. Putting objects into sets also provides the ground work for data handling, such as making graphs and charts. This activity can also be extended with older or more able children to provide an introduction to place value as objects are sorted into sets of ten, identifying for example that 24 is made up of two sets of ten plus four more units.

Treasure hunts indoors and out are an enjoyable extension on this idea as children search for chosen items, for instance, three wide leaves, four small stones. You can build on children's understanding of prepositions as they search for treasure placed 'under', 'on' and 'behind' items.

Dice games

Dice games aid number recognition and counting skills. They can be as simple as traditional

snakes and ladders or use technology such as Roamer or Pixie, which can be programmed by the children to move forward, backward, up or down, a required number of spaces.

Children enjoy games whereby numbered pieces have to be collected to build up a beetle or house, for example. You can make up similar games based on popular songs and rhymes, for example 'Incy Wincy Spider', who moves up the spout on the correct throw of the dice, and falls back down if a six is thrown. Introduce a dice with numbers on to aid recognition of written numerals. These are widely available but it is easy to make your own with sticky labels.

Songs and rhymes

Children enjoy rhymes which can be acted out or require counting down on fingers, and a number line based on 'Ten in a bed' (see below) is fun to use as well as effective in reinforcing name and order of numbers.

Sue Fisher

Paper plate faces made by children, on lolly sticks.

If children show a genuine interest in any character, be it self-generated or commercially produced, capitalise on it, says Dawn Lyell. Use it to encourage, motivate and develop a child's understanding and make learning exciting and enjoyable

Counting with a **favourite character**

To count, children need to be able to say numbers in sequence and to understand that there is one number for each item counted (one to one correspondence). The following activity creates opportunities for children to use number language to count to ten, to join in reciting number names in order, and uses rhyme to develop an understanding of number.

Most young children respond positively to a character who inhabits the learning area. Mine is a cuddly penguin who squeaks when squeezed, and provided the initial stimulus upon which I have built a collection of activities.

Children were asked to think of a name for the penguin and then given opportunities to make him squeak. Counting squeaks formed part of a question/answer language session - one squeak for yes, two squeaks for no.

We then made large iceberg shapes for him to jump forward and back along (made out of white card with blue shading to give a 3-d effect) and a counting box.

How to make a penguin counting box

You will need: one large cardboard box, one penguin outline, clear Coverlon (large enough to cover the front of the box).

What to do:
Cut out the beak shape in the penguin outline to create a posting hole. Glue the penguin onto the cardboard box.

Cut a hole in the cardboard box for the posting hole. Cover with Coverlon (this prolongs the life of the counting box).

To make the fish shapes you will need a fish template and some wrapping paper. Cut out up to ten fish using the template. I use holographic (shiny) wrapping paper and then laminate them (this means they are quite flexible but sturdy). Check that the fish are small enough to fit through the beak!

Keep all the fish together in a plastic bucket or net (supermarket orange nets are ideal).

Encourage children to feed the penguin and count the number of fish that are posted. Children can think of a name for the penguin and use it in the following rhyme:
This is .... penguin.
His/her beak is open wide
I know he/she is very hungry
Let's pop some fish inside.

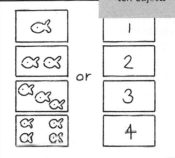

Children then count one, two, three as each one is posted.

You can take this a stage further by making cards with fish or numerals on (see above).

Fix the cards to the penguin's tummy using Blu-tack for the children to post the corresponding number of fish.

Matching icebergs
The icebergs were reduced in size to form an independent activity. Each iceberg had a number assigned to it and a corresponding number of penguins. By cutting each iceberg into two, matching them together provided a self-correcting activity. Children could then put them into the correct sequence.

Dawn Lyell

Joan Craven sometimes turns up for work wearing odd socks, two different earrings and even shoes that don't match! She's not eccentric - just giving her Reception class the chance to talk about 'same and different'!

Understanding
same and different

Children's ability to sort and classify is an important aspect of maths and science. A lot of early number work is based on sets of objects - counting them, matching the correct number to the set of objects, making a set of objects to match a given number. In science, children will be comparing, noting similarities and differences, describing observations and explaining their findings.

Children need substantial practical experience of 'same' and 'different' before they can sort and classify in more complex ways. The activities here do not involve making sets but are intended to develop the following skills and understanding:

• observation
• knowledge of material, function, mathematical attributes (eg size, shape)
• vocabulary
• understanding that objects can be the same and different simultaneously
• understanding that objects can be the same in more than one way
• understanding that criteria can change
• understanding that whilst an object can be included for one criterion it will be excluded for another
• understanding that something can belong to two sets at the same time

A good way to begin is to ask two children to stand side by side and ask the rest to see if they can find something the same or different about them. The children love doing this when the areas identified are joined using a coloured lace and paper-clip. Keep adding a child to the line and finding something else the same or different. This is a good activity for helping children to see differences about each other in a positive way.

Listening and looking game
Choose an action, such as clapping, and say 'Do the same as me' or 'Do something different to me'. The children really have to focus on whether it is 'same' or 'different'.

Changing places
Sit the children in a circle. Hold up an item, such as a black shoe, and say 'Change places if your shoe is the same colour as this' (or it could be a different colour to this). Again this focuses the children on the vocabulary of 'same' and 'different' and encourages them to look at an object for a specific criterion.

Find someone the same as you (or who's different to you)
The children sit in a circle. One child skips around as the others sing to the tune of 'Here we go round the mulberry bush': 'Find someone the same as you, the same as you, the same as you, Find someone the same as you on a cold and frosty morning'. At which point the child has to choose someone and say how they are the same (or different). The child who has been chosen continues in the same way. The similarity (or difference)

often starts off as gender but becomes more and more complex as the children's understanding grows and will extend to hair and eye colour, clothes, and so on.

Odd sock day
The children become fascinated by 'same' and 'different' when I come to school wearing brightly coloured odd socks (and earrings)! It stimulates lots of conversation about how they are different. I ask them to come in wearing odd socks the next day for more discussion on 'same' and 'different'.

Washing line
The odd sock day can be extended so that children can sort independently. This is much more fun if they are given a washing line, some pegs, a small washing basket and a selection of items to hang on the line. I usually start with socks, and although children initially put identical pairs together they often begin, if they have had enough experience with other activities, to put together socks that are long, short, striped and so on. Different items of clothing can be added to encourage sorting for colour, kind and fastenings.

Children find all these activities much more exciting than being asked to 'make a set'. All the suggestions can be done in a short space of time with a group of children and keep their interest because they include quite a lot of movement. They may be games but if a different activity is chosen each week they will have a noticeable impact on the children's understanding and form a sound basis on which to build a more formal approach to sorting and classifying in the future.

Joan Craven

There are endless opportunities to develop mathematical skills outdoors, using a variety of resources, many of which are either inexpensive or free. Cash in on these opportunities and meet the needs of all your children!

Matching activities **outdoors**

Planning for matching activities outdoors allows the children to revisit and refine skills that they are learning indoors with a totally different approach and covering all areas of learning. Through this, you are also making sure that children who thrive outdoors are getting the same learning opportunities as their peers who prefer to be inside.

The bear trail

This is a popular activity which ties in with a topic on 'The Three Bears'. It introduces matching by colour, shape, size and pattern, develops observational skills and is great fun to play. You need to design a sheet with pictures of bears on it. Each bear needs to be different in some way (see illustration right and activity overleaf). Make copies for each child so each can have their own master sheet. Cut out the same number of corresponding bears. Hide the bears in the garden (remember where you have put them - it's easy to forget where they are!) and then the children, armed with clipboards and pencils, have to find them and match them to the ones on their master sheet.

Playing postman

This is an ideal matching game to link to a topic on 'People who help us'. Turn your trucks and bikes into delivery vans by putting 'Royal Mail' labels on the sides of them and label parking bays with identical signs. Provide a graphics area where children can write letters and wrap parcels. Allow opportunities for emergent writing with addresses and numbers and provide numerals to stick onto the letters. The postman can then deliver the post to the letter boxes (made from cereal boxes, painted a variety of colours) that have numerals on them and match the address to the corresponding number. Use postman hats and sacks to complete the role play.

The garden centre

Collect plastic and silk flowers (ask at your local florists if they have any old ones from displays) and set up a flower shop. Make a price list for the different varieties of flowers and provide a till, plastic money, a technology area containing paper, scissors and tape dispensers for wrapping bouquets. The children will soon become engrossed in matching the colour, shape and price of the flowers, comparing them to the price list and charging their customers accordingly.

Set up a cafe in your garden centre using your outdoor house or just a corner of the play area. Provide menus, notebooks, pencils, a till with money along with utensils, cups, saucers, plates and food. The waiters and waitresses develop their matching skills through setting the table, making sure each customer has a chair, a place setting and a menu and then by taking the order using emergent writing skills can match the food to the price and charge accordingly. The children will be using mathematical language and one to one correspondence in their play and will be recognising prices and numerals on menus and lists.

Number games

Draw a large number line (a row of squares numbered 1 to 10) on your playground using chalk. Encourage the children to walk around the edge of the number line in time to music. When the music stops, the children have to stand on a number. You can then ask the children questions, differentiating by ability, to include all in the activity. Questions could include:

❑ Who is standing on 1?

❑ How many children are on 4?

❑ If you are on 5, move onto a square which is a higher (or lower) number.

This game can last as long as the children's concentration and is great fun. If you don't have a tape recorder, use outdoor musical instruments or simply clap a rhythm.

Playground games

Using playground chalk, draw number and shape trails and lines of varying size and colour. You can then ask the children to do a variety of tasks, such as find the red square and jump onto it, walk along the zig-zag line and run to the blue circle. Children can throw coloured bean bags onto shapes drawn from a matching colour, for example throw the blue beanbag onto the blue triangle. Once you begin these games, you'll be surprised at how many you - and the children - can think up yourself.

Tidying up

Tidying up at the end of a session

provides natural opportunities to develop matching skills. By careful use of large signs (pictorial and print) in appropriate areas, children can return equipment to its rightful place as part of their everyday routine.

Ann Clay and Maureen Mercer

With the recent emphasis on mathematics in the early years, there's a danger that adults might resort to inappropriate, formal methods involving paper and pencils, rather than the practical mathematics that young children need, says Hilary Faust

Maths through story-telling

Here's an enjoyable way to make sure that you are introducing children to mathematical concepts and language in ways that really make sense to them. Stories with props hold and focus attention as well as engaging young children's thinking and problem-solving abilities. They allow us to teach in a direct way that is appropriate for under-fives.

You will need a collection of about six soft toys. Mine consists mainly of animals of different sizes, from a large sheep to a tiny mouse, but they don't have to vary in size. Charity shops are a wonderful source of new characters.

Decide on the mathematical concept that you want to introduce (size, weight, counting, simple addition and so on). In the 'Teddy's Box' example (see box) the concepts are size and capacity. Sometimes children's preoccupations may guide you, for example spaceships or an interest in height. The idea is that the adults model and demonstrate aspects of mathematics through the vehicle of a story, making the chosen concept clear and accessible. It's best to stick to one main idea at first, you can always embellish the stories when you retell them, which the children will certainly request!

Simple story line

❑ Think up a simple story line to convey the main concept clearly. The best stories often involve an element of suspense and a problem to be solved, as well as lots of repetition. Children also enjoy deliberate mistakes. It works best if you can easily use the props to get the concept across. Sometimes it helps to use a favourite book to get you started.

❑ Collect your resources. What props will you need? In the example of 'Teddy's Box', I use a small bowl and a range of

five different sized boxes, only one of which fits the bowl. Later I add a calendar and a clock.

❑ Decide what language you want to use. Giving the children useful and precise words is important to enable them to think and talk about the concepts and scenarios. In 'Teddy's Box', Teddy repeats 'This box is the wrong size! The box is too small, the bowl's too big, it won't fit!'

❑ Practise your story using the characters and props, working out the moves and giving it lots of dramatic expression.

❑ Tell your story, perhaps first to a group, and later to the whole class. Some stories work better in a smaller group as you can involve the children more easily, for example asking them if they think the bowl will fit (prediction) or involving them in problem solving. (How can the character get his ball out of the pond?)

❑ After you have told the story, leave out all the characters and props to allow those who want to play out the new ideas and language, assimilating them and making them their own. You may find that it's necessary to have duplicate sets of some props. (For example, boxes in 'Teddy's Box', because they don't last long!) It can be useful to observe these play sessions to assess individual children's responses, as well as sensitively intervening if necessary.

❑ Provide more structured follow-up activities to ensure that the mathematics is consolidated.

You will be delighted with the children's involvement and enthusiasm as they make sense of new information about their world, learning new concepts, skills and language.

Hilary Faust

Teddy's Box
Concepts: Size, capacity

Story line: Teddy wakes up, has breakfast and suddenly remembers that it's his cousin Brian's birthday tomorrow, and he needs a present to send. Searches and eventually finds bowl (for porridge). Realises that he needs a box to post it in, but can't find one! Very upset! Mouse appears, offers box, goes to fetch it, teddy tries it but it's too small. Duck and crocodile bring increasingly larger boxes but still too small. Sheep brings box which is too big. Dog saves the day with a box that is 'a perfect fit, it isn't too big and it isn't too small, it's just the right size!' Can go on to wrap box (lots of comparing size and shape and so on).
Language: Too big, too small, wrong size, won't fit, right size, fits.
Resources: Animals, boxes, bowl, calendar (for spotting date), alarm clock, wrapping paper.
Follow-up: Different sized bowls and boxes, parcel wrapping, different shaped items to fit into different shaped boxes, making simple boxes.

Mathematical Development

Learning which colour is which and attaching the correct label to each can be confusing for many young children. Lesley Button explains

Exploring **colour**

The range of understanding within the pre-school age group is enormous. For those children who are having difficulty with colour recognition it is important to focus upon one colour at a time.

Hold a colour day or week

Organise it well in advance and involve parents so that, if possible, children and adults wear something in the chosen colour. You can have a colour table with a collection of items in the chosen colour or make a colour book using catalogue pictures, fabric scraps, and so on. Use food colouring so that even the water and Playdough match!

Have a colour activity table. Choose only the red Duplo/Lego, red sewing cards, red bus puzzles, red beads for threading, red crayons/felt-tips, and so on. Because of the very nature of the equipment you will also be introducing shades of the same colour.

Craft involving only one colour does not limit you to red paint. You can explore texture using different fabric or paper all of the same colour. Colour pasta by cooking it in water with food colouring added and then allow to dry. Sand and wood shavings/sawdust can be coloured in the same way. Or try a taste/smell activity and collect foods in the chosen colour - not a good idea for blue, but it works well for most others!

Start with primary colours

Start your colour activities with the primary colours: red, yellow and blue. For those children who are beginning to recognise colour then sorting by colour, playing colour games, choosing the odd one out and colour matching activities are all part of the consolidation process.

You can even reinforce colour recognition through physical activity. Use carpet samples or card in primary colours to play a form of musical bumps - when the music stops sit/stand on a red/blue/ yellow square (double their use by cutting the samples into different shapes and use as a shape recognition game). Have a collection of dressing-up clothes (hats, coats, gloves, jumpers) in a mixture of colours and play a similar game - when the music stops put on something red. This is good for dressing skills, too, and great fun.

Mix and match

Progression can then be made to secondary colours - purple, green and orange which can be made by mixing. You can do this in a variety of ways. Mix your paint so that it is fairly runny and let children pick two of the primary colours, paint a portion of the paper in each and then a part in both - what happens when the two mix? Encourage children to predict the outcome or, at a later stage, guess which two colours you started with. Try painting non-porous paper with water and then sprinkling with dry powder paint in the two chosen colours. You can also cut paper to fit a tray or lid and drip two colours onto it. By turning the tray, the droplets run and mix to form new colours and fascinating patterns.

Place two different coloured paints under a sheet of clean perspex or cling-film. Children can press and smooth the colours to blend. This can also be done as a messy but fun finger-painting activity.

Go on a treasure hunt looking for items of a particular colour - green leaves, cars, front doors, shop signs. Ask the children which colours they see most or least and make block graphs to illustrate this. (You can use the same method to record favourite colours or colours of clothes.) Sort fruit and vegetables by colour. Many fruits and vegetables produce coloured liquid when cooked which can be used for tie dying or creating coloured boiled eggs.

There is an enormous fund of scientific knowledge and information to be gained when looking at colour. Colour your own flowers by putting food colouring in water and placing the stems of white flowers into it. Carnations and narcissi are particularly good for this.

If you introduce white into your craft activities you move on to shades and tones. Make caterpillars with every segment a different shade of green or mix colours to create different skin tones.

Lesley Button

There are many books to support a colour theme. *Brown Bear, Brown Bear, What do you see?* by Bill Martin Jur (Puffin) ISBN 0 140 50296 3 is particularly good for the early stages, as is *The Blue Balloon* by Mick Inkpen (Hodder) 0 340 75738 8.

When Dad did the Washing (Puffin) ISBN 0 140 54422 4 Dad does the washing while mum's at work and everyone ends up with pink clothes!.

There are several titles in the *Elmer* series by David McKee (Hodder).

You could try: *Colour* in the Usborne *First Learning* series ISBN 0 7460 3800 3.

Introducing **colour** to **young children**

Some people plan to 'do' a colour a week, and blitz the children with a colour table, painting activities, collage and so on, then expect all children to have 'got it' in a week and then move on to the next colour!

Although this approach has some benefit in helping children notice a certain colour, I would prefer to see a much longer term project on colour in its entirety. I would not put emphasis on children learning to name the colours (although some will of course), rather on learning 'about' colours. This could be far more stimulating and interesting for all concerned.

Colour is one way of seeing differences and similarities between objects, and because of this can aid a child's mathematical development, for example in sorting a group of items into sets according to colour. However, there are also many other ways to sort objects - by type, by function, by material, by size, and all are equally valid. So I feel colour is often wrongly labelled as part of mathematical development.

Colour fits more neatly under Knowledge and Understanding of the World as part of scientific understanding, for example how colour is made; rainbows, prisms, crystals and how colours can be mixed to make new ones. Also in building up an understanding of the environment and people and objects around us, it is advantageous to be able to describe things as clearly as possible. Colour is obviously one of those descriptors. Children may want to talk about different colours of skin among their friends during discussions about colour. Use it as an opportunity to promote positive attitudes to skin colour.

Colour has an obvious place in Creative Development with providing paints, crayons and papers of different colours and introducing children to the principles of colour mixing. In close observational drawings children are encouraged to look at things very closely to represent them, and being able to describe and mix colours to match is important.

Organising activities on a colour theme

Colour is one of many things that young children are learning so it is best taught through an informal approach in everyday experiences, for example 'Look, your coat is red like Jamal's', or 'Oh! you've built something using only blue bricks!' Of course it is worthwhile to plan some special activities on colour, just don't expect all the children to learn them at once, because they won't! Some will be ready and that's fine, others will benefit from the experience in other ways.

Planning a topic on colour

Draw a spider chart (or topic web) with 'Colour' written in the centre. Divide the page into six sections, one for each area of learning. At a planning meeting start to fill in each section with ideas for activities related to colour that fit the area. After each activity, explain exactly what you want the children to learn from it; be as specific as you can. Then find a way to fit these ideas into your regular weekly planning. Be prepared to allow activities to be repeated over several sessions and possibly weeks if the children are enjoying them and are still benefiting and learning from them. One useful way of checking this is to hold a daily evaluation session to discuss how the

activity went, what you think the children are gaining from it, what extra input it might need the following day and so on. At the end of each week do an evaluation sheet to review how well the plans are going, what the children are learning, and what changes, extensions, additions might be necessary to carry the plans forward into the following week.

An example spider chart might include:

Knowledge and Understanding of the World

A discovery table with colourful things to look at such as kaleidoscopes, colour paddles, colour screens (large colour filters mounted on a stiff frame that children can look through to see their world turn a different colour), holographic papers of various designs, some prisms and cut glass crystals that break light into rainbows (with adult supervision only). If you have the table by a window you could stick different coloured cellophane to the glass for children to look through.

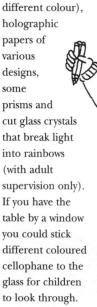

Learning outcomes

From this children will have the opportunity to investigate, discover and explore the articles available. They will talk about their observations and will so increase their communication skills and possibly their vocabulary (adult input required). They will be learning and asking questions about how things work - a kaleidoscope, a prism - and about how we can change the appearance of things by looking at them through different coloured screens. They may begin to learn how colours can be changed when two are put together, for example if the blue and, yellow paddles are put together they make green. They will be socialising and taking turns, and selecting and using resources independently.

You may notice that although the heading is Knowledge and Understanding of the World, many of the learning points cover other areas of learning. This just goes to remind us that young children do not learn in compartments called 'subjects' but through whatever captures their interest.

Creative Development

Colour mixing can be done with a variety of different colour sources - powder paints, food colourings in water, coloured chalks on the playground (then add water using a watering can to see what happens),

wax crayons, pastels, oil pastels, water based printing inks. Demonstrate different methods of mixing, for example mixing with water, with a brush, with a spoon, mixing dry, on the paper, in a palette, smudging with a finger, a sponge, a cotton bud.

Learning outcomes

From this children will have opportunities to learn physical control and manipulative skill, how different materials can be combined in different ways, that new and original colours can be created through mixing, aesthetic and design skills by making choices about how to express themselves artistically.

Gill Hickman

Personal, Social and Emotional Development
Colour song:
What's your favourite?
Learning objective:
Working in a group, taking turns, caring for others.

Mathematical Development
Sorting coloured objects
Learning objective:
To develop skill of matching like with like (essential before colour names can

Communication, Language and Literacy
Talking about colours
Learning objective: Children will begin to learn about colours and some will learn colour names.
Following instructions
eg find something blue
Learning objective: To listen, attend and act on instruction.

Colour

Knowledge and Understanding of the World
Display about colour
Learning objective: Children will enjoy discovering that they can change the way things look by looking through different colours - kaleidoscopes - crystals - prisms - coloured perspex

Physical Development
Playground games
Draw chalk circles in different colours in the playground.
Ask children to 'stand in the red circle' You can also use hoops for this.

Creative Development
Colour mixing
Learning objective: Children to discover how colours can mix together to make others- paints - chalks - crayons - coloured perspex.
Songs
Learning objective: That songs can help them to learn about colour

Resources for colour

Books

Start with Art: Developing Creativity in Young Children by Su Fitzsimmons (Nelson Thornes) 0 7487 2395 1

Primary Colours 1: Teaching in Colour by Ron Adams (Nelson Thornes) 0 7487 1798 6.

These books have suggestions for general art activities and include some specifically on colour. Be wary though, as some have good ideas, but present them in an adult directed way.

Planning for Learning through Colour by Rachel Sparks Linfield and Penny Coltman, (Step Forward Publishing) 1 9024 383 11 6 Mini-themes on red, yellow, blue, black, and white, and mixing colours - with a rainbow party as the grand finale!.

For collages

Collect as many items of different colours as possible; get parents to help you.
Scraps of material, wool, paper of all types, plastics, printed materials in certain colours, (from magazines) pipe cleaners and so on.
Store each colour separately, so it is easy to access 'just reds' when you need them.

For colour mixing

For the colour activity (see below) you will need powder paints in the double primary colours:
a warm red - a cool red
a warm blue - a cool blue
a warm yellow - a cool yellow
Pots for water, paint brushes of various thicknesses, palettes for mixing paint.
White paper for painting on – not too thin, preferably cartridge if you can get it.

For drawing

Drawing implements of many different types for example:
Pencils, pastels, wax crayons, felt pens, chalks in as many different colours as possible.
Some of these can be used with water for colour mixing.

For a display about colour

Anything transparent and coloured, for example:
Hang a crystal in a sunny window and have hundreds of rainbows all over the walls. Sheets of coloured acetate, coloured plastic bottles, pieces of transparent coloured perspex, children's sunglasses with different coloured lenses.
Make a colour telescope - use the inside of a kitchen towel roll, and stick cellophane over one end. Kaleidoscopes and other viewing toys. Books about colour; Dorling Kindersley do a lovely series, each of six books focus on a single colour and are filled with stunning photographs. (Red, blue, green, yellow, brown and orange.)

Colour mixing with powder paint

This is intended as a long-term project, to take place over a term at least, and possibly to replace the usual ready mixed paints that are put at the easels.
Provide; brushes, clean water, a sponge, small quantities of powder paint and a palette for each child. Teach children the four step method:
1. Dip brush in water.
2. Dab off excess on the sponge.
3. Dip brush in the colour chosen.
4. Mix paint in palette.
This makes initially a minute amount of paint so show them how to repeat steps 1 to 4 until the required amount is mixed. Start by providing just two colours, say yellow and red and let the children experiment. They will soon discover what a fabulous range of different oranges they can make. Then gradually introduce more colours until you have blue, yellow, red and white. This is known as the 'single primary' set.
After several weeks, when children are working confidently with this you can go on to the 'double primary' set which consists of a 'warm' red, blue and yellow plus a 'cool' red, blue and yellow and white. By mixing these colours together in different quantities, so many wonderful shades and tones can be created! Children will gain a much deeper understanding of colour and their paintings will beautifully reflect their skills and knowledge.

Back to our colour theme
Then at any point after the introductory period you could plan several activities around one colour at a time, for example blue water, blue dough, blue collage materials, blue drawing implements. This should well take longer than a week to do it justice, otherwise it becomes just a whistle-stop tour! Under-threes can particularly benefit from this kind of planning and over-threes can also benefit if they are allowed time to really get their teeth into it and as long as the planning is responsive to their needs.

Cross-curricular

Get used to using the correct terminology, says Lesley Button. If you describe three-dimensional beads as spheres, cylinders and cubes this is what children will learn

Learning about shape

The aim of all these activities is that children should be able to recognise and know the properties of common shapes and use language to describe their shape and size.

Introduce children to the basic shapes, look at them and keep naming them. Gather some together - lids, toy wheels, large buttons (make sure that they are not swallowed - count them all out and all in!) Talk about the properties of the shapes, in other words, how many sides or corners do they have? Do the sides have straight lines? Look for shapes around you - the doors, windows, table tops, the wheels on toy cars and prams. Look at books and name the shapes you can see in the pictures.

Have an interest table or, if you work in a setting which has to be cleared after each session, use a box. Collect relevant items. You could have a 'circle table' with bracelets, boxes, lids, magnifying glasses. Encourage children to add to the collection and to talk about it at home.

Shape in craft
Rectangular paper is almost always used for painting. Try varying the shape, for example, cut the sheets into triangles.

Use shape in printing. Cut pieces of sponge or potatoes into a shape to make print blocks. Make patterns of different sized circles/triangles/squares.

Bubble painting illustrates circles well. Mix washing-up liquid with fairly watery powder paint and place in a dish or bowl. Blow through a straw until the bubbles are above the surface and then place a piece of paper over the top.

Use triangles, circles, squares and rectangles in a collage to make a variety of figures or objects - a clown, a house, a ship - or use materials of

different textures to make patchwork patterns, rough next to smooth, dull next to shiny. You can also begin to ask 'What happens when...?' as you place squares or triangles next to each other. Two squares can form a rectangle, four squares a larger square. Triangles can be joined to make a square, diamond or a larger triangle.

Don't forget to keep repeating the names of the shapes you are using all the time.

Matching and sorting
You can extend your equipment easily using card and felt tips to make your own matching cards to work alongside beads and shapes of all types.

Make large sorting hoops for whole group or circle activities by sticking together strips of card and bending to the desired shape. Use the display box or table and ask children to choose an item and place it within the correctly shaped hoop - the bracelet inside the circle, the margarine lid inside the rectangle. Only one child should choose at a time but the whole group will benefit by watching and listening.

Language activity
Cover some boxes in coloured paper and use them as a language activity by placing different objects inside. Ask a child to describe what is inside the circular box or the square box without actually naming it.

Let the other children try to guess what it is. 'It has four legs, is black and white and says moo'. You can also use the boxes simply as containers for sorting activities using beads or plastic/card shapes.

Shape games
You can buy shape lotto or make your own. This is a good game to play using a feely bag. Rather than asking 'Who has a circle?', ask the children to put their hand in the bag and feel a circle. This helps to reinforce the properties of each shape.

Story and role play
There are many books written to illustrate shapes, but you can ad-lib with others. Try the Mr Men books - the characters come in every shape and size.

Let children make their own or group shape books. They could use ready-made scrap books and cut out pictures from cards or catalogues or make their own concertina books. If a colleague or parent has a talent for storytelling try making up stories linking the random pictures!

It is worth keeping a collection of pictures of different shaped objects mounted on cards. They can be used as flash cards for a large group - 'What is it?' 'What shape is it?' - or as matching and sorting cards for a smaller group or individuals

Most of all, enjoy the activities and don't forget that Early Learning Goals are not an end product. Just as you have children within your group who need to learn about basic shapes you will also have those ready to move on to the three-dimensional. Many of the activities mentioned are easily adaptable for this next stage.

Lesley Button

Examples of two-dimensional shapes can be found all around us. Learning to spot them and discussing their properties are important early maths skills for young children, says Rebecca Taylor

Exploring two-dimensional shapes

Children are surrounded by shapes and it is often difficult to know whether we should start by teaching about three-dimensional shapes because we live in a three-dimensional world or with the two-dimensional shapes.

The trouble with a two-dimensional shape is that, strictly speaking, it is not possible to pick it up on its own. Even a flat, oblong piece of paper is really a cuboid. Thankfully children accept a circular piece of paper or plastic as a circle and not a flat cylinder.

Many educationists argue that for very young children it is best to start with the names of two-dimensional shapes because the children need to have these established before they can start looking at the properties of three-dimensional shapes. A cube, for example, is made up of squares and children need to know this before they learn the names of three-dimensional shapes.

Getting to know the shapes

Your children need not only to look at shapes but to feel and manipulate them and be surrounded by them. A great starting point is to give your children stringing laces and Plasticene and encourage them to manipulate them into shapes. They need to discover for themselves that a straight line

can be manipulated into a curved line which in turn can be manipulated into a circle. They need to have experience of painting and drawing straight and curved lines.

Learning the names

Once children have felt and manipulated straight and curved lines they are ready to start learning the names of the two-dimensional shapes: square; circle; oblong/rectangle and triangle. Many people refer to oblongs as rectangles, which is correct, but squares and oblongs may both be classified as rectangles. It is important,

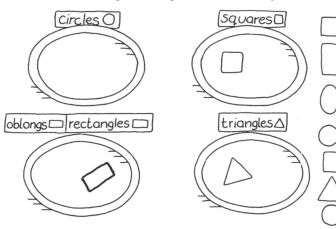

therefore, that you use both terms to name the shape in front of the children. You may find that some children know the two-dimensional shape names but need to be able to distinguish between them and learn about their properties.

Give a small group of children four hoops and four individual signs that say the shapes' names and a picture cue (see above).

Provide the children with a collection of two-dimensional shapes made in different colours and sizes from stiff paper, card or plastic. Can they sort the shapes into the right hoops? Once they can, help them to find out how many sides the different shapes have.

Shape books

Making group shape books is a fun activity. Cut out the pages of each book in the relevant shape. Encourage your children to draw around a variety of corresponding shapes in different materials and sizes. This will give the children their first insight into the area of shapes. Display your shape books alongside your shape display.

By giving the children straws and strips of paper you will be encouraging them to construct their own two-dimensional shapes. This will help them focus on how many sides a shape has.

Pandora's bag

A wonderful activity to end any session with is 'Pandora's bag'. Create a fabric draw-string bag and sew a face on it. Put inside it a variety of two-dimensional shapes - all different shapes and sizes. Begin by saying: 'I have lots of two-dimensional shapes in this bag. I'm going to put my hand in and see if I can guess which shape I have in my hand just by feeling it. And I'm not going to peep!' Say your thoughts out loud, such as, 'It has corners and I think it has three. It also has three straight sides, so I think it must be a triangle.' Encourage other children to have a go and predict what shape they are holding.

Rebecca Taylor

Useful definitions

Rectangle
A plane figure with four right angles and four straight sides, opposite sides being parallel and equal in length.

Circle
A perfectly round plane figure whose circumference is everywhere equidistant from its centre.

Square
A plane figure with four right angles and four equal straight sides.

Triangle
A plane figure having three sides and three angles.

Children live and play in a three-dimensional world. It is important that we help them to develop their vocabulary of shape and recognise the properties of 3-d objects that they touch and see every day, writes Rebecca Taylor

Learning about **3-d shapes**

Many children will have only experienced 2-d shapes by looking at outlines in books. However, 3-d shape is a concept that young children will experience before they begin pre-school or nursery and so this is a great topic for the early years.

There are seven primary 3-d shapes which you can use to help your children enhance their knowledge of maths and shapes. Cube, cuboid, triangular prism, cylinder, pyramid, cone and sphere are all 3-d shapes that your children will recognise and have fun experimenting with.

You may find the following definitions useful:

- A cube is a prism with six square faces all of the same size.
- A cuboid is a prism with six rectangular faces; opposite faces are the same size and shape.
- A triangular prism is a solid with equal parallel triangular ends of the same shape and rectangular lateral faces.
- A cylinder is a solid with a circular face and two equal parallel circular ends.
- A pyramid is a solid with a straight-edged base (of any number of sides) and sloping triangular faces which meet at a point.
- A cone is a solid with a flat circular surface coming to a point.
- A sphere is a solid with a surface on which every point is the same distance from the centre of the solid.

Using toys

Toys are a great starting point for your 3-d shape work. Balls, bricks, Lego, Duplo and post-it boxes all provide opportunities for children to begin to establish their early concept of 3-d shape.

You could start off by asking your children to bring in their favourite toy from home and describe its shape. Then ask them to take two toys and describe the similarities and differences between them.

Construction toys such as Lego, polydrons and wooden bricks are an ideal way to help children manipulate 3-d shapes. Set a theme and a purpose for their play, asking questions such as: 'Can you make a castle out of the wooden bricks?' 'Can you stand some cylinders up for the doors?' 'Can you put cones on top of them to make the castle look grand?'

As the children play, encourage them to roll the 3-d shapes down an incline. They will begin to realise that curved objects will roll and that straight ones have sharp edges and won't roll.

Touching and feeling

A lot of food packaging comes in 3-d shapes. Tins are cylinders; cereal boxes are cuboids. However, it's worth investing in some more hard-wearing plastic or wooden shapes as well as you want children to be able to handle them as much as possible to help them discover their properties. (They are available from most good educational stockists.)

Create a 3-d display table and encourage your children to add examples from home. You will find that they notice how many faces 3-d shapes have just by handling them. Encourage them to count the faces: a sphere has one face; a cone has two; a cylinder has three; and a pyramid has four or more.

Make a feely box and put an example of a 3-d shape inside. Pass the box around the circle and get each child to say how it feels, whether it has smooth or straight edges. Children will begin to develop their knowledge of 2-d shape alongside their 3-d knowledge and start to observe their environment using mathematical vocabulary.

Words to describe shape

Some children find the vocabulary of 3-d shape hard to grasp. It will take time. It is more important at this stage that they are able to recognise the properties and describe them.

Capitalise on every opportunity to spot and identify two-dimensional and three-dimensional shapes when you go out for walks or on trips or even when looking at pictures in books. With a little bit of help you will soon be surprised how many shapes they can spot and name.

Rebecca Taylor

Recognising and recreating patterns is one of the important aspects of mathematical understanding which help to provide the foundations for numeracy. Jean Evans suggests some ways of exploring patterns

Let's look for patterns

One of the Early Learning Goals for Mathematical Development is 'Talk about, recognise and recreate simple patterns'. It is one of the important aspects of mathematical understanding which help to provide the foundations for numeracy. We can help to develop this understanding by encouraging children to look for patterns in their surroundings and by giving them opportunities to copy and create patterns of their own through practical activities.

Patterns are a fundamental part of mathematical relationships. There are patterns in numbers and in the way shapes relate to each other. By extending children's experience of patterns we can help them to understand that some relationships are consistent and can be predicted and recreated. Every pattern recognised, created or copied will be added to the child's store of experience in this area and used and applied to help solve future mathematical problems.

Why not start to explore patterns by looking for examples in your setting? Examine the floor tiles, the curtains, bricks, window panes and ceiling. Get the children to investigate patterns in the fabric of the clothes they are wearing. Can they find stripes, checks or dots? Look at off-cuts of material and wallpaper samples in your collage store. Many will have repeat patterns. Look closely at equipment. Can the children see patterns in the climbing frame and slide, construction equipment, puzzles or board games?

Take the children outside and continue your search. Look at buildings. How are the bricks and roof tiles arranged? Are the chimneys in rows or groups? Look at the pavement slabs, fences, walls and the zebra crossing. Can you find rows of vertical, horizontal and diagonal lines? Watch the sequence of traffic lights, or listen to the repetitive noise of the pelican crossing or a reversing vehicle.

Look for patterns in nature either by direct observation or by referring to books and pictures. Children recognise many animals and plants by their external patterns. Find pictures of a striped tiger or zebra, a segmented worm, or a spotted ladybird or dalmation. Examine the leaves of a dandelion or cut some fruit in half and examine the arrangements of the seeds.

Children love stories and rhymes with repeated sequences and wait with anticipation for the familiar words and phrases when they can join in. Let them listen for repeated sounds using percussion instruments and try to find patterns in pieces of music with a rousing chorus.

Making patterns

Once children have explored patterns around them give them opportunities to create patterns of their own. Provide a selection of threading objects such as beads, cotton reels, pasta tubes and milk tops or objects to print with such as sponge shapes, vegetables, small bricks and yoghurt pots. Fill a paper cone with salt and attach it to some string tied to a broom handle. Swing the cone in a circle and watch the spiral pattern the salt creates as it pours on to a dark piece of paper. Print patterns in sand, snow, dough and clay with fingers, hands, shoes and various small objects. Explore the patterns you can make in role play by plaiting hair, setting tables and hanging up clothes. Create patterns by making marks on paper using brushes, pencils, chalk and crayons. Experiment with musical patterns using tuned instruments such as a xylophone or keyboard, or beat regular patterns with percussion instruments.

When children have experimented with creating their own patterns why not encourage them to recreate patterns using various media? Start by using small objects such as plastic bears, beads, bricks and plastic links. Make a simple sequence with just two variables and see if the child can copy this alongside. You can buy cards ready printed with patterns of shapes or make your own and get the children to match the objects on top of the shapes on the cards. Try copying the patterns of a brick wall using plastic bricks. Many construction sets supply plans for models which can be mounted on card and used for copying. Children always enjoy playing 'Follow my leader' and this is an excellent way of copying patterns. Try copying sound repetitions as part of your work with sound recognition. For example, 'Sh, sh, sh, sh' or 't, t, t, t' and tapping or clapping rhythms.

You could develop the idea of patterns further by looking for examples of symmetry, mirror images and tessellations. Making butterflies by painting half a butterfly on one side of a sheet of paper and folding it over to print the other half is a favourite activity in most groups. This can be extended by painting a series of shapes on one side of the paper and folding it to create an identical pattern on the other side. Muslim art work has some beautiful examples of symmetry and geometric patterns which older children will enjoy.

If you are lucky enough to have a computer many programs contain opportunities for children to create, copy and continue patterns and you can then print out copies to add to a display or to make your own book of patterns.

Jean Evans

Understanding the concept and the language of length is one of the basics of developing mathematical understanding. Barbara Garrad gets you started

The concept of length

At nursery school age, children are usually able to compare the length of two or three objects, placed side by side. They can decide which is shorter or longer than the other. They do not, however, realise that the comparison requires the objects to be aligned. If one is pushed forward of the others, they will decide that that is the longest, whether true or not.

The most important concepts for measuring length with under-fives is for them to become familiar with descriptive language: long, short; big, little; tall, short; wide, narrow; thick, thin; with comparative language: longer, shorter; taller, smaller and so on: and to be able to make ordered arrangements of the objects being considered.

Many activities arise in the course of the day. Dolls and teddies can be compared and placed in order of size. You can make use of the children and their belongings. Peter is taller than Mark; Ranjit's scarf is longer than Tom's; Jenny's feet are shorter than Isaac's. You can mark their heights on a strip of paper attached to the wall, then again a month later to compare their growth. Let them compare crayon/pencil lengths and place in order of size. The setting environment is a good resource - which is the tallest/shortest tree/window/door in sight? Is the playground longer than the field/lawn/flowerbed?. Which are the tallest/shortest flowers? Each activity should be accompanied by discussion and the use of the language of length, width and height.

To make more accurate measurements, the children can use simple measuring devices. Bricks, Unifix, cuisenaire, Stern rods, counters or hand spans are suitable for measuring small items. Sticks/canes of the same length, balls of string or lengths of tape, footsteps and strides can be used for measuring and comparing longer lengths. Gradually the children will begin to realise

that a standard measure is required, but this can safely be left, except for exceptionally bright children, for the primary years.

When standard measures are introduced, they should be simple. Many manufactured rulers contain too many numbers and divisions. I don't agree with using a trundle wheel with very young children. To appreciate length, I think that they need to place the measuring objects end to end.

Have some fun! Get the children to each draw and colour a snake. By placing counters along its length, they can decide whose is the longest/shortest snake. Cut them out and mount as a display. Build towers with bricks - record how tall each tower was before it fell. Whose tower was the tallest/shortest? Who can make the longest Plasticine snake? Use handspans to measure the length of bookcases or tables; feet or strides to measure the carpet or the room. Always discuss the results and try to make a pictorial record for future reference. Use the children themselves as measuring sticks - how many, lying head to feet, cover the length of the hall? Compare the children's pets - Peter's dog is taller than Jo's, Jenny's mouse is smaller than Tom's guinea pig.

Whilst encouraging children to use various items as units of length, do not neglect to let them have their own ideas about ways they can measure length, width, and height. Sometimes they can surprise you - like a group who insisted on using their lunch boxes as a unit of measurement, and then were ready to start eating!

In the pre-school years, our most important contribution is to develop a child's understanding of the language involved, both descriptive and comparative. If you

achieve that before sending them on to their primary school, you have done a good job. If you have had fun doing it, so much the better.

Barbara Garrad

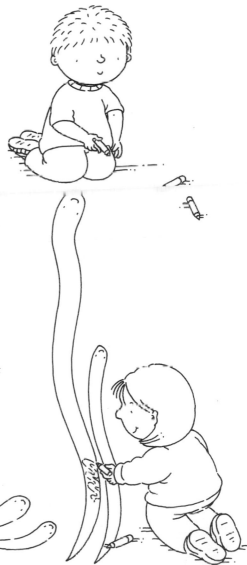

Ofsted inspectors will be looking for evidence that a setting provides activities which involve the comparison of measures. Caroline Jones looks at the concepts of 'heavy' and 'light'

Understanding **heavy** and light

Some activities which involve the comparison of measures will occur as children play naturally, for example encouraging children to compare the height of brick towers. Other chances may arise from regular pre-school activities such as making cakes.

Settings should aim to provide a balance between child-initiated activities where children can consolidate and experiment and concepts 'taught' through adult-directed activities. The adult plays an important role in promoting mathematical language and thinking, as it is often the adult who introduces new concepts and associated vocabulary. Effective questioning allows children to develop their understanding of comparison of measures in a meaningful context.

Heavy and light
A useful starting point is to introduce the words and concept of 'heavy' and 'light' to children.

❑ Sit a small group around a table or on the carpet in a circle.
❑ Take two objects, one heavy and one light, for example, a stone and a feather.
❑ Let each child pick up both objects at the same time and ask them to say which is heavy and which is light.
❑ Put an assortment of light and heavy objects in a box or bag.
❑ Ask the children in turn to take an object out of the bag.
❑ Encourage each child to say whether their object is heavy or light.

This can be done firstly with a few objects which are easily compared. Then reduce the discrepancy between the objects and increase the number to select from.

Role-play areas can be equipped to support children's learning with a plastic measuring jug, baking or bathroom scales in the home corner, a tape measure in the 'haberdashery shop', scales to weigh the goods in the 'farm shop' or parcels in the 'post office'.

To assess children's understanding, set up a group activity sorting the objects into heavy and light or ask children individually to select a heavy object or a light object from a new group of objects.

Children could record their observations by drawing or sticking pictures into heavy and light sets.

For those who learn more quickly ask challenging questions such as:

❑ Which do you think is heavier?
❑ Which is lighter?
❑ Which is lightest?

Check understanding in the abstract by asking if they think an elephant is heavy or light. It is this type of adult questioning which encourages children to think mathematically and to become familiar with the use of mathematical terms.

In a practical way the concept of comparison could be extended to sort or order groups of three objects into heavy, heavier, heaviest or light, lighter, lightest. Children could then choose their own objects to create a heavy and light interest table which would stimulate further learning.

Balance
Once children understand the concept of heavy and light, move them on by encouraging them to hold two objects, one in each hand, so that they use their hands as a balance and feel which is heavier/lighter. You can then introduce them to balancing scales and weighing familiar objects such as conkers, marbles, sticklebricks or toy cars. Allow the children to 'play' emptying, filling and balancing the buckets. Let them experiment pouring sand or sugar through a plastic funnel into the scales and seeing what happens. Ask questions such as 'Do we need to put more conkers in or less?' 'Do we need to make it heavier to make it balance or lighter?' In play or cooking sessions mathematical vocabulary such as 'weight' and 'grammes' could be introduced. Set up a display of different types of weighing scales which might include simple balances, various kitchen scales, bathroom scales, a spring balance and digital display baking scales.

Caroline Jones

Effective questioning allows children to develop their understanding of comparison of measures in a meaningful context. Caroline Jones explains

Comparing **measures**

Comparison of measures is often overlooked in the pre-school. However, it is an important element of early mathematical experiences which will lay the foundations for a whole range of concepts in science as well as in mathematics. More importantly children will learn that mathematics can be fun!

Comparing height

A variety of construction toys can be used to investigate and compare height. Small groups could build towers and compare heights achieved between groups. Or each morning at snack time, a child could add another brick to a communal tower so they would all see it getting higher each day. Other towers could be built of different heights and displayed.

Another way of comparing measures is to compare the children's heights. Make a height chart - a beanstalk or ladder - and children can mark off each other's heights. Staff can ask questions and introduce terms such as metres and even centimetres. Compare the height of a child and an adult. Use the story of 'Goldilocks and the Three Bears' to reinforce the language and concept of comparison.

When sunflowers or broad beans are planted, you could chart their growth. Make the most of every opportunity, such as on the climbing frames and throwing balls up in the air, to talk about height. It is the quality of questioning which will challenge the children to think about the concepts.

Length and width

A trundle wheel is fun for measuring metres in the garden as it clicks and the children can count the metres.

Plastic Unifix cubes are invaluable for measuring length. Children could be introduced to a metre rule or laying bricks in long or varying length lines. This can be recorded by drawing long and short lines with chalk on large sheets of paper outdoors.

Capacity

Comparison of capacity is best achieved through water play and activities with small groups using a water tray. Different size plastic bottles, coloured water with a plastic funnel are extremely effective. Alternatively, use a variety of plastic containers of varying shapes and sizes such as yoghurt pots and margarine cartons. Maintain the balance between adult-directed and child-initiated activities, allowing children to experiment as well as teaching them through questioning and joining in. Observe as children fill and empty bottles, asking 'Which one holds the most?' Encourage children to pour from one container to another and use words like 'empty' and 'full'.

Caroline Jones

Playdough activity
❑ Sit with a group of children
❑ Show them how to make snakes by rolling out a ball of Playdough into a long thin sausage shape
❑ Display all the snakes in the middle of the table

❑ Ask more questions:
❑ Which do you think is the longest snake?
❑ Which is the shortest?

Children could record this by arranging the snakes on the Playdough board or table mat in order of length.

Mathematical Development

The Early Learning Goals require children to 'find out about past and present events in their own lives and in those of their families and other people they know'. Pam Taylor gives you some starting points

Developing a sense of time

Young children are egotistical and the key to promoting an interest and understanding is to start with them. The topic 'All about me' lends itself perfectly to developing young children's understanding of the passing of time.

Growing up

All children love looking at photographs, especially of themselves, so start with a board 'Look how I've grown' and get parents to bring in photographs of their children as a baby and now. The children will talk to each other about their photograph and be more than willing to talk about themselves in a group situation, developing speaking and listening skills.

From these photographs they can begin to talk about what has happened to them in the past, that is birthdays, staying at home with mum, being in a pram and so on, to talking about what is happening today, going home for dinner/tea, going to bed, to what might happen in the future - going to school, growing up to be a firefighter, or a police officer.

Baby talk

Ask a mum with a new baby to bring their baby in with a collection of baby things - nappy, bottle, dummy, toy rattle. Talk to the children about when they had a bottle. Why don't they need one now? Set up a time line with four drinking cups, for a baby - bottle, toddler - feeder cup, nursery child -

plastic cup with handle and a glass for an adult. Get them to put the cups in order. Talk about why each one is suitable for the particular age group. Can they match and sort baby, toddler and a nursery children's clothes. Look at size of shoes, socks, gloves and other clothes.

Develop this simply by getting children to bring in a photograph of themselves, their mum or dad, grandma or grandad. Perhaps a grandma/grandad could come into nursery to talk to the children, bringing in more photographs of when they were a child. Look at how they dressed and if the photographs are black and white, talk about why. (The problem today is that grandparents are getting younger!)

Toys are an obvious link but it's not always easy to get hold of examples of old toys. Your local museum might have a display of old toys that you could go and see or perhaps your local education authority has a loans service of toys from the past. It's always better if the children can have hands-on experience of playing with old toys, even if they are reproductions. Point out how simply they were made and how few children had to play with. They wouldn't have had computers, remote control cars, robots, or

dolls which talk. Nor would they have had the variety and amount that children have today. Perhaps you could make a simple wall chart of toys the children have and those that their mums and grandmas might have had. I doubt if mum or grandma would have had a computer, and I doubt if the child has a spinning top .....

Remember, children's experiences of the passing of time are:

❑ Celebrating my birthday

❑ Looking at baby photographs and seeing how I've changed

❑ Grandma telling me stories about when she was little

❑ Looking at and talking about old toys, and other objects and being able to recognise that they are different today.

Pam Taylor

Mathematical Development

Introducing graph work to young children may seem daunting but it can be done quite easily as an extension of their sorting work, says Rona Catterall

From **grids to** graphs

First we need to look at three aspects of data handling:

- processing
- representing
- interrogating

Start with sorting as it is a mathematical skill we are constantly developing and refining in our children. Sorting is a fundamental skill of life. To be able to sort we need to recognise attributes for it is one (or more) of these we use to sort into sets, whether it be to sort the blue from the red beads or the cups from the saucers. This sorting is known as processing the data. Once we have sorted our objects we rearrange the information so that we can see at a glance the result of our sorting. As an adult this representation may take the form of a list, chart or diagram while for children it is often a picture. The aim of sorting and representing data is to gain information, to find answers to questions more easily or even raise questions, to interrogate the data.

We do a great deal of processing with young children (sorting) - then we stop. We do not take advantage of the opportunities which would allow them to represent and interrogate the data they have handled.

Suppose we are working with a small group of children. Using a box of nine bricks (five red and four blue), tip out the bricks and the children sort them out into a pile of red and a pile of blue bricks. What then? Our questioning is going to be very limited.

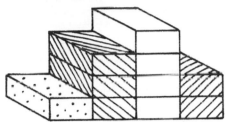

However, if we ask the children to put the sorted bricks into towers and stand the two towers side by side we have a clearer representation, a simple three-dimensional block graph. Now we can ask a variety of questions - comparison questions, number questions, counting questions such as:

- how many red bricks are in the tower?
- how many blue bricks are in the tower?
- which is the taller tower?
- which is the shorter tower?
- which tower has more bricks?
- which tower has fewer bricks?

We do not ask all these questions at once but introduce them gradually as we repeat the activity using two towers of different colours and different numbers of bricks.
When the children can build the two towers and answer many of the questions we extend the work to three towers and later maybe four, but no more. The questions would be as before but more searching questions could be asked:

- which is the tallest tower?
- which is the shortest tower?
- which tower has the most bricks?
- which tower has the fewest bricks?
- are any of the towers the same height?

Towers compare easily as they stand on a base line. As children sort objects which will not stack, such as toys, we need to make a simple grid to aid comparison. On a large sheet of paper (sugar paper) draw a two-column grid making the sections large enough to hold each object (about 10x10 cm).

Again, we sit with our group of children and some small toys, say four boats and three cars. The children sort them, then one car is placed in each space in the first column starting at the base, the boats go in the second column. When our graph is finished we label the bottom of each column with the corresponding word. We ask the same type of questions as with the two towers.

The activity can be repeated varying the task by using different objects, buttons, material pieces, pictures, shapes, and so on. There are lots of possibilities to add variety and interest. Each time the activity is repeated the children take more responsibility for making the graph without help, while we encourage the children to tell us about their graph, to answer or to ask questions.

When moving to a grid of three columns and maybe four (but no more) it is important to remember that using more than two sets of data will challenge some children. Again the questioning can be more searching.

So children have developed from sorting into piles to showing us how to represent data in a clear, graphical way from which they can extract a lot of interesting information. We have provided them with opportunities to practise many of the mathematical aspects asked for in the Early Learning Goals - count, compare, sort, discuss and use mathematical language. At the same time we are providing a sound foundation for later, more abstract graph work.

Rona Catterall

You don't have to be an artist to help your children develop their own drawing skills. You simply need to be able to show the children what to do and how to do it - a different thing altogether from producing great works of art yourself, says Hilary White

Developing drawing skills

Start off by leaving your youngest children free to explore with wax crayons and pencils. Don't worry about acres of 'scribble' at this early stage - far from wasting paper, the child is learning to become comfortable with a pencil and, at the same time, refining his fine motor skills.

Little by little, the random scribbles become representational. As the child develops his hand control and realises that a drawing can represent something in real life, so he starts to produce pictures of people, houses, animals, aeroplanes, wherever his fancy takes him. He may be the only one who can identify the subject of his drawing but that doesn't matter - he has grasped the *idea* of representational drawing. At this stage, you can introduce observational drawing.

Observational drawing
Show the children the outline (shape) of a particular object and explain that you are going to look very carefully at that object so that you can draw it. It's a good idea to carry out the activity yourself so the children can see what to do, emphasising all the time that you are closely observing the object as you draw. Always remember that your own picture does not have to be expert, as long as your demonstration clearly shows the children how to do the activity for themselves. Similarly, don't expect realistic results from the children. The point of this activity is to enable the child to understand and go through the process, not to achieve a perfect end product.

What to choose
Begin by choosing objects with a clear, simple outline, such as geometric shapes, leaves, shells, ornaments, toys. As the children's skill develops, you can introduce more complex objects with lines, splodges and other details - the model of a cat with interesting markings, the pattern of veins on a leaf or each other. If you have a child who

needs encouraging, offer an object geared towards his or her particular interests.

Using your pencil to shade
As well as drawing lines, the artist needs to be able to shade. For the young child, this means having the skill to use and control your pencil so that you can cover an area of the paper. There are a number of techniques you can introduce:

Zig-zags:
MMM MMMM
short tall
MMM MMMM
tight loose

Hatching: ///// ||||

Cross-hatching: ▦

Dots:
loose tight

Zig-zags - this is the easiest shading technique. Once the children have got the hang of it, encourage them to experiment with short, tall, loose or tight zig-zags (see diagram).
Hatching and cross-hatching - these are proper artistic terms for shading with short, separate lines or with criss-crossing. Hatching is less challenging than cross-hatching.
Dots - dotting with the pencil is noisy and great fun. It is more successful with a blunt, soft pencil. Experiment with sharp and blunt pencils. Introduce soft drawing pencils (B or 2B grade) and show the children how to smudge lines and marks with a finger. Pressing hard or gently on the paper will

also give different effects, as well as helping the child to think about and develop pencil control. Older children can try using a rubber on an area of pencil shading.

Drawing in colour
All of these activities can be done in colour, using various media such as wax crayons, coloured pencils or chalks. You can also introduce some of the following techniques to create special effects:
❑ Two colours can be used one on top of the other, starting with the darker/stronger colour.
❑ Explore making marks with the different parts of the wax or chalk - the round end, the pointed tip, the entire length of the stick.
❑ Stabbing with chalk or wax gives lovely dots or short lines.
❑ Chalk marks are very effective if smudged with a finger.

Using your drawing skills
These activities and techniques are not an end in themselves. The aim is to give the children new skills that they can use in their free drawing. Remind them to use their shading techniques in their drawings to add pattern and texture. Encourage them to choose objects in the classroom or garden to draw, and give them magnifying glasses to help them observe closely.

Once the children have become familiar with the drawing pencils, chalks, wax crayons and coloured pencils, make them freely available. Include a choice of different coloured papers and encourage the children to select the most suitable coloured paper/medium for the subject of their drawing. For example, chalks on black paper is particularly appropriate for fireworks or Christmas lights. Skin tone paper and crayons are important for drawing people accurately.

Hilary White

Young children love using wax crayons. Brightly coloured and easy to grip, they are the perfect tool for early drawing and mark making and a versatile resource for introducing new ideas and possibilities to your budding young artists

Using wax crayons

There are many different types of wax crayon to choose from. Buy the best quality you can afford and introduce variations such as glitter or fluorescent crayons. Triangular shaped crayons are worth looking out for if you want to do rubbings. Avoid crayons described as 'washable' or 'paint sticks'; these are water soluble and not suitable for making scratch cards or wax resist pictures.

Children need time to explore and enjoy using wax crayons at first. When they have developed sufficient hand control, show them some different ways of using the crayons.

Offer older children a variety of coloured papers to work on and encourage them to experiment with just one or two colours at a time. Sometimes, the same wax crayon can look completely different depending on what colour paper you are working on. For example, the yellow crayon that looks dull on white paper can look bright and fluorescent on black. Encourage the children to think about which effect they

prefer, to help them realise that they can choose different materials to create different effects.

Rubbings

When the children are able to use the crayon along its length, show them how to take rubbings. Place a piece of paper over an object with a raised pattern and rub the crayon over it to reveal the pattern. Combine this with a sticking activity - give the children shapes cut from thick card to glue onto a background. They can then take rubbings of their own pattern. Try using more than one colour to create a rainbow rubbing.

New colours

Wax crayons can be combined to make new colours. Always start off with the strongest colour, blue before yellow for example. Show the child how to colour in an area with the blue, pressing lightly. Colour over the blue with the yellow, this time pressing hard. You can then show the child how to draw onto the wax layer with a sharp pencil to reveal the blue underneath.

Wax resist

Ask the children to make a drawing or pattern with chunky wax crayons. Encourage them to cover a good proportion of the paper, pressing as hard as possible. Next, paint over the whole picture, using a thin colour wash and a thick brush. The original wax drawing resists the watery paint so that the colour shines through. Mix up the colour wash in advance by combining one part

liquid or powder paint with 20 parts of water.

Scratch cards

Even very young children can use this technique to create an eye-catching picture. Work on A5 sized cartridge paper or thin card and colour the whole card with wax crayons, using a variety of colours. Cover the paper so that no white is showing through and then paint over the wax layer with thick black paint. If you have ready-mixed paint, use it neat from the bottle rather than diluted. You may need to paint two coats, leaving the first one to dry before starting the second. When the paint is dry, the children can use a sharp pencil to scratch patterns into the paint, revealing the bright wax layer underneath. Involve the children as much as possible with each stage of making the cards.

Stained glass windows

Give the children circles of greaseproof or tracing paper to work on and encourage them to draw and colour in areas of colour like a stained glass window. Another variation is to crayon onto white typing paper and then paint over the back of the picture with cooking oil. Involve the children as much as possible in painting on the oil; older ones will be fascinated to see how the oil changes the appearance of the paper and wax colour. Tape the pictures onto the window so that the sun shines through, bringing out the glowing, jewel-like quality of the wax.

Save any chunks or shavings of crayon from sharpening or cutting notches. Fold a piece of white typing paper in half and show the children how to sprinkle the wax inside the paper. Cover the folded paper with an old tea towel and press over with a warm iron to melt the wax. Paint the back of the paper with oil and tape it to the window.

Hilary White

Different effects

❑ Pressing lightly gives a faint, shadowy effect.

❑ Pressing hard gives a strong, rich colour.

❑ Jabbing the crayon on the paper gives dots and flecks of colour (and lovely sound effects!).

❑ Using the whole crayon along its length is a good way of colouring in a large area. (As a variation, you can cut notches into the side of the crayon. Choose the thickest crayons you can find and don't cut in further than the centre of the crayon. Use lots of different coloured crayons and vary the size and spacing of the notches - good for creating patterns on backgrounds or wrapping paper.

❑ Older children can experiment with using the flat bottom of the crayon as well as the side. Give them thinner crayons to explore or sharpen a crayon to give it a pointed end.

Early art and craft activities create the ideal time for talk and action to complement each other. By exploring ways of working with paint you are encouraging discussion between adults and children in a secure setting

Experiments with paint

Simple experiments with different techniques give children the opportunity to have control over the work they are doing and the confidence to talk naturally about work in progress. All these ideas need to be introduced through a structured session – children need to know the rules and boundaries of working in a different way. Some of them may be old favourites but sometimes we forget how the simplest ideas can give children pleasure and a sense of achievement.

Printing patterns

You can print with anything - natural or made - and make the most wonderful patterns or abstract pictures. There is no right or wrong way, whatever the children produce is individual and created by them alone. Make up the paint to a creamy consistency in a shallow dish. Dip the shape into the paint and print onto the paper. Use hands, dib and dab with fingers – children love getting messy for a purpose! To introduce a mathematical dimension, make up pictures of all circles, squares and so on or repeat colours. Talk about where they might have seen patterns used in this way – what about wallpaper or wrapping paper? Bring some examples in for them to look at. How could their patterns be used? Get them to comment on each other's work. Who'd like a jumper with Tara's pattern on it? Which ones do they like best and why? Do they have a favourite colour?

Bubble painting

Add washing-up liquid to a thinnish powder paint in different size containers. Get the children to blow through straws into the paint until the bubbles froth over the top of the container. Place the paper on top of the bubbles and gently press down. Fill the whole of the paper in this way and then cut around the shapes of the bubbles to create lovely bubble creatures. The children can add eyes and a mouth with felt pen.

Note: It's a good idea for the children to practise blowing through a straw before using the paint. Ask them to blow a ping-pong ball across the surface of a table - that way they learn the purpose of blowing and enjoy the fun of making the ball roll without touching it. You can then take this a step further.

Blow a picture!

Put a small spoonful of mixed paint onto the paper. Get the children to blow gently across the paper to produce lovely spidery effects. What happens if they blow gently? What if they blow hard?

Flick and splatter

Children love the freedom of being able to flick paint onto paper without worrying about the consequences! Flick it or dribble it onto one side of paper and then fold it in half to give you a butterfly painting.

Feathers for brushes

Use different size feathers to dip into paint and move across paper to make interesting patterns.

Using string

Use lengths of thick wool or string and dip into medium mixed powder paint. The children can wriggle the string around on the paper to create a pattern or place the string flat on the paper into a shape then carefully lift it off to see what they have created.

Painting with marbles!

Use black sugar paper and bright fluorescent paint for a dramatic effect. Place the black paper into a shallow tray and drop a paint

covered marble into it. Get the children to tilt and rock the tray in different ways to send the marble around the paper leaving behind a trail.

Display

It's a good idea to have several of these activities set out on tables in one session or choose one a day over a period of a week. That way the children can get a real feel for the huge variety of effects they can achieve with the same basic materials - it just takes a bit of imagination. As their confidence grows you'll find them coming up with their own suggestions for techniques to try!

When you've finished, make a big display to show all the different effects and talk about which you like the best. Perhaps parents could join in and try to guess what their children used to make the pictures.

Pam Taylor

Observational art work sounds like a tall order for four-year-olds, but Janet Gilbert suggests you set aside time for children to study their environment and learn to see things as they really are

Observational art work

Children's drawings have a universal appeal. We all enjoy looking at their drawings of parents with green and orange hair or the blob labelled 'mummy'. These imaginative interpretations of the world form an important stage in children's development. However, children also need to learn to see things as they really are and how to make accurate observations of their environment. Close observation work is a method of developing visual awareness in the framework of art and craft sessions.

In a close observation class children are given an object and asked to draw or paint it. This may sound a tall order for four-year-olds, but the importance of the session is not so much in the actual painting but in the observation carried out before the painting begins. The children are encouraged to look at the object closely and discuss its various attributes. Only after this do they begin their painting, with the clear aim of painting the object as it actually is and not as an imaginative response to it.

The first close observation classes can be very labour intensive as the children will require a lot of guidance and supervision. However, as their visual skills develop they will need less help from you.

A session consists of two parts: the observation and the painting or drawing. The first is carried out as a class activity, the second individually. Each child will need help at first so it is easier to supervise a small group of about four children at a time. You will need to engage the rest of the class in other absorbing activities that require minimal supervision.

What to paint
The object must attract the children's interest, be relatively uncomplicated and have a clearly defined outline. Any patterns should be simple so that the children can try to reproduce them. The object can be related to a class topic. Here are some popular ones to try:

❑ flowers - tulips and daffodils have some good shapes and vases can have simple but bold patterns on them.

❑ fruit and vegetables - a chance to introduce more unusual ones from other countries; cut them in half to reveal patterns made by seeds.

❑ pets - cat, dog or rabbit. (One of our children included her nits in this category and brought some to class in a magnifying jar!)

❑ objects and artefacts from different cultures.

❑ small objects and mini-beasts viewed through magnifying glasses.

❑ a bicycle - the wheels provide easy recognisable shapes and serve as reference points for the painting.

❑ percussion instruments - drum, triangle, tambourine and recorders.

Decide which materials are suitable: paint, charcoal, pencils or wax crayons. Paint may be the best medium for young children new to this activity. Most children are familiar with using paint and the results will be big, bold and colourful. Only put out the paint colours that are necessary for the exercise - when they are more experienced you can encourage them to experiment by mixing their own colours.

Class observation
Place the object in a prominent position on a clear surface so that the children will not be distracted by surrounding clutter. Tell them that they are going to look very closely at the object before drawing a picture of it. Ask questions which prompt them to look closely and draw their attention to details. Let the children touch the object if appropriate.

This observation and discussion period is the key to the learning outcome. Ten to fifteen minutes is enough time to spend on the initial session. It is often helpful to demonstrate the painting, asking the children to give you instructions.

When you are ready to begin, choose four children. Ask each child where they are going to start on the paper and what colour they are going to use. Keep an eye on their progress and ask questions to prompt them when necessary. As the children become used to this type of work they will require less supervision and you will be able to increase the size of the group. When the paintings are finished they can be framed and made into an attractive wall display.

Children find close observation work absorbing. It promotes concentration as well as developing visual skills. The children also take great pride and pleasure in the pictures they produce. It is a very rewarding activity, both in terms of learning outcomes and in the pleasure and enjoyment of the class during the sessions.

Janet Gilbert

You can respond to great works of art at any level. You might like a painting because of the colours used or because of how it makes you feel - and children are no exception. Dianne Irving shows how children as young as three can learn to be art critics

Using works of art

Art plays a part in everyone's life - creative images are all around us in books, on television, on advertising hoardings and in magazines. We are sometimes attracted to the images we see and sometimes they provoke moods or feelings in us that at first we don't really understand. It is important, therefore, that we equip children with the tools and thought processes that they need in order to analyse these images for themselves.

Many early years practitioners are frightened to introduce children to the work of famous artists partly because they are unsure about their own feelings and understanding of the artists' work. There is a great deal of pretentious snobbery among adults where art is concerned.

If you are at all worried or anxious about how children will receive a piece of art work then rest assured that the early years setting is an excellent place to dispel any anxieties. When young children are introduced to a piece of art they are free of any pre-conceived ideas about the work or the artist. They will react from gut feelings and enter into some excellent discussions.

Start your collection

If you would like to introduce children to art then begin by collecting reproductions of paintings that appeal to you. Excellent resources are available through your local library, art club and art gallery or high street print shops as well as on the Internet. Encourage parents to join in - you will be amazed at how rich and diverse a collection of prints can be put together in a short time.

At first, introduce children to a piece of artwork that you like and feel comfortable sharing. Each setting will have to decide upon what artwork they consider appropriate

for sharing with young children; work containing nudity or strong religious images may not be suitable! But do introduce art from a range of cultural backgrounds.

What can you see?

To begin, gather your children together and show them the image you have chosen. Explain what the composition is called and tell children a little about the artist. Make this information relevant - it may only be necessary to give children the artist's name.

Ask the children to look carefully at the picture and describe what they see. Encourage them to look at the colours in the painting. Count how many different colours have been used. Is there any particular part of the painting that catches their attention or draws their eye?

How does it make you feel?

Ask the children to consider how the painting makes them feel. Try to encourage children to put their own feelings into words as this gives a far more honest response than if we lead them into saying things such as 'It makes me feel happy', and so on.

❑ Imagine being able to get inside the painting. How would you feel? What could you see all around you? What noises would you hear?
❑ Why do you think the artist chose to paint this particular image? After these discussions, ask the children to consider if they like the painting or not.

Don't be afraid to share how you feel about the painting. If you have an opinion, then it is worthwhile and valuable. If a painting makes you feel angry, frightened or sad, take some time to consider why you feel this way. In many instances if you feel like this, it was the artist's intention!

Share other works by the same artist with children and encourage them to begin seeing similarities in style between painting. Look at artists with distinctive styles such as Gustav Klimt. Look at a selection of paintings and try to identify all those painted by a particular artist. Work with children to try to paint their own pictures in a similar style to the artist they have been studying.

Dianne Irving

Suitable paintings to start you off:
The Sailor - Picasso   *The Kiss* - Gustav Klimt
The Soul of the Rose - John William Waterhouse
July, the Seaside - L S Lowry
Flaming June - Frederick Leighton
Thanksgiving - Doris Lee

How about a group of children building their own farm? It will give you a great display and - more importantly - it will help children understand three-dimensional shapes, the properties of materials, and teach them to work with one another

Introducing **three** dimensions

Through making models from recycled materials children develop understanding and skills in several areas. There is a great deal of exploration of two- and three-dimensional shape: circles, oblongs, squares, cylinders, cubes and cuboids. There is exploration of the properties of the shapes: 'Can you make the cylinder stand on the box?' 'Which of the shapes will roll?'

Children will also develop familiarity with the properties of the materials they are handling. 'What could you use to make some soft wings for your bird?' 'Could you give the rocket a shiny nose cone?' Such skills contribute to Knowledge and Understanding of the World and are an important aspect of 'junk' modelling, but they are only part of the story.

Social skills

Modelling recycled materials is a creative occupation. You only have to listen to the conversation around a modelling table to tap into the flights of imagination taking place. It is also a forum for the development of social skills, sharing scissors, taking turns with the glue, or holding the wobbly piece still whilst a friend wraps the sticky tape around it.

In the early years children's ideas will mostly be 'materials led'. In the same way in which busy adults will decide what to make for tea having viewed the contents of the fridge, children will decide what to make having looked at the materials on offer.

Something about a particular plastic box will inspire the making of a boat or a pond. The long cardboard tube will suggest a magic wand or a telescope. It is only as familiarity with the materials grows through experience that children will begin to be able to 'design' before making. (To return to the catering analogy, imagine, as an adult, being asked to plan a menu using unfamiliar ingredients.)

Sometimes, as a result, children get into a rut, sticking to the tried and tested ideas which they know are successful. Every visit to the modelling table for a fortnight produces yet another aeroplane!

Working together

One way to break this cycle is to ensure that the selection of materials offered varies as much as possible. Another is to plan a large scale collaborative model environment.

Start by choosing a theme for your model, selecting an idea which is relevant to the children. You might link it to a recent visit to a playground, park or wildlife reserve, or you could introduce a story linked idea such as the *The Village of Round and Square Houses* by Ann Grifalconi, the Three Bears' wood or the farm from *Rosie's Walk*.

Explain to the children that they are going to work together to make something. It will be bigger than anything they could make on their own! Talk about the place they are going to make. What sort of things might

they find there? Encourage the children to offer as many ideas as possible. In a park, for example, children might suggest a play area, some seats, trees, a cafe, paths and fencing. Explain that everyone is going to make something to go in the model layout. They can make individual contributions or work in small groups.

Materials

Present the children with a wide range of modelling materials. You could use entirely recycled materials, a selection of construction kits, including wooden blocks, or if you are working with older children, a selection of both. It is especially useful to have a few props in the form of appropriate model people, animals and/or vehicles. You might also find it useful to have a prepared base such as a large piece of green fabric to help in setting the scene.

Encourage the children to look carefully at the materials and to think about what they would like to make. You could start by making a few suggestions - 'We could stick some of these lolly sticks in Plasticine to make a fence', or 'This box would make a wonderful barn'. As the layout grows the children become more and more motivated and excited by their achievement. Conversation becomes increasingly technical, 'You need to make the slide more slippy!', 'Who's going to make the tables for the cafe?'

Co-operation, language, creativity, planning - a wealth of developing skills, all of which will be relived as parents are brought in to view the marvel and to hear the story of its construction.

Penny Coltman

Using cardboard boxes

The brightly coloured, shiny surface on the outside of most household packaging boxes is difficult to hide when modelling. So turn the boxes inside out! Open up the seam down one of the long sides, and carefully undo any remaining glued edges.

Reverse all the fold lines on the box, joining it back together with double-sided tape, masking tape or staples. (Ordinary adhesive tape can be used, but it is difficult to paint over.)

The result is a box with plain, matt sides which can easily be decorated using paint, felt pens or crayons.

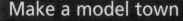

Make a model town

Cereal boxes painted to look like houses, a toothpaste box with wheels and windows drawn on to look like a coach, smaller square boxes with wheels as cars and smaller houses ....

Diwali, the festival of light, is a happy time in the Hindu year when people decorate their homes with diva lamps, lights, garlands and special traditional patterns or rangoli. Why not decorate your nursery, too?

Decorating for **Diwali**

Diva lamps

You will need: air-hardening clay, small candles or nightlights, clay tools.

Let the children handle the clay at first until it softens. It may help to have a small pot of water that they can dip a finger in and work into the clay. Form the clay into a small bowl shaped like a teardrop. Make a hole in the centre using a small candle or nightlight. Be careful that the base of the holder is flat so that it doesn't wobble! The surface of the clay can be decorated using clay tools. The children can scratch patterns into the clay or even push small dry pasta shapes into it. You might like to paint the finished lamp using brushes or spray paint.

You could paint pictures of diva lamps onto the windows using ready mix paint. If you add a drop of washing-up liquid to the paint it makes it easier to clean off later!

Rangoli patterns

These geometric patterns are made on the floors and doorsteps of houses to give thanks and make visitors feel welcome. During Diwali competitions are often held to design rangoli patterns. Traditionally they are made using coloured rice flour and follow elaborate designs that often include flowers The rice flour also serves as food for wild birds, squirrels and even ants.

Try making your own pretty rangoli patterns. You can use lots of different materials such as seeds, rice, cereals, coconut, sand, mixed with powder paint or food dye for colour. Make the patterns on strong pieces of card and place them on the floor or in the doorways. First apply glue in the required

shape and then sprinkle the dry materials on top. The children could also make rangoli patterns using coloured chalks on an outside play area or pavement. You could have an exhibition of all the rangoli patterns.

Dressing up

At Diwali people enjoy wearing new clothes and decorating their hands and feet with mendhi patterns. Mendhi is made from henna and is a brown dye. Hindu brides also wear these traditional decorations. Ask the children to draw around their hands on paper and design some mendhi patterns. Cut out the hand shapes and display them on the walls. Get the children to experiment with making the mendhi patterns on their own hands and feet. They can use washable brown felt pen or paint and cotton wool buds. Can they make the patterns match? Is it easier to paint each others hands? How does it feel? Does it tickle?

Dancing

There are many dances associated with Diwali. One of the simplest to try with young children is the dandia raas. This uses dandia or decorated sticks.

You will need: 30cm lengths of dowelling, coloured sticky tape, paints.

Ask the children to choose two different colours of tape or paint and decorate the sticks. Help the children to find partners and stand facing one another. Can they tap the sticks together above their heads? Try tapping each others sticks. Ask the children to turn around and tap the sticks together again. Can they dance around their partners? Try and find some Indian music for the children to dance to or provide a simple drum beat. The dandia raas music starts slowly and gradually gets faster. Try inventing some simple moves of your own. As the music speeds up take care not to hit your partner's fingers by mistake!

Fireworks

Any Diwali party would not be complete without some fireworks. Remember the fireworks safety code and talk to the children about keeping safe around fireworks. There are lots of creative activities connected to fireworks. Try making a group firework picture on black paper using fluorescent paints, glitter, silver and gold stars, and shiny paper. You can use toothbrushes to spray the paint effectively like sparks. Run your finger or thumb towards you, down the head of the toothbrush. (Try it the other way and you will get covered in paint!) Children will enjoy working together on a big painting to display on the wall.

Judith Harries

This season cries out for something glittering to be made and taken home, says Rhona Whiteford. Here's a simple printing activity made special with dribbled glue and glitter. It can be a greetings card or a decoration

Christmas craft

This sort of structured art work, which has a series of steps to follow, helps the children develop their concentration. It is also a great opportunity to talk together about the task in hand, to develop dexterity and that difficult skill of hand-eye co-ordination.

Although everyone makes the same decoration, each child is able to express their creativity by choosing their own colours and printing blocks and making their own glitter trail. It is almost a group activity because everyone is following the same procedure and later groups can watch the pioneers do theirs. This does help develop a sense of community, encourages the timid ones and also helps the children to feel that they are learning and growing like their friends.

Make a glittering stocking

This glittering stocking involves some simple printing. Have your own stocking ready made as an example and also be prepared to do one with each group. Children can see what they are aiming for and can work with a sense of purpose. Yours can stay as decorations (maybe round a Christmas noticeboard) when the children take theirs home.

You will need: some thin white card or good white cartridge paper; ready mixed paint in red and two shades of green; some things to print with (polystyrene shapes, sponge stars, cotton reels, tubes); flat containers for paint with a thick layer of foam in each; PVA glue and spreaders in small containers; silver glitter; cotton wool; red parcel ribbon.

Preparation

This activity is done in two stages, with the printing first and the dribbled glue second. You need a drying area for the printing or do the activity at two sessions.

Cut out the stocking shapes in advance to roughly A4 size. You could cut simple circles or diamonds so that those with other faiths can add them to their decorations. Prepare paints in trays and have bottles nearby to fill up as you go. Put only enough paint in the tray to be absorbed by the sponge so that the surface is not too wet. Choose printing items that have enough space for a good hand hold.

For the glue dribbling you need two separate ends of a large table, each with a large sheet of paper, one for the gluing and one for the glittering operation. Put the glitter in a saucer and after each child has finished pour the remaining glitter from the paper back onto the saucer.

The printing

Put each child's name on the back of their stocking before they start. Show the children how to print by dipping the block into the paint, then scraping off any excess on the side of the tray. Place the printing block down gently to get a good image. Encourage them to make their own artistic choices - let them just use one colour and shape if they want, making any arrangement they like. Talk about the different shapes, sizes and colours and about what we use Christmas stockings for or about decorations in general. Let the paint dry thoroughly.

Glue dribbling

Put the painted stocking on the glue table and, using a glue spreader, take up a fair load of glue. Holding it about 30cm above the stocking, show the children how to let the glue dribble in a spidery pattern over the paint. Move the spreader around to direct the glue. Young children are sometimes so fascinated by the dribble they forget to move the line around!

The glitter

Now move to the glitter area and put the stocking on the paper. The children can do all this themselves with a little guidance. Using their fingers, they need to pick up small piles of glitter and cover all the dribbles thickly, without touching the glue at all. Tip the stocking and tap it lightly to remove any excess and reveal the glittered lines over the bright paint. Save the remaining glitter before the next child comes.

Finishing off can be done by the children on a different part of the table, but needs care if the glitter dribble is still wet. Glue cotton wool to the top edge of the stocking. When everything is dry, you can staple on a ribbon loop for hanging and add a greetings label on the back.

Rhona Whiteford

Creative Development

If you are building up an instrument collection from scratch, it can be quite bewildering knowing where to start. Anne Hunter gives an idea of what you might need and what you can get for £100. And if you don't have the funds, you can always make your own

Choosing musical instruments

The first thing you will discover is that musical instruments are expensive. Don't be put off by this. Any toy or game that is going to survive frequent and boisterous handling will need to be of good quality and therefore not cheap. The same goes for musical instruments.

Save up

It is well worth saving up for some decent, sturdy instruments that will stand the test of time. You could have a special fund-raising event dedicated to this purpose. Why not have a sponsored sing? Get the children to collect sponsors for the number of different songs or rhymes they can sing in, say, 20 minutes. Write to local shops and businesses for sponsorship. (Write down the songs in a list before you start - don't rely on inspiration!)

You will probably need about £100 to buy a new collection of, say, 25 instruments. If you are attached to a school, county council or any other large establishment that is VAT registered, you will be exempt from VAT. If you're not, seek out your local music shop and browse through their catalogues. You can place your order through them and many will be happy to give you a discount if the goods are for educational use. (You will need to produce proof of where you are from, like a letter on headed paper or an insurance certificate). Don't be afraid to ask!

You can buy ready made-up boxes of a range of suitable instruments, usually called something like Early Years/Key Stage 1 Collection. While I can see the attraction of these, I prefer to pick my own. I think you can save money this way, as well as being able to choose instruments that suit your own needs.

You will probably come across instruments 'especially for pre-school children' which are designed to look like monkeys, frogs, and so on. In my experience, children do not need to have musical instruments disguised in order to want to play them! They are thrilled to play 'real, grown-up instruments'.

Four main categories

You will need a good mixture of instruments to give your children a wide range of musical experiences. There are four main categories to choose from. Try to have some from each. Don't be confused by fancy names - you will recognise them all when you see them in the shop or catalogue!

Wood:	Woodblocks; castanets; claves; agogos; octochimes; guiro.
Metal:	Triangles; Indian bells; finger cymbals; bicycle bell; chimes; cymbals.
Skins:	Drums; tambourines; tambours; bongos.
Shakers:	Maracas; tambourine sticks; bell trees; cabasas.

There is also a large range of unusual instruments from different countries available. These will add interest and extend the children's experience. Here is a sample collection, which would be fine for a group of 25 children. I have costed this at just under £100 (including VAT), from any reputable typical music retailer:

- 6 pairs of wooden castanets
- 2 pairs of claves
- 1 two-tone woodblock
- 1 large woodblock
- 1 bicycle bell
- 2 pairs of Indian bells
- 2 pairs of finger cymbals
- 2 triangles
- 2 sets of hand bells

- 2 large maracas
- 2 tambourine (or 'jingle') sticks
- 1 tambour
- 1 tambourine

I realise that some groups might struggle to raise £100 in one go, but I would urge you not to stint on quality. Cheap, plastic instruments from discount shops will not last and could be dangerously sharp if broken. As with toys, your instruments need to be safe. It is far better, in the long run, to add to your collection gradually, supplementing it in the meantime with your own home-made instruments, which can be effective as well as giving children a sense of achievement and of course being great fun! Here are two simple ones to try:

Cabasa

Thread coloured beads or small pasta tubes onto pieces of string or elastic. Tie or tape these in rows around an empty, lidded tin (you could use any size tin, for instance golden syrup, coffee or powdered milk). To play, either hold firmly while shaking with a wrist twisting action - this is a lot less complicated than it sounds - or hold firmly in one hand while pushing the beads around the tin with the fingers of the other.

Claves

Buy some thick dowelling from a DIY shop and cut it into equal lengths of around 6 inches or 15 cm. Make sure the ends are well sanded. Let the children decorate them with brightly coloured paint (you may want to varnish them with non-toxic clear varnish to stop the paint from rubbing off onto sweaty little hands). Hold one in each hand and tap (carefully!).

Anne Hunter

Anne Hunter hopes to convince non-musicians that they can create worthwhile, positive musical experiences for their pre-school children without the need for a formal musical education, the ability to play an instrument or access to a specialist music teacher

Organising a **music session**

Although there will be times during the day when singing fits nicely into your schedule - often at the end of a session or just before drinks time - it is important to set aside times for designated music sessions as well.

Some of you may have a visiting music teacher and therefore will have a regular time for music. The rest of you have an advantage - you can be a little more flexible in selecting a good time. If you plan, for instance, an instrumental activity that requires a reasonable level of concentration, and the children are overexcited because they have been stuck inside on a rainy day, then you can postpone it. As a visiting music teacher, I cannot be postponed at such short notice! Nevertheless, in that situation I would probably decide to do something less taxing, like a favourite songs request session.

The best time
Children of this age tend to be more alert and responsive during the morning, so aim for this if at all possible. I once had a regular 1.30 pm slot at a nursery: the children had recently had lunch, followed by a lengthy, energetic outside play. As you can imagine, some of them were more ready for a snooze than a music session!

Size of group
There is no clear cut answer as to how many children should be included in a music session. Much will depend on your level of staffing, whether you have volunteers or students to support the children and, of course, how many children you have. Ideally, some musical activities (particularly instrumental work, when you may occasionally want to hear each child individually) work best in smaller groups, say up to twelve. This is primarily because children of this age can become impatient and restless while waiting for their turn.

Accepting that this will not always be possible, do try to have as much adult support as possible, even if this means encouraging parents to come in and help.

Where to sit
In an ideal world, music sessions should be in a quiet room, away from the main play area. As this is rarely possible, always have a good tidy beforehand to make sure that there are as few distractions as possible.

You will have your own ideas about which seating arrangements work best for your children. I find that sitting in a circle on the floor is most successful. The children have easy access to their instruments without having to bend down from a chair, and they have a clear view of you.

How much time?
The ideal length of a music session will vary according to your needs and resources. If you have a new group of very young children, you will probably find ten to fifteen minutes is enough.
A good way to get them used to sitting still and keeping their interest at this stage is to sing a 'hello' song. Try singing, to the tune

of 'Twinkle Twinkle Little Star':
'Hello Matthew, how are you? It's so nice to sing with you.'

Start with sounds
Before introducing instruments, help the children to become aware of the many ways they can use their voices and bodies to make sounds and rhythms. Experiment with different types of vocal sounds - high/low, sweet/growly, loud/soft, long/short. Try clapping, stamping feet, rubbing hands, drumming fingers, and so on, and discuss the different sounds they make.

Listen to environmental sounds, either real or taped (try your local library for sound-effects tapes or CDs) and imitate them in various ways. You could take the children outside to see how many different sounds they can hear. This is useful for developing listening skills; they have to be very quiet!

Clap simple rhythms and see if the children can imitate you, first as a group and then individually. One single clap is hard to copy; two or three seem simpler for some children. A good way to help a child really tune in to sounds is ask them to clap their own name. See how many names have the same number of sounds (for example, Paul and Sam, Robert and Jodie, Ravinder and Christopher). Think of words from your current topics and see whose names fit with them (for example, Sam, snail; Jodie, spider; Christopher, millipede; Gabriella, caterpillar).

Introducing instruments
When the children seem to be confident with this concept, you can begin to introduce instruments. Start the session with a couple of songs as this focuses the children. (You might also feel ready to increase the duration of the session.)

Before giving each child an instrument, choose one and demonstrate it yourself. Talk about the sound it makes and whether or not they like it. Then pass it round and let everybody have a go - perhaps they could try and play their name.

Add another, contrasting instrument and repeat what you have just done. Which do the children prefer?

Choose instruments that make different sounds, for instance a wood block, a triangle, a shaker and a drum. How might the children describe them and the sounds they make? This is excellent for language development, as well as teaching the children that not all instruments make the same noises, and that they can be played quietly as well as loudly.

When you feel the children are ready, they can each have their own instrument. You will need to have a few strategies up your sleeve here! Young children simply love to hold and play percussion instruments but the noise they produce can be deafening, as well as not very productive musically!

Try not to be too strict too soon. Imagine the frustration of being given an exciting instrument to play and then immediately being told to be quiet! Let each child 'test' their instrument first of all, to check that they know how to play it and to 'make sure it's working'. Then they need to be able to place their instruments gently on the floor in front of them. Insist on careful handling; musical instruments, like books, are worthy of special respect. It will take time for some children to achieve this kind of discipline with the instruments, but it is well worth persevering. Try to leave time for a couple of songs or games where the children can bash away happily without restraint - this is a good incentive for attentive behaviour.

There are various ways to hand instruments out and the methods you use will depend on the time you have and your objectives. I often display the instruments on a table or large cushions on the floor at the beginning of a session; this allows the children to see what is available (rummaging around in a box can be noisy and frustrating).

Pass the teddy

A fun game you could try (if your numbers are fairly small) is 'Pass the teddy'. Pass a teddy round the circle while you sing a song; whoever is holding the teddy when the music stops gets to choose an instrument. Carry on until everyone has an instrument. You could sing, to the tune of 'Baa baa black sheep': 'Pass the teddy, round and round and round. When we stop you choose a sound.'

Tappers and shakers

Another way is to pre-select groups of instruments with similar sounds, such as tapping and shaking. Ask each child to choose an instrument that makes a particular sound, then divide the group into tappers and shakers; this often adds an element of healthy competition to see which group performs their task best (a simple 'stopping and starting' test is good to start with). Add further dimensions with tinging and banging sounds!

Try to have some sessions where there is genuine free choice so the children can experiment with different sounds. There will inevitably be the occasional scuffle over some instruments, just as there are with particular toys. You will need to exercise your much practised mediation skills here! Also, there will be times when it is more appropriate simply to hand out the instruments randomly; this is fine too! It's really a case of achieving a balance.

Signs and signals

From the very first time you introduce the instruments, it is important to establish definite signs for starting and stopping (stopping being the most tricky to control!).

Choose signals you feel comfortable with; I generally use an emphatic, downward point to indicate 'Go!' and a policeman-style outstretched, flat hand to mean 'Stop!' The children will need a lot of practice, but they have great fun achieving this particular skill!

Experiment with tempo and dynamics.

Puppets are useful here. I have an ostrich who likes loud music and a sheep who likes quiet music. When I raise each puppet, the children play their instruments accordingly. The same can be done with fast and slow.

There are many other ways for children to have fun while learning basic music concepts. The most important factor at this age is for them to learn to love music, both listening to it and making it

Anne Hunter

Children can have a lot of fun listening to all sorts of music, and there is no reason why you should exclude classical pieces. We help you decide which pieces to choose and suggest how you might use them in a music session

Listening to **classical music**

It can be difficult to decide which pieces of music to use in the nursery. Here are some keys to success:

❑ Choose a piece for a specific musical reason. Listening activities should help children to understand how music works. For example, go for music which has clear contrasts in it, such as obvious changes in the musical elements, ie dynamics (loud/quiet), duration (long/short), pitch (high/low), tempo (fast/slow), texture (several sounds played or sung at the same time/one sound on its own), timbre (contrasting instruments/sounds), and structure.

❑ Use these musical elements to teach your usual type of curriculum (based on activities in *High, Low, Dolly Pepper,* for example - see resources over page), and supplement these learning tasks by playing some recorded music which focuses on the same teaching point.

❑ Focus on just one aspect of one of these elements at a time.

❑ Link the listening directly with performing/composing activities in each session.

❑ Choose music which evokes a particular mood or atmosphere, or which is topic related.

❑ Experiment with any music (in any style), that you think the children may like. Let them help choose pieces.

❑ Keep the musical extract short, to maintain interest.

❑ Keep all of the children actively engaged in listening to it, for example by marking out the beat of the music on different parts of their bodies (perhaps copying a leader's actions); by asking the children to move/dance to the music; by using circle activities.

❑ Use the listening activity to complement the work elsewhere in the music curriculum.

❑ Always use good quality recordings (live music would be an added bonus). If you like, you can select a 'Piece of the week' and play it every day that week - familiarity can increase enjoyment and understanding.

❑ If possible, provide opportunities for children to choose and listen to music of their own choice. Set up a listening corner with tapes/CDs and headphones. Include the 'Piece of the week' in the selection offered.

Just for fun

Sometimes listen to music simply for fun, for example, to introduce or follow on from a story-telling session. Collect musical examples from radio, television or your own general listening. Never underestimate your broad knowledge of music. Ask at your local library for advice on choosing pieces or, perhaps, for the titles of works

Good first pieces to try

The Four Seasons - **Vivaldi**
Danse Macabre - **Saint-Saens**
Carnival of the Animals - **Saint-Saens**
Peter and the Wolf - **Prokofiev**
Sorcerer's Apprentice - **Dukas**
Symphony No 1 - Slow movement - **Mahler**
Concerto for Orchestra - **Bartok**
Clarinet Concerto - **Mozart**
Trumpet Concerto - **Haydn**

Creative Development

that you have listened to and would like to use. Classic FM is a good source of ideas.

Here is an example of how you might use listening materials in a typical music sessions.

Example session plan

Aim: to explore loud and quiet sounds in contrast, to create an atmosphere.

Equipment: a tape/CD player; a recording from the list below; a variety of instruments; different sorts of paper (tissue, sugar paper, ordinary paper, cardboard, newspaper, wrappings from chocolate boxes).

Activities:
❑ Talk together about the weather and the sounds of different types of weather (light rain, heavy rain, thunder).

❑ Listen to a tape recording of the rain or a thunderstorm (see if you can get hold of a BBC sound effects tape from your local library). Or, on a rainy day, listen to the rain on the windows. Discuss sounds and children's feelings.

❑ Ask the children to make the sound of light rain by tapping gently on the palm of their opposite hand. Hold hands up to one ear to amplify these quiet sounds. Can the children think of other ways of making the sounds of light rain? (transfer pitter-pattering to the knees, other parts of the body, or to untuned percussion instruments or the paper). Explore sounds, listen, refine, discuss.

❑ Ask the children to think of ways of making the sounds of heavy rain (stamping on the floor, using instruments). Here they should explore louder sounds.

❑ Make up a signal to indicate when the children should switch between making light and heavy rain sounds. Carefully fine-control the volumes within each by raising/lowering your hands. Invite a child to take over and become the conductor. He or she is now also the composer and can decide how the weather piece develops.

❑ Listen to an extract of one of the weather pieces listed below. Ask the children to respond to the loudness of each part of the music by raising/lowering their hands.

Example weather pieces
Ask at your local library for these recordings:

Mussorgsky: *Night on a Bare Mountain*
Beethoven: Symphony No 6, *The Pastoral* (storm)
Britten: *The Four Sea Interludes* from *Peter Grimes* (storm)
Chopin: *'Raindrop' Prelude*
Takemitsu: *November Steps*

Associated listening/performing
'Singing in the rain'
'Raindrops keep falling on my head'

Extension work

Suggested pieces for other topics:

Toys
The Nutcracker Suite - Tchaikovsky
Radetzky March - Straus
William Tell - Rossini
Symphony Fantastique - Berlioz
Rite of Spring - Stravinsky

Animals
Carnival of the Animals - Saint-Saens
Peter and the Wolf - Prokofiev
Galop from Jeux d'Enfants - Bizet

Water
Fingal's Cave - Mendelssohn
Water Music - Handel
Swan of Tuonela - Sibelius
Swan Lake - Tchaikovsky
Finlandia - Sibelius
Sinfonia Antarctica - Vaughan Williams

Festivals
Festival Overture - Shostakovitch
Firework Music - Handel

Music from other cultures
Music by Nikhil Bhanerjee (India)
Nemangolia, Song with Neikembe (Congo)
Music by Chinese classical Orchestra (China)

Your local library will usually have a good selection of music from around the world.

Similar ideas for integrated composition work on the topic of the weather appear in the following recommended publications:

High, Low, Dolly Pepper Veronica Clark (A & C Black) pp 6, 10, 11, 12, 21, 48, 76, 77, and 91

Sounds Topical, Oxford Music Course J Holdstock and C Richards (OUP)pp 180-191

Sounds of Music G Odam *et al* (P1: nursery and reception) (Stanley Thornes) pp 16-19 and 74-77

Practical Ideas for Use in the Primary Classroom J Rothschild *et al* (The Birmingham Advisory and Support Service, Music Team publication; available from BASS: 0121-428 1167) p 51

Three Singing Pigs K Umansky (A & C Black) (dynamics) pp 40-45

Feedback from parents
Lots of parents have reported the fun their children have in responding to all sorts of different kinds of music. Letters and e-mails read out on Classic FM on the school run (usually after 8am, weekdays), often share ideas and successes in using classical music with children. Recently, one parent wrote in and asked to listen to Saint-Saens' *Danse Macabre*, because their children enjoy play-acting along to it: they pretend to be skeletons in a graveyard, dancing until the 'crow' sounds the dawn near the end. They enjoy playing to the music!

Some say that listening to music like Albinoni's *Adagio* can help children to concentrate better. You could test this out for yourself by sharing this (or practically any other Baroque-type piece) with your children! Works by Mozart or Haydn are supposed to be good, too. Try them out. Be guided by your children's likes and dislikes, but go for variety (choose any music you like) and enjoy!

You don't need lots of space or a large hall to do drama. It can take up a few minutes at snack time or a whole session. Judith Harries offers some general guidelines on how to get started and gives some more detailed ideas to try on an Easter theme

Introducing **drama**

Drama is difficult to define and in many ways, you can pick and choose the bits you feel able to tackle with the children in your care. It can involve quiet activities, that develop concentration, and more boisterous games, that help children learn to co-operate with each other, as well as opportunities to develop self-confidence by speaking in front of people.

The Early Learning Goals for Creative Development do not use the term 'drama', instead they state that children should be encouraged 'to use their imagination' and 'express and communicate their ideas, thoughts and feelings by using imaginative and role play'. They also recognise that 'being creative enables children to make connections between one area of learning and another' and drama is a useful vehicle for this.

The opportunities for children to respond to and make up their own stories and poems are an important part of language development. Drama also helps children to express themselves imaginatively and to recreate roles and experiences through which they can gain insight into personal and social development.

A lot of simple drama activities can be incorporated into an ordinary session without too much difficulty and many of you are probably doing lots of drama already without realising it. Singing time at the end of the morning often includes rhymes or songs which can involve some actions or 'acting out'. When Humpty Dumpty falls *carefully* off the wall how are we going to put him back together? 'Five currant buns' is more fun and memorable if the children can put on a hat, pick up a shopping bag, and

pretend to walk to the shop with their money and buy the bun! What happens when the shop runs out of buns?

Using stories and poems

If you are focusing on a particular story or book what better way to do it than by acting it out. *The Blue Balloon* by Mick Inkpen is a good example of where to start. Not only can the children watch you try to blow up the blue balloon as big as the one in the story, but they can try to make their bodies 'blow up' like balloons and then shrink into a crouch as the balloon deflates. What happens to them when you let go of the balloon? Can they pretend to hold an 'indestructible' balloon and try lots of different ways to pop it?

A lot of drama work can be developed in the role-play corner. Take time to design and create with the children different scenes, for example a park, magic cave, under the sea, garage, farm, and so on. Alongside the normal pretend play that these inspire try adding some 'drama'. Take the farm - the children have to choose jobs or activities to do in the farm and mime them. Make a list of their choices and help them, within reason, to stick to their role rather than switching as they would when simply playing. Select a role for yourself, such as the farmer, and use a simple prop such as a hat so the children know when you are in role.

Introduce a problem or dramatic situation - a runaway horse, a shortage of water - and work with the children to solve it. Help them to discuss solutions and try to avoid always

resorting to magic! You can narrate an ending to tie up any loose ends.

In a small group at snack time you can try some simple mime. Ask the children to pretend to pass a ball around the circle. Remember to keep the size and shape of the ball constant. Now try passing a pretend hot cup of tea, being careful not to spill it! Pretend that you have something fragile in your hands such as a baby bird or an egg. Can the children think of something else that they can pass around?

Who, where and when?

All of these activities work well with children between the ages of three and five either in small groups or the whole class. When working with younger children take care that your starting material (songs, stories, poems) is suitable for that age group. Drama does not need lots of space or a large hall to work in. It can take up five minutes during the session, a few minutes at snack time or a more extended activity can involve the children for up to 30 minutes. You can adapt activities to work in the space and time available. In other words, please don't let logistics put you off!

The following ideas make up a

An Easter drama session

sample drama session for you to try on the theme of Easter. Don't feel you have to work through all the ideas, just pick those that suit your group. This format is one I often use and you can easily adapt it to other themes by changing some of the activities.

Warm up or wind up

Begin with a circle time when the children are encouraged to relax by playing a few simple games.

Who am I? Ask the children to introduce themselves and answer a simple question: 'My name is .... and my favourite colour/toy/fruit is ....'

All change places Change places if you're wearing red/have brown hair/walked to nursery this morning/like chocolate eggs, and so on.

Magic carpet This is a good way to introduce a new theme for the drama session. Ask the children to sit on the carpet or rug with you and close their eyes. Many find it easier to cover their eyes with their hands. You can then ask them to imagine that this is a magic carpet, flying you all away somewhere. Try to describe the scenery and events in some detail. The places they can visit are limitless from their bedrooms to fetch a favourite toy to the local supermarket to choose an Easter egg - all in the imagination. Some children find this activity hard to do but with practice you can help them all to use their imaginations more effectively.

Physical games

Here are a couple of physical games to get the children in the right frame of mind for drama.

Greetings and hugs All the children walk around the room, weaving in and out, saying hello to everyone. Change the greeting to shaking hands, rubbing noses, hugging, saying 'Happy Easter' in funny voices, and so on.

Beans Every time a different variety of bean

is called out the children perform a different action, for example runner (run), string (stand tall with hands in the air), baked (curl up), broad (legs and arms wide apart), jelly (wobble) - or think up your own actions. I have also tried this with minibeast movements (bees - buzz, flies - fly, frogs - jump) and Mr Men characters.

Mime and concentration

Mime - action without words - is a good way of encouraging children to concentrate.

What's my mime? Ask the children to mime a specific activity, either together or for the other children to guess, for example making a sandwich, stroking an animal, brushing teeth.

Mirrors Sit the children in pairs facing one another and number them one and two. All the number ones have to pretend to unwrap and eat a melting chocolate egg and the number twos have to copy them exactly.

Drama focus

This can be structured around acting out a story or adding actions to a poem or song, anything where the children can be encouraged to express themselves imaginatively. Or you could try a more improvised style of drama which works well with four- to five-year-olds especially. The important rule is to listen to the children's suggestions and ideas so that the finished drama is their work and not just yours!

The mystery egg

I tend to use very few props (just the egg) and rely on the children to pretend and mime their way through the drama. Hide a large polystyrene egg somewhere in the room before the children come in.

Who? They are a group of children who are going on a picnic one fine spring day. You can be the teacher or parent going with them. Ask the children what they need to take with them, for example food, drinks, rug, map, compass, ball, fishing nets. Make a list of all the children's favourite picnic food. Assign the children tasks to prepare for the

picnic - making sandwiches, buying fruit, finding a map.

Where? Decide where you are going for the picnic. How are you going to get there? If you are walking the children may need to put on special clothes. Some of the children could draw a map. You can make the journey as easy or as difficult as you wish, in other words up and down hills or through a wood.

What's up? Help the children to find the egg and then gather round and discuss what they think should happen next. Suggestions I have received vary from 'Take it home' and 'Leave it alone' to 'Cook it!' Use your discretion as to which solution you choose but here are some endings you may like to narrate:

❏ On closer investigation the egg was found to be made of chocolate and so we all shared it.

❏ We waited quietly behind the trees and after some time heard a noise in the bushes. A huge prehistoric bird came up to the egg and sat on it carefully. We all left the scene quietly and carefully so as not to disturb them!

❏ We took it home wrapped up in a coat in the picnic basket and several days later it hatched. To our surprise out came a small crocodile/monster and when it saw us it thought we were its parents!

Wind down

It is important at the end of a drama session to allow time for the children to talk about what they have just done, how they felt, and so on. You may prefer to wind down with a simple game.

Throw that feeling Throw a bean bag or soft toy to one child in the circle and say happy/sad/angry. They have to pull the appropriate face before choosing someone else in the group and throwing the bean bag to them.

Judith Harries

Using rhymes and poems in drama gives children the chance to develop their ability to speak clearly, audibly and with an awareness of the listener. These ideas on a fishy theme can be worked through as a complete session or dipped into at any time

Drama through rhymes

Young children enjoy rhymes. They respond to the pattern and rhythm inherent in rhyming words. Many picture books use rhyming text and even very young children can be helped to fill in missing words in a story or poem if they rhyme. It's easier to learn words if they have metre and rhythm and so you can encourage children to recite simple poems and rhymes with increasing confidence and expression.

Using rhymes and poems in drama gives opportunities for young children to develop their ability to speak clearly, audibly and with an awareness of the listener. The older child may concentrate on the annunciation of the words in the poem, whereas younger children will naturally present it as a more interactive experience. They are generally happy to add actions and interpret the poetry in a more physical and dramatic way. Look out for poems which lend themselves to adding actions, have a simple refrain which the children can quickly learn to recite or simply make them laugh.

Good poetry books

Twinkle Twinkle Chocolate Bar, Rhymes for the very young Compiled by John Foster (OUP)

Whizz Bang Orang-Utan Rhymes for the very young Compiled by John Foster (OUP)

Tasty Poems Collected by Jill Bennett (OUP)

Noisy Poems Collected by Jill Bennett (OUP)

Commotion in the Ocean by Giles Andreae (Orchard Books)

Rumble in the Jungle by Giles Andreae (Orchard Books)

My Song is Beautiful by Mary Ann Hoberman (Little, Brown & Co) - poems from around the world

First Verses - Action Rhymes, Chanting Rhymes, Counting Rhymes, Finger Rhymes (OUP) Series of new and original poetry for young children, chosen by John Foster.

Musical cassettes are also available.

When introducing poetry to young children it's good to begin with nursery rhymes. They are familiar and safe and can usually be spiced up with actions.

The one that got away

Sparkling in the sun
A shiny fish swims by,
Darting through the water,
Trying to catch a fly.
Unaware of danger
Lurking in the deep,
Where very, very slowly,
A shark wakes from its sleep.
Jellyfish move gracefully,
With a wobble here and there.
Crabs scuttle sideways,
Not taking too much care.
Shellfish curl up safely
Inside their crusty homes.
Starfish stay quite still,
Much too tired to roam.
Beneath the shiny fish
Dark shadows can be seen.
The shark, feeling hungry,
Glides through waters green,
Great jaws open wider,
But I'm happy to say,
Shiny fish darts quickly.
He's the one that got away!

by Judith Harries

Rhyme games

Begin by playing some simple games to help the children explore and experiment with rhyming words.

Rhyme time: Sit in a circle and ask each child to think of a word that rhymes with cat as you go round the group. When the rhymes dry up, choose a new starting word. Sometimes young children will say a nonsense word that still rhymes. You can choose whether to allow this or to stick to real words.

Fill the gap: Choose a well-known nursery rhyme or poem and recite it leaving obvious gaps for them to fill. Try this with

more unfamiliar rhymes and see which words the children contribute.

Physical games

These ideas are designed to get the children thinking, miming and moving.

Rhyming boats: This is a cross between musical chairs and sardines! Each child starts with a mat or boat to sit on. On your signal, a shout of 'Jump!', they leave the mats and pretend to swim in the water. Remove some of the mats so that when you shout 'Bump!' they have to find a boat to share with a friend. Continue the game until there are a few overcrowded boats! Shout 'Sink!' and everyone falls out of the boats and lies completely still on the floor.

Fishes' wishes: A variation on 'beans' - every time a different type of sea creature is called out the children perform a different action, for example, starfish (make star shape with body), shark (make hands snap like jaws), crab (move sideways), flat fish (lie flat on floor), jellyfish (wobble), whale (make themselves as big as possible). When you call out 'Any fish you wish!' they can choose their favourite action.

Dramatic poem ('The one that got away')

This poem can be used as a drama or mime activity. Before reading the poem talk to the children about how fishes and other sea creatures move. Fishes' wishes will also give them some ideas of how they can move in response to the poem. You may find it simplest to allocate the roles of 'shiny fish' and 'shark' to individual children while organising groups of jellyfish, crabs, shellfish and starfish. Encourage the children to make suggestions for how they can interpret the poem.

Judith Harries

Creative Development

Dance in the early years - where do you begin? Chrys Blanchard's ideas for movement and physical fun give children the chance to explore and enjoy their physicality

Bodyworks ~ **first steps in dance**

Unless you are lucky enough to have a hall the thought of attempting a movement session can be daunting. However, you will be surprised at what you can achieve if you pile up all the chairs and tables. Don't forget to use outside space, too.

What about music?

Don't panic - you don't have to be an accomplished musician to lead a movement session, but you do need to be aware of the role of music or sound. It provides an important stimulus.

Music falls into two categories: pre-recorded and live. Pre-recorded music is useful for activities where you want to create a mood or establish a theme. Listen out for both popular and classical music from a range of cultural traditions that fit the topics you are doing - the 'clocks' from Pink Floyd's *Dark Side of the Moon* for a waking-up, rubbing eyes and yawning sequence or Ragtime piano music (Scott Joplin) for lighthearted and comical movement. Live music, however, is usually best.

Well-known classical pieces include:

Pictures at an Exhibition - Mussorgky
Includes the rather 'scary' music that depicts the story of Baba Yaga the witch.

Carnival of the Animals - Saint Saens
Contains several pieces depicting chickens, donkeys, elephants, fossils (great if you are doing skeletons - well-known xylophone music).

Peter and the Wolf - Prokofiev
Characters are depicted by different orchestral instruments. The whole piece is a story. Good for different qualities of movement and recognition and response.

Don't forget the waltzes by J Strauss and Chopin, which will provide lots of lilting music, and marches by various composers, often played by military bands.

Fairground music: there are recordings available of steam organs.

Song is ideal. If we sing as we move we are not only co-ordinating skills, but we are also in control of tempo (speed), pitch (high or low) and we can stop and start when we want to.

Sound is also useful - banging a drum for giant steps, shaking bells for wiggles or shivers. 'We haven't got any instruments!' I hear some of you cry. Don't worry, improvise. Find something to beat a rhythm on - a saucepan and wooden spoon is surprisingly effective, as is a bucket, wastepaper bin or washing up bowl. To make jingly sounds, try a teaspoon in an empty cup. With your 'instrument' in your hand you are right there with the children and can move around with them whilst keeping control of the pace - stops and starts, volume and character of the sound.

Session format

Adapt the basic format of a familiar game such as musical chairs/statues/bumps. You will need to decide what you want to happen when the 'music' stops.

The options are many:
- sit on the floor;
- make a statue (of an animal/sports player/scary statue);
- find someone to hug;
- stand on a large central mat/circle/carpet (or you'll fall in the water);
- stand on your spot (marked by chalk circle, small mat);
- stand in a hoop.

Explain that NOBODY will be out. This game is non-competitive, thus removing any anxiety of failure. The fun is in the challenges that arise from the types of movement you include.

Getting started

Choose your source of sound/music. Each time the music starts tell the children how you want them to move until it stops (adjust your 'percussion' to fit the style of movement): jump up and down, walk on tip-toes, creep quietly, take giant steps, walk with wiggly legs, stick out your tummies, tiny steps, twirl around (making the sound of wind blowing and swishing), move like a cat/lion/mouse/ rabbit, move like a spaceman on the moon, march like a soldier.

Note: hopping is quite tricky for very young children, and skipping is often not achieved until the age of five or so.

When the children have responded to the STOP in the music that's the time to give them the next instruction - 'Next time I want you to jump like a kangaroo ' or 'Let's do giant steps again'. (You could say 'Fee, Fi, Fo Fum' as you do this one.)

It's important to do each type of movement several times to give the children chance to get the hang of it. Children like to repeat things, so keep it going as long as they want - and you can bear!

Chrys Blanchard

Chapter 3

Unit C11: Promote children's language and communication development

About this unit

Unit C11 is all about helping children to develop their language and communication skills, including speaking and listening, and non-verbal communication. In this unit, you will need to assess children's stage of language development through carrying out some child observations. If you don't feel confident about writing observations, read the chapter on C16 – 'Observe and assess the development and behaviour of children'(pages 150-170). That will give you some helpful hints. You will also need to show the activities and experiences you provide, and how you communicate with the children, in order to promote their language development

If you have already completed C10, you may have covered some of the evidence you need. If you have not yet filled in your cross referencing sheet, have a look at each element and see if you can identify things you can cross reference from C10, and make a note of them. Check which PCs, range and knowledge evidence they cover and pencil them in to your assessment records if you feel confident to do this, and then check them with your assessor.

Values

All of the elements place particular emphasis on the welfare of the child, learning and development, equality of opportunity and the reflective practitioner. The first element emphasises the value of working in partnership with parents when assessing the children's stage of development, so you will need to be aware of your setting's procedures for gathering information from parents about their child. Elements 2 and 3 focus on anti-discrimination and celebrating diversity through providing activities and books which prevent stereotyping, and reflect the varied experiences and cultural backgrounds of the children. You need to be aware of this when choosing books and activities and writing your evidence. You should also promote a positive awareness of language by including bilingual books, and using signs and labels in more than one language where appropriate. Children also find it great fun to learn songs in different languages.

Throughout the unit, make sure that you are aware of appropriate ways to help children who use more than one language. For instance, does your setting have a member of

staff who can speak to the child in their own language? If not, do they have access to the local intercultural support service, or a parent who can help? Read the article on bilingualism later in the chapter for more guidance. You will also need to show how you would help children who have difficulty in communication for other reasons, such as hearing and speech impairment, and emotional difficulties. Some of the articles later in the chapter will help you with this.

Getting started

In this unit you are aiming to show that you can:

◆ Identify the stages of language development

◆ Provide activities to extend children's language and communication

◆ Share appropriate books, stories and rhymes

◆ Provide opportunities for communication

◆ Interact with children

This unit lends itself to cross referencing across the elements. For example, Elements 2, 4 and 5 are closely linked, and one activity could provide evidence for all of them - by providing the appropriate activity, being there and encouraging the children to talk, and showing that you can interact effectively with them. Elements 3, 4 and 5 are also closely linked, and could be covered together - if you use your story time as an opportunity for children to recall and discuss the story, and listen to each other's comments.

If you find it helpful, use the personal skills profile on page 21. If not, go straight into your planning, with your assessor if possible. Try to plan for the whole of this unit on one assessment plan, and discuss with your assessor which bits you can cross reference.

Remember to check whether you have any evidence from the past you can use, especially for things you have done but you don't do in your current work role. Remember, too, that if you have difficulty with a lot of written work, you can discuss with your assessor other ways to provide your evidence, such as oral questioning or taped reflective accounts.

Try to include as much knowledge evidence as you can in your activity plans, child observations and other evidence. If there are still gaps, write a short assignment to fill them, relating it as far as possible to your own work practice. The resources in this book will help you with your underpinning knowledge, but you may also need to arrange with your centre to attend appropriate training or read the study materials and recommended books.

The rest of this chapter gives some suggestions and resources for each element, to help you with your planning.

Element C11.1 Identify stages of children's language and communication development

Key issues

This element is about you identifying the children's stage of development in language and communication. You may already have been involved in completing language development records for the children in your setting. If so, ask if you can photocopy some examples for your portfolio, but remember to remove the name on your copy in order to maintain confidentiality. Write a note with it to explain how you use it.

If you have bilingual children in your setting, you should assess them in their home language as well as in English. They may lack confidence in their second language but be fluent in their first. It's vital that you distinguish between language delay and lack of confidence because the child is learning a second language. Consult their parents about their use of their home language, and ask for support from your local intercultural support service if you need to. There is a section which deals specifically with assessment of the home language in the article on bilingualism on page 117-118.

Which type of evidence?

If you look at the evidence requirements for this element, your assessor only needs to observe two PCs to ensure that you are recording observations accurately and responding appropriately to children's use of home language and local dialects. Most of the evidence for this element will be your *child observations*. It's useful to have a tape recorder to record children's language, because it's difficult to keep up with what they're saying unless you can do shorthand! It's also a good way of listening to yourself interacting with children, to judge whether you're interacting effectively.

Your assessor will need to observe one aspect of each range context, too. Read the notes on this element for an explanation of the range statements. Note that non-verbal communication is included in the range, so make sure you refer to it. The third context may be difficult to observe, if you don't have any children with special needs in your setting. If so, find out as much as you can about how to support children with speech and hearing impairment, and emotional difficulties, and write about them, using examples from your past experience if you can. Check what you need to include in the knowledge evidence, and include that information, too. There are several articles later in the chapter which will help you.

The related *knowledge evidence* statements for this element are 1, 2, 5, 7, 8, 11, 30, 31, 32. Read through them, and note which ones are linked to other elements too, so that you can include all the evidence you need to. If you have already done a piece of work on stages of development, you will be able to cross reference to that. If you evaluate your *child observations* well, you will cover most of the knowledge evidence at the same time.

> **Remember!**
> To look at the chapter on child observation if you need help with how to carry out observations.

Element C11.2 Provide activities, equipment and materials to extend and reinforce children's language and communication development

Key issues

Many of the activities you have used in C10 will be equally useful for this unit. Include as much free play as possible when you are organising activities for children. Play often provides a far more relaxed situation where children who say very little in more structured activities will feel confident enough to talk more freely. Build time into your programme for observing and talking with children while they play. Let them lead the discussion, don't take over. If you are working with babies and very young children, one-to-one play and talking with an adult is particularly important for them.

Remember to give the children a play environment which reflects a range of cultures, abilities and social backgrounds, and which gives all children equal opportunity to take part in the full range of activities. That sometimes means taking positive action to encourage children to take part in activities which they may not choose to do. For example, if a child is reluctant to sit and read a book or use writing and drawing materials, they may need some encouragement to do this by linking it to an activity they particularly enjoy.

When you are supervising children for a structured activity, listen and respond to their comments. Sometimes, adults get so involved with the organisation of the activity that they forget to listen to the children, or they talk so much that the children don't have a chance to speak! Try taping an activity and see how much talking you do, and how much the children do. You might be surprised!

Which type of evidence?
If you look at the evidence requirements for C11.2, you will see that your assessor needs to observe all but one of the PCs and one aspect of each range category. If she has gained enough evidence from the activities you did for C10, you may be able to cross reference this element.

If your assessor doesn't think there is enough evidence, plan with her which activities she will observe. You may do an activity plan if you wish. Think about the language skills you want to reinforce with the children.

Remember!
To refer to the knowledge evidence when you're writing your evidence to show that you understand why you do things the way you do, and how the children will benefit.

If there are other activities you have carried out which have extended and reinforced children's language and communication, write a *reflective account* about them, or reference appropriate activities in your diary. Make sure that your account covers all aspects of the range not covered by direct observation, and try to cover the knowledge evidence, too. Note that this element also refers to written communication, so write about how you encourage children's emerging writing skills. You will find some interesting articles about the development of writing skills on pages 142-148.

For C11.2 the related *knowledge evidence* statements are 1, 2, 3, 6, 7, 11, 14, 15, 16, 24 and 32. Remember that the resources in this book will help you, but you may need to use other recommended books to ensure that you have the breadth of knowledge to cover the requirements. You will need to be aware of the section on Communication, Language and Literacy in the Early Learning Goals and the *Curriculum Guidance for the Foundation Stage*, and also of the National Curriculum, and the National Literacy Strategy. Your employer or the assessment centre may have this information, or you will probably be able to find it in your local library.

If you haven't covered all of the knowledge in your other evidence, fill the gaps with a short written assignment, trying to include examples from your own work practice.

Element C11.3 Share books, stories and rhymes to extend children's language and communication development

Key issues
It's never too soon to share books with young children. Babies from as young as three months love to sit on your lap and look at bright, colourful picture books. If you encourage a love of books from an early age, you will help children to develop a skill which will benefit them for a lifetime.

When sharing books with children, you need to think about whether they reflect good practice in terms of preventing stereotyping and promoting positive awareness of gender, disability, and social, cultural or religious groups. Some traditional stories are not acceptable in today's society, and others will raise issues about equality. You need to make a decision about whether a book is worth keeping, and discussing with the children where it raises issues about equality, or whether it is totally unacceptable, and should be removed.

If you feel that the range of books in your setting is limited, visit your local library, preferably with the children, and choose some books. When buying books, always buy the best quality you can. Look for good illustrations in a variety of styles. Include fun books, poetry and rhymes and information books as well as a good range of both traditional and modern story books. Some educational book companies have some lovely story books with positive images of children and adults with disabilities, with people from different ethnic groups in leading roles, with women and men in non-traditional roles, with untypical families, and inner-city situations as well as the many traditional story books. They also provide books which help children to deal with their anxieties, from going to the hospital to bereavement, and tackling issues like dealing with bullying. Some of the best-loved children's stories are now available in dual languages. It is good for children to see languages other than English, especially in settings where there are no children from minority ethnic backgrounds.

Many stories can be used as a good lead in to drama and role play. Try getting the children to make up stories. Give them some props and see what they come up with. Puppets are one of the best ways of helping children to make up their own stories. You can act as scribe and write or word process the story; make a book and let the children do the illustrations. They'll love going back to it over and over again.

The articles later in the chapter have some good practical ideas for using stories and rhymes with children.

Which types of evidence?

You will notice from the evidence requirements that your assessor will need to **observe** all but two of the PCs for this element, and one aspect of each range category. She may also wish to inspect the range of books in your setting, and the way they are displayed.

Read the range and the notes on this element to get a picture of the range of books you should include, and methods of storytelling you need to show you can do. A good piece of evidence for this element would be a **reflective account** about the range of books you have in your setting.

Plan with your assessor which evidence you will aim to cover through **direct observation** and **inspection**. Remember that this element includes rhymes as well as stories, and telling a story from memory. You should also try to include some visual aids - this works particularly well if you are telling a story from memory, and can easily develop into some drama or role play. For example, if you provide the three bears, their dishes, spoons, chairs and beds, the children will have endless pleasure in re-enacting the story. Visual aids are important if you are reading to a child with a hearing impairment. For a child with a visual impairment, sound and touch are important.

You may want to prepare an **activity plan** for the storytelling session. We have already suggested a **reflective account** about the range of books you have in your setting. You may want to make reference to **diary** entries about successful storytelling sessions, or include these in your reflective account. Remember to look at the requirements for the knowledge evidence, and try to include this information in your evidence.

Don't forget!
To cross reference evidence wherever you can, to avoid repetition.

The related **knowledge evidence** statements for this element are 9, 18, 19, 20, 21, 25, 26, 27, 28, 29, 33. Hopefully, you will have already covered most of these in your other evidence. Fill any gaps in your knowledge evidence by writing a short assignment. Don't forget to include examples from your own work practice.

Element C11.4 Provide communication opportunities to enhance and reinforce children's language and communication development

Key issues

It's important that you take every opportunity to talk with children. Notice that we use the word 'with' rather than 'to'. That emphasises the importance of two-way conversation, rather than the adult talking all the time. Read about the different techniques for encouraging talk, such as open-ended questions which need more than a yes or no answer - like 'What do you think about..!' or 'I wonder why that happened?' If you have already recorded yourself talking with the children, listen again, and find out whether you are asking open-ended questions. If you haven't, do it now. Don't overdo your questions, though, because it can become tedious for children. Try to make it a proper conversation like you have with adults, with a two-way exchange of comments and discussion. Read the article on 'Making time for meaningful talk' on page 115 for guidance on strategies for encouraging talk.

Circle time is often the time when children have the opportunity to talk and listen to other adults and children, but it is difficult for young children to sit and listen for long, and some children are not confident to speak in a big group. Think about how you organise your circle time. Does one person have the whole group? Why not split the children into smaller groups so that they all have a chance to speak? Many early years settings have key workers, and each has their own small group of children at certain times during the session. This is much more manageable, for both children and adult, and gives more time for each child to communicate in a less daunting situation. Children with difficulties in communication are likely to need individual support.

In your activities and routines, keep reinforcing the link between the spoken word, reading and writing. Put labels on to children's work - perhaps a caption which they have given you to go with their picture, which you can read back to them. When you're reading a story, sometimes follow the print with your finger - big books are especially useful for this. Put writing tools in other play areas, like the shop and the home corner. You will probably be able to think of lots more ideas, and you will also find the articles on emergent writing later in the chapter (pages 142-148) helpful.

The way you talk with children, the attention you give them individually and the respect you show for their language, accent and family background will have a great impact on their level of self-esteem. You need to know the child's home background, within the constraints of confidentiality, so that you can communicate more effectively by encouraging talk about their past experiences. Have a look at C5.3, 'Develop children's self-reliance and self-esteem', and you will see how closely it Is linked to this element. Remember to cross reference any appropriate evidence.

Which evidence?

This element is about showing how you allow children the opportunity to talk within everyday routines and situations, as well as in planned activities. You will see from the evidence requirements for this element that your assessor will need to **observe** all of the PCs and at least one aspect of each range category. Of course, if she can observe more, so much the better. She probably already has some evidence of how you promote children's communication from previous observations.

Read the notes on this element to help you to plan what range of evidence you need to provide. Plan with your assessor what she still needs to **observe** - she may want to see some of the routines of your setting, to see what opportunities for talk there are for the children. Plan what other evidence you need to provide - perhaps a **reflective account** or **diary** account of how you have provided opportunities for talk. You may wish to include a **child observation** or a taped recording of conversations between children, or between yourself and children. Look at the knowledge evidence to see what you still need to cover, and try to include it in your accounts.

> Take every opportunity you can to widen your experience by working with children of different ages and in different settings where possible.

The related **knowledge evidence** statements for this element are 1, 2, 3, 4, 7, 11, 14, 17, 22, 23, 24, 32, 34, 35, 36. Check your evidence to see how much you have already covered, and fill any gaps if necessary with a short assignment.

ElementC11.5 Interact with children to promote their language and communication development

Key issues

This element is so closely linked to all of the other elements in this unit that it is most likely that you will already have covered all the evidence you need. It focuses on your own skills and ability to interact with children, like the tone and volume of your voice, body language, the way you show children you are listening, and so on. You have already been made aware of these things in the other elements, but perhaps this is a good opportunity to reflect on your own practice, and identify whether there are areas where you could improve your skills. There are no activities particularly related to this element which have not been discussed already.

Which type of evidence?

Your assessor will need to **observe** all but one of the PCs and one aspect of each range category, but she has probably already done this as part of the other elements.

The related **knowledge evidence** statements for this element are 1, 4, 10, 11, 12, 13. Check your other evidence to see whether you have covered it already, and fill any gaps with a short assignment, linking it to your own work practice as much as possible.

The Early Learning Goals for Communication, Language and Literacy focus on children's developing competence in talking and listening and in becoming readers and writers. Gay Wilkinson translates this into good early years practice

Communication, Language and Literacy

One of the most important ways in which children learn about themselves, others and the world about them is through seeing, hearing and using language - talking, listening, reading and writing - and of these talking and listening are the aspects which they master first and which will form the foundation for later reading and writing.

Meaningful conversation

Parents and carers do not develop a formal structure to teach their children how to construct language — they don't give them lessons to teach them new words. Instead, from the moment of birth they behave as though the child is a language user; they respond to the baby's gestures and sound as though it were part of a meaningful conversational exchange and talk back.

As the child begins to acquire words and try them out they listen to their efforts, interpret and add other words in order to help them sustain the conversation and continue to do so as the child becomes more competent. Above all, they use talk to accompany the everyday activities of family life and engage the child in conversational partnerships as part of these, providing a context within which the child can construct and extend their understanding of the world.

As a result of being in this rich and supportive language environment, by the age of four most children are already sophisticated language users. They have mastered the basic grammatical rules in spoken language, built up an impressive vocabulary, learned that language can be used to make meaning and can communicate meaningfully with others. In situations which interest and are of relevance to them they are able to use language to talk

about the things they see and hear, express their feelings, ask questions, predict likely events, reflect upon their experiences, past and present, share their ideas and imaginings and take part in extended conversations.

Awareness of print

As well as becoming confident and competent talkers, by the time they are four young children have already begun to learn things about literacy - reading and writing. At home and in their community they have seen print being used by parents and other adults as part of real life. They

have begun to recognise and remember the shape and pattern made by certain words in their environment and know the sounds associated with each pattern, such as their name, particular shop names, street names, titles of favourite television programmes and story books. They will have also seen writing and reading being used for a variety of real purposes and even taken part in some, for example writing their name on birthday cards, and have an understanding that these skills are important for conveying and sharing meaning.

It is important to remember, however, that

parents have not set out to teach children to use language and be literate and children do not learn about language and literacy as a subject. The learning that they have acquired is not ordered in any particular way and is closely bound up with all the experiences they have had before they join the early years setting. It has been acquired as part of the social context in which they live - a tool to make sense of the world around them - and they cannot describe what they have learned in subject terms. It is the responsibility of the early years setting to build upon what children have learned informally and through management, organisation and planning help children to make sound progress in language and literacy.

The early years setting

Children need to be involved in practical, first-hand and interesting activities in order to use language. Is there a wide variety of activities available from which children can choose which will both engage their interest and provide real opportunities for talk? Imaginative play is recognised as being particularly valuable for promoting children's talk. A well-equipped home corner which has resources which mirror those in the home will support them in taking on roles and allow them to engage in the variety of conversations which they have heard at home and extend their understanding of how talk is used to develop and maintain relationships, manage situations and solve problems.

Opportunities to talk

As well as promoting talk through sensitive intervention and participation in children's spontaneous play you can also provide special times when children are encouraged to talk about themselves and events in their lives and learn to listen to what others have to say. Instead of having 'talk time' with all the children together, put them into small groups, each with an adult, so that each child has a real opportunity to talk and listen without having long waiting times. Invite parents, grandparents, older children and young people and other people from the community to come in to listen to and talk with the children. The children will benefit from having more opportunities to engage in conversation with a wider variety of adults. For children for whom English is an additional language it is particularly important that they have opportunities to talk frequently in their first language with other children and adults, as well as being involved in activities which help them to begin to learn English.

Parents and community members who use other languages can be a significant help to you and the children and should be invited in whenever possible.

Words and sounds

Children need to be helped to become more aware of the sounds within words and the similarities and differences between words. This will contribute to later reading success. Regular opportunities to hear and join in with saying or signing nursery rhymes, songs and poetry will both develop their listening skills and strengthen their awareness of sounds. Rhyme is especially important in helping children to recognise the similarities and differences between words. There are a large number of delightful story books written for young children which use rhyme, for example *Each Peach, Pear, Plum* by Janet and Allan Ahlberg (Puffin) and these can be read to them. Once they are familiar with what rhyming means, play a game with such stories by encouraging them to guess what word might come next which has both a matching sound and fits in with the sense of the story.

Range of materials

How does your environment reflect the importance of reading and writing in the way the world outside the classroom does? Are there labels attached to resources? Are there signs which give useful information and which will help children make sense of the environment? Do play activities reflect the richness of literacy opportunities that children may experience in their own homes and in their community? Does your home corner encourage them to engage in literacy behaviour by providing opportunities for reading and writing as a real part of their play? Is there a range of different reading materials - magazines, comics, newspapers, cookery books, car maintenance manuals, telephone directories, letters, bills? Is there a range of materials which will support writing - writing paper and envelopes, message pad by the telephone, memo board, shopping list blanks, birthday cards, birthday invitation cards, postcards? Does other role play provision developed as part of a theme promote literacy behaviour? For example, a garden centre provided as part of a theme on 'Spring' or 'Growth' could have a range of reference books on plants, seed and bulb catalogues, blank order forms and invoices, headed note paper for official letters, blank plant labels and tags, labels denoting different sections of the centre, seed packets and advertising posters.

Planned activities

In addition to these experiences children need to have specific opportunities to take part in activities which will promote reading and writing development. As well as being able to choose to look at and share books in the book corner they should have daily opportunities to hear stories read and told as part of a group activity, in pairs or individually - parents and other adults can be useful for such activities. It can be helpful to identify a small number of books which particularly appeal to young children and to use these specifically to develop early reading strategies. By reading and re-reading these with the children they will become familiar with the language used in books (which is very different from spoken language), familiar with how these particular stories work and eventually be able to relate the spoken text with the printed words and read them on their own.

A number of publishers produce books in both a large book format for group activities as well as normal book size. You might consider purchasing some large format story books as well as several copies of the same stories in the normal size so that children can participate in small group activities followed by the opportunity to either have the same book as their friend and read together or read on their own.

As well as the informal writing opportunities provided as part of their play children also need planned opportunities which will encourage them to think about writing. You could consider developing a writing area in your room which has a range of writing tools available, different papers of good quality, blank books in different forms and models of handwriting displayed which children can refer to when undertaking a writing activity. At this stage in their development as writers it is more important that children write for themselves rather than copying from a card or blackboard. However they do need to be helped to think about how words can be written down and how to organise writing. A useful activity can be to bring a small group of children together to create a story. In deciding features of the story you can help them to think about how stories work, how using different words can enhance the story, introduce new vocabulary. Once each part of the story has been finally agreed then you can write it down in front of the children so that they can see how writing works as well as providing opportunities to talk about and demonstrate different features of print, punctuation, word patterns, letters and letter formation and presentation. At this stage in their development your emphasis should be on promoting their confidence in themselves as writers and helping them acquire the skills of organising their thoughts and ideas so that they can effectively share them with others.

You will need to be aware of what each child is able to do in all the aspects of language and literacy and what new knowledge and skills they need next in order to make progress and grow in competence. You will need to observe and assess regularly their language and literacy behaviour in both their spontaneous play and as they participate in the more structured activities you provide. These assessments should then be used to help you plan what further opportunities you need to provide which will extend children's skills as talkers, listeners, readers and writers.

Gay Wilkinson

Recall time is an important part of the daily routine in High/Scope settings. Sue Hedley explains why it's so valuable and offers some guidance on how to get started

Making time for meaningful talk

It is our aim and responsibility to help children become confident communicators in their world. We present a powerful model of language use to children, yet often our talk is perceived by them to be mainly about management - we tell, command or judge when we speak to children and often give them too little time to respond to our questions. To encourage children to use talk as a means of learning, we need to be good listeners. We need to give children our full attention when listening, indicating that what children say has value.

If appropriate experiences that include using speaking and listening are planned and included in the daily routine, then effective talk arises. The planned activities need to be organised with the intention of extending particular aspects of children's language, in other words, questioning in a way that is relevant to the child's interests, needs and ability. This way, there is more likely to be productive interaction between children.

One way in which we develop children's oracy skills and the use of questioning and evaluation is through recall time. The results are significant.

What is recall time?

Recall time is part of the daily routine in our early years unit, where children come together in small groups of 13 to share their experiences of a planned activity they have carried out at work time. Although this is a consistent part of the daily routine in a Highscope setting, anyone providing an active learning environment where children are making choices and decisions about their own ideas and work, could enjoy the significant benefits children gain from reviewing their work.

What are the benefits?

Recall time is a wonderful opportunity for children to receive recognition for the things they have done, to use language to describe their actions, to remember, to represent, and to reflect on what they did and learned. This repetitive process helps to enable children to draw upon their experiences for future learning situations.

Through recall time children are talking to each other about personally meaningful experiences. Children choose an experience

'Enjoy listening to and using spoken... language, and readily turn to it in their play and learning.'

to share, something they want to talk about based on their own interests and ideas. Having the opportunity to say something about their own experiences is more important than which experience they actually recall. Recalling involves social interaction on a personal level, reflecting an experience and finding the words, actions and gestures to convey their meanings to others. It's almost a kind of personal storytelling in which they, as narrators, are the major characters. Because this

storytelling is a shared experience, based on concrete experiences, other children want to listen - they are the audience and often want to find out more information through questions and answers.

Your role

For children to get the most out of recall time the adult role is very important.

❑ First, you must provide a place for children to meet together as part of their daily routine.

❑ Organise the group preferably in a circle where children can see and hear each other.

❑ Provide a table, box or bench in the area for children to put their finished work on, so they can select what they would like to talk about.

❑ Join in and converse with the children at their physical level.

How to start

Start by inviting the children to talk about what they have done. This can be through:

❑ a comment - beginning the conversation with a personal comment or observation about a child's work time experience, for example:

Adult: 'I saw you were driving in the block area today, Luke.'

Luke: 'I was taking Sam and Jenny to the hospital. Guess what happened?'

This immediately captures the children's interest and invites them to ask questions.

❑ a direct question: 'Kate, would you like to tell us where you have been working today?'

For children to develop the skill of asking questions, you must role model questioning on a consistent basis. The questions must be questions that help children think!

> *'Use talk to organise, sequence and clarify thinking, ideas, feelings and events.'*

Different types of questioning
Divergent questions

These have more than one right answer. They encourage children to express their ideas, feelings and predictions.

'What do you think would happen if . . .'

'What do you think is in the box?'

'How can we try to get the seeds out of our pumpkins?'

Thought-provoking questions

These have a right answer that is based on children's direct observations of materials they are using or experiences they are having. Thought-provoking questions encourage children to classify, use numbers, or observe the relationship of space and time.

'What did you do in the art area today?'

'How many red blocks are there in your tower?'

'Which one of your clay balls is the biggest?'

Minimal response questions

These questions call for yes or no answers.

'Is that a triangle?'

Learning from role models
Through your role modelling of divergent questions children begin to ask each other questions. The child recalling often says 'Would anyone like to ask me a question?' The children who want to ask a question put their hands up and the child recalling chooses two people. This puts the child in control of their own learning and by the end of the year the children are managing recall time themselves and I am a spectator!

To begin with the questions tend to be limited to 'What's that bit there?', leading to 'How did you get that tube to stick?' and 'What did you use for the base of your model?'

As the questioning skills are role modelled, developed and practised, children begin to evaluate their own and each other's work in a constructive, positive manner. They might ask 'Did you have any problems?' or 'What do you like best about your picture?' Often an observant child who has noticed no wheels on a model of a car might ask, 'Why did you not put any wheels on your car? Will you put them on tomorrow?' Children also use comments to evaluate each others work: 'I like the way you have used ribbon and pasta on top of the paint'. This encourages other children to make positive comments and discuss what they like about the picture.

At recall time, new ideas are often shared, especially if they have come from home, for example stencil painting: 'How did you make your pattern? Can I do one? Will you show me how to do it?' The learning process from this experience becomes spontaneous, meaningful and rapid. For me and the children recall time is invaluable. It allows me to keep track of the children's interests and abilities and how to provide more challenges for each individual child.

A special time
Recall time is a special time in our daily routine. It is when we are a cohesive family group. One child often says to me, 'Mrs Hedley, can we have a cosy cosy recall?' This is when we all sit close together, sharing our thoughts, ideas and achievements in a warm and cosy atmosphere. Through this children gain confidence from each other. They gain respect for each others ideas. They gain recognition for their work. Putting all these skills together, children gain acceptance into *their* social world for who they are and what they are - unconditionally, without being right or wrong!

Sue Hedley

Many children who are developing bilinguals are expected to shed their own language and culture in order to become integrated into our society. Rubina Din highlights the dangers in this and explains the importance of using a child's home language as a tool for learning

Bilingualism: a help or a hindrance?

Bilingual children start learning a language from the day they are born. They have been interacting with their parents so are sophisticated language users when they arrive at nursery or pre-school. But for many of these children this is when their cognitive development becomes delayed.

Research has shown that this happens because it takes children five years to learn a language, and when these children start school their language learning is interrupted at a crucial stage in their linguistic development. This is not taken into account. These children are held back because they don't have the language in English to continue their thinking skills.

Damaging effect

Adults learning a second language expect to use the skills they have in their first language to do this. Children, on the other hand, are immersed in language they don't understand or see the reason to learn, in an alien culture. The whole thing is such hard work for the child that it is easier to switch off.

If the child is expected to discard his or her own language, what are the messages that they take away about themselves, through the hidden curriculum? It can have a damaging effect on their self-esteem and motivation.

Your role is to provide the children with a good solid start in life so that they have a clear and strong language through which to build up a picture of the new language. Parents also need to be aware of ensuring that the children are being encouraged and supported in educational pursuits in their home language to give children a solid language base to start with.

Tool for learning

Children need their home language as a tool for learning.

You need to find ways in which children can be encouraged to develop and use skills they already have. Parents know their children best. Ask them to tell you what their child is capable of.

Gather information on the languages spoken at home by the children. This gives the parents a sense of value for their language and gives you the opportunity to talk to the parents about expectations for their child and how the parents can support the child's thinking skills by encouraging the child to use their own language at home.

Parental support

This is a fundamental area which holds the key to educational success for all children. You need to give the parents a structured programme to follow. You can talk them through a book and any book skills you want them to work on, in home language. Get them to talk about the pictures, laugh with the children, ask them to say what might happen next. All of this will help the parent become more confident in supporting the child who is continuing to develop his/her thinking skills which otherwise would be delayed.

> 'Gather information on the languages spoken at home by the children. This gives the parents a sense of value for their language.'

Books

Books which the children are using need to be culturally appropriate. If the children are being expected to talk about things completely outside their experience then they will find this difficult. It may even turn them off books because they are not related to anything in their lives.

Displays

Displays need to reflect the languages in the groups. You can ask parents to write up simple labels in home languages for you. If parents do not have the equipment at home then give them the pens, card, paper they need. After tea/coffee mornings, parents can be asked to produce labels for the work they do with their children.

Role-play areas

These areas are paramount to the development of the children's thinking skills, social skills and children's own self-concept. It is important that children are involved in working in areas where they can see and play with things they can relate to. Make sure that you have items in your play areas which will help the children to play creatively using the experiences they have had at home. This will help to bring school and home closer together. For example, if you have lots of children with an Indian/Pakistani background in your group then you will need to have items in the home corner such as a chappatti stick, griddle, pans, plastic onions, peppers and other such things which children will see at home.

A writing corner

The writing corner will provide children with essential experiences of developing concepts about the purpose of writing. It is important children see their own languages as serving the same purpose as the English writing. You can make a collection of writing from different languages - magazines, posters from films, newspapers, video cassette covers. Children will automatically go to the writing that they may have seen in their homes and attempt to write in that way. They will be keen to talk about the writing they have done and why their families may write. This kind of dialogue will be a good starting point for discussion about the purposes of writing. Children can be encouraged to bring in items of writing they see at home.

We all know that we need to build on what children bring to a situation, but it's easy to forget that some may be learning through an alien language.

Rubina Din

Assessing the home language

Assessment of the way in which children use their home language is important in deciding what kind of support they need next. A comfortable and culturally appropriate environment will help the children with a stress free start to their lives in the nursery and will ultimately be conducive to learning.

Assessing a home language is a specialised area but, with some help, you should be able to build up some sort of picture. If you are a local authority school then there may be an LEA bilingual support service who can help you. If not try your early years partnership - see if they can point you towards someone with the appropriate skills.

The aim is to see that the children are as capable in their home language as you would expect first language English speakers to be. Of course, unless you are bilingual, you won't be able to understand them. If there is no one in your group who speaks the child's first language you are going to have to gather the information about the way they speak.

Get the child, or children, to talk to you about a personal experience using their home language. You could tape record this chat for a third person to listen to.

Write down what you hear - using the English script - so recording what they are saying. After this you can sit down with someone who speaks that language and analyse the way in which the child has constructed the speech. You will need to check whether the responses are what you would expect of a child of that age group. This will give you an insight into the way in which the child is functioning and will help you decide the support needed.

Alternatively ask a bilingual assistant or one of the child's parents to help take down a sample of speech then use the same technique. This is a quicker way of getting a speech sample as the person taking the sample will be able to analyse the information as the child is discussing their experiences with them.

There are other ways in which the children can be assessed. In order to find out where the children are developmentally you could ask them to:

❏ Retell a well-known story;

❏ Sequence events (using pictures);

❏ Talk about a personal experience (as above).

This selection will provide you with a clear picture of a number of different ways in which the child can use language. This will need to be carried out in the home language. The main purpose of this is to see whether the child can articulate language appropriate to his/her age, in order to give you a starting point for support. Children do not start at zero - no matter which language they speak as their mother tongue.

By the time a child is three, they should have mastered all the skills necessary to communicate with the adults and children in their environment. However, studies show that approximately seven per cent of all children in the UK do not develop those skills. We look at one specific area of development that contributes to children experiencing communication difficulties - speech and language impairment

Communication delay

What is a communication problem?

Early years workers are likely to come across children with varying degrees of impairment in communication. Broadly-speaking, a speech and language impairment means that a child may have difficulty in:

❑ how they say their sounds;

❑ how much they understand what you say;

❑ how much they can say, that is the size of their vocabulary, how many words they can string together to form a sentence.

Types of impairment are:

❑ Specific language delay/disorder (differential diagnoses will be discussed later)

❑ Phonological delay/disorder

❑ Phonetic delay/disorder

❑ Developmental dyspraxia

The term impairment includes children who have a delay or disorder. If a child has a delay, we would expect her speech and language to be similar to a child of a younger age - that means that the child is acquiring skills at a slower rate. A disorder exists where skills are not being acquired within the correct/known developmental sequence. Speech and language development is different from the sequential norm.

Prevalence and causes

Speech and language impairments occur more frequently in boys than girls. It is not always clear why a child has a speech and language impairment. He may be born with it, or could have acquired a speech and language difficulty. Apart from this, the causes aren't clear-cut. A distinction should

be made between innate and environmental causes. There are, however, some at risk factors to look out for such as:

❑ Family history of speech delay/disorder;

❑ Traumatic pregnancy and/or birth;

❑ Recurrent ear infections/glue ear;

❑ Sensory deprivation;

❑ Feeding/swallowing problems;

❑ Emotionally deprived/unstable environment;

❑ Limited exposure to good models of language at critical points of language development.

How speech and language impairment manifests itself

A speech or language impairment can affect a child in three ways:

❑ behaviourally;

❑ educationally;

❑ emotionally.

Behaviourally, children with speech and language impairment can be withdrawn and quiet within the class environment or, alternatively, extremely active with poor concentration. They often have difficulty following adult-directed activities, for instance story time, and they tend to respond poorly to verbal instructions. There are children who remain confident speakers in spite of their difficulties; these are generally more outgoing by nature.

These children may display a number of educational characteristics.

❑ Make limited contributions to activities that require verbal skills, such as telling a story and during show and tell sessions;

❑ Have poor listening skills - instructions need to be repeated a number of times before they are able to carry them out, or they are easily distracted by noises in the classroom;

❑ Mispronounce words;

❑ They compare well with others on non-verbal tasks;

❑ Have limited amount of speech;

❑ Have limited range of vocabulary;

❑ Have difficulty in acquiring new words;

❑ Find it difficult to find appropriate words to express themselves;

❑ They mainly use simplified sentences, single words or sounds;

❑ They put words in the incorrect word order;

❑ Have difficulty in understanding abstract concepts such as emotions and time;

❑ Make consistent/inconsistent substitutions of sounds.

The emotional effects could be:

❑ Have difficulty when playing with their peer group;

❑ Get frustrated which results in temper tantrums when they can't make their needs known or when they are misunderstood;

❑ Poor self-esteem;

❑ Poor integration into their peer group.

The practitioner's role

If you suspect that a child has a speech and language impairment, the parents or carers must be informed. They, in turn, should tell their GP, health visitor or local child development clinic and ask for a referral to a speech and language therapist.

The child will need an assessment so recommendations on therapy can be made. Therapy can be given on an individual or group basis.

Liaison between the therapist and the pre-school is essential in addressing the child as a whole.

In the classroom

❑ Create a good listening environment by using soft furnishings to absorb sound.

❑ Keep comments short.

❑ Use as many senses as possible to aid in learning.

❑ Have a variety of activities available for the child who has poor attention control.

❑ Vary activities that are challenging, for example listening to a story, with fun and more active types of activities such as painting, outside play or musical chairs.

❑ Physical contact, such as sitting in a worker's lap, can be a great help for children who struggle with attention control and listening.

❑ Use lots of animation at story time, and tell the story in short sentences rather than reading it word for word.

❑ Music is a powerful tool in gaining children's attention and stimulating listening and language skills by action songs, for example.

❑ Using a musical tone of voice can also help.

❑ Do not make the child talk; instead, follow their focus of attention and comment on what they're doing. The likely response is that the child will naturally want to tell you about his/her interests.

❑ Regular discussions with parents or carers are helpful when it comes to activities that involve talking within the group. Find out what the child's or family's interests are and when there's a special occasion in the child's life.

❑ Repeat the child's utterances back to him and model the correct form to him.

❑ Do not put the child in the spotlight, such as in show and tell activities.

❑ Avoid asking 'testing questions' like 'What colour is this?' or 'What is this?'. Children with a language impairment feel tested and will naturally withdraw. When you find yourself wanting to ask a testing question, use that moment to *tell* the child what the answer would have been - 'It's a blue truck'.

Reserve time, even just a few moments per day, in a quiet and relaxed environment where you can spend quality time with the child and focus solely on *playing* with him.

Relationship with parents

A trusting relationship between parents and practitioners is invaluable. Parents are useful sources of information, to help us see and address the child's needs as best we can, taking all aspects of child development into consideration. Specific times need to be set aside to meet with parents. As children with speech and language impairment often struggle with generalisation of concepts, words and skills learned, parents need to reinforce activities at home. Speech and language impairment influences many other areas, social interaction and behaviour and parents frequently need some practical advice on how to assist their little one at home. Strategies are often put into place in the early years setting that can be successfully applied in the home environment.

Tania Crampton-Hayward, senior paediatric speech and language threrapist at The Speech, Language and Hearing Centre, Christopher Place, London.

Where to go for help

■ Royal College of Speech and Language Therapists, 2-3 White Hard Yard, London SE1 1NX. Tel: 020 7378 1200. Email: info@rcslt.org

■ AFASIC, 69-85 Old Street, London EC1V 9HX. Tel: 020 7841 8900

■ ASLTIP, 58 Cheshire Street, Market Drayton, Shropshire TF9 1PR. Tel: 01630 655 858. Email: asltip@netcentral.co.uk

■ The Speech, Language and Hearing Centre, 1-5 Christopher Place, Chalton Street, London NW1 1JF. Tel: 020 7383 3834. Email: info@speech-lang.org.uk

■ Your local education authority

Five per cent of all children under five stammer at some point. This means that most early years professionals will at some time in their career need to be able to recognise the early signs and know what to do to help the child and support their parents

Stammering in young children

Speech is a skill which develops rapidly during a child's first two years as he learns to make meaningful sounds and words. We often take for granted that a child will learn to talk easily and freely but, like learning to walk, there will be bumps, stoppages, starts, faltering first steps and then, with practice, children learn to co-ordinate all the necessary skills and walk steadily.

Although all children repeat words and phrases, pause between words with ums and ers, and often hesitate, some children will stammer and have more difficulty than others in learning to talk smoothly. There has been a commonly held belief that young children who stammer simply grow out of the problem if it is ignored. However, stammering is a complex problem and parents often wonder if the stammer will get worse, whether they should do something and if so, what help they should seek.

combination of factors is involved. In about 60 per cent of cases, there is a family history of stammering, or other speech and language problems in one or more relatives. However, other factors can affect a child's ability to speak fluently, including their language and motor skills, environmental, social, emotional, and psychological factors.

What is known about stammering?

Five per cent of all children under five stammer and just over one per cent of school age children. Stammering occurs in all cultures and social groups and affects three times more boys than girls (therefore this text uses 'he' instead of 'she'). It most commonly begins between the ages of two and five years old - the average age of onset is 32 months. Fortunately, most of these children will not continue to stammer into school age, but around two in five are likely to continue to stammer unless they receive help early from a speech and language therapist.

It is not known why young children begin to stammer but it is recognised that a

How will you know if a child is stammering?

If you look after a child who is stammering there are several things which you may notice:

❑ that the child's speech does not seem to flow smoothly - it may sound tense and jerky;

❑ the child is putting extra effort into saying his words;

❑ the child is aware that he is finding talking difficult or shows signs of being frustrated;

❑ that the child gives up talking half way through a sentence or a story.

Or you may hear the child do one or more of the following things:

❑ repeat part of words and whole words; for example 'Ca-ca-ca-can I have a drink?' or 'I-I-I-I want a story';

❑ lengthen sounds; for example, 'He is ssssssssitting on the chair';

❑ block - this is where the child knows what he wants to say but gets stuck on a particular word; for example 'Where's . . . . daddy gone?'

Stammering varies a great deal from child to child so you may hear some or all of these things when the child is talking.

One of the features of early stammering is that it tends to come and go. Children can often have days, weeks or months when their speech seems to flow easily and smoothly and the stammer seems to have disappeared, and other times when the stammering is more noticeable and the child finds talking difficult again. Even within one day you may notice that a child's stammering varies:

❑ it may be more obvious when he is feeling tired, unwell, excited, or anxious;

❑ it may change depending on who he is talking to, for example other children, adults, carers or strangers;

❑ or according to the situation, for example if it is noisy, quiet, rushed or relaxed.

What should you do?

Because you are with the child regularly you hear him talk at different times of the day and in different situations - when he is playing alone or in a group, first thing in the morning or when he is more awake. You are in an ideal position to be able to notice if a child is stammering or finds talking difficult.

If you think a child you look after is stammering the first thing to do is to discuss this with his parents or carers. If stammering is identified and treated early enough, therapy is effective and can help the child overcome the stammering. Therefore if a parent/carer is concerned in any way it is important that they do not delay in asking for a referral to their local NHS speech and language therapy (SLT) service either through their health visitor or GP, or directly, by contacting the SLT department.

Practical ways of helping

There are many things adults can do which help a child who stammers to talk more easily.

❑ Listen and respond to what the child wants to say not how he says it.

❑ Don't look away from the child when he stammers.

❑ Be patient and allow the child time to complete his thoughts and to speak rather than finishing the child's sentences or interrupting him.

❑ Reduce the number of questions you ask, and make sure you give the child time to answer one before asking another.

❑ Slow down your own rate of speech slightly - this is more helpful than asking the child to slow down or to stop and start again. Slowing down helps the child feel less rushed when they talk.

If stammering is identified and treated early enough, therapy is effective and can help the child overcome the stammering.

❑ Wait a second or so before responding to a child's comments or questions - pausing like this helps children feel less hurried when it is their turn to talk and gives them time before answering.

❑ Praise and encourage the child for what he does well. This helps build confidence.

❑ Treat a child who stammers in the same way as other children regarding their behaviour - discipline should be appropriate and consistent.

Children who stammer respond well to a less hurried lifestyle and in a structured environment and a routine.

If the child needs to tell you something, give him your full attention. If you are doing something else at the time, explain why you cannot stop, but give him your full attention later.

Where to go for more help

If you suspect a child you look after is stammering, it is important that his parents or carers seek professional help from a speech and language therapist (SLT) as soon as they become concerned - preferably from an SLT who specialises in stammering. Stammering can be prevented from developing if it is treated early enough. Parents and childminders can contact the British Stammering Association's Information and Counselling Service to receive a free information pack, details of their local NHS speech and language therapist service and whom to contact to make a referral.

Copies of the leaflets *Does Your Young Child Stammer?* and *Stammering in the Under Fives* are available free to all pre-school workers from the BSA.

Other useful books include *Helping Children Cope with Stammering* by Trudy Stewart and Jackie Turnbull and *Stuttering and Your Child: Questions and Answers*.

Elaine Christie, Specialist Speech and Language Therapist, British Stammering Association.

You can contact The British Stammering Association on 0845-603-2001 (local rate call) or write to them at: British Stammering Association, 15 Old Ford Road, London E2 9PJ. Main office number:

0208-983-1003

Kate Griffin explains what it means to be autistic and offers some advice on detecting early signs and on meeting the needs of a child with autism

Working with an autistic child

Take a moment to imagine what it would be like to live in a world where words, gestures, facial expressions and displays of emotion mean almost nothing to you. This is the isolating experience of more than 500,000 families in Britain whose lives are touched by autism.

What is autism?

Autism affects the way a person communicates and relates to people around them. The term autistic spectrum is often used because the condition varies; some people may have accompanying learning disabilities while others are more able, with average or above average intelligence.

Asperger syndrome is at the more able end of the spectrum while Kanner syndrome, sometimes referred to as classic autism, is at the less able end. However, despite wide-ranging differences, everyone with the condition has difficulty with social interaction, social communication and imagination.

Early signs

Parents are astute judges of their child's development and most often it is they who notice that 'something is not right', usually when their child is around two to three years old.

Distressingly, in some cases a child may seem to be developing quite normally and then suddenly appears to start losing the skills that he or she has acquired.

The signs of autism are varied. Parents and carers might notice that

their child takes no interest in creative or imaginative play, preferring to repeat the same activity time and time again. Perhaps they find that their child repeats actions or words, behaves in public in ways that are odd or inappropriate, fails to make eye contact or has an almost obsessional interest in a particular subject or object - it has not been unknown for children to become fascinated by household appliances like vacuum cleaners!

In addition, a child with autism may become very distressed if routines are altered - for example, if mum varies the usual walk to the shops, or decides to serve the evening meal at a different time.

Relationships can be difficult and not only for parents. Children with autism can sometimes appear to be disruptive, rude and indifferent to other youngsters when playing or socialising. Occasionally their behaviour in public can be misunderstood by onlookers as a display of temper or

naughtiness - the resulting comments made can be distressing and hurtful for parents who are doing their best to cope in a difficult situation.

Diagnosis

Early diagnosis is vital to ensure that the child and family receive support and educational guidance as soon as possible as this can have a positive impact on the future.

Most parents who suspect something is wrong approach their GP. They may also contact their local education authority to ask for an assessment of their child's needs. However, although awareness of autism is increasing, some families still experience frustrating delays before their suspicions are finally confirmed and a diagnosis obtained. (Occasionally, some of the more able children with autism, including those with Asperger syndrome, are not diagnosed until they are in their mid to late teens - sometimes even later.)

Support for parents

Once a firm diagnosis is obtained, a prime question for parents is education. A key aim is to overcome or reduce the disabling effects of autism by providing a broad and relevant curriculum and giving extra help in the areas of communication and social skills as well as compensating for difficulties in imagination.

In the early years setting an autistic child will need specialised assistance targeting these areas and to help them cope with the school environment generally. It is accepted that early intervention can make a real difference to the life of both the child and their family.

The National Autistic Society has set up a project known as EarlyBird which aims to support parents in the period between diagnosis and school placement. As part of the project, therapists work with parents to establish good practice in applying a knowledge of autism. They are shown techniques to put them in control of their child's development at an early age, to help pre-empt inappropriate behaviours and realise their child's potential.

Remember that you are trying to improve the quality of life for the child, helping him or her to behave in a more socially acceptable way so that others respond better and so that the child is happier.

❑ Make sure that the day is predictable and safe by establishing meaningful routines. Children with autism learn best through practical activities that are meaningful to them, for example routines for putting on clothing, eating, play.

❑ Keep calm and avoid using a raised excited voice. Use gentle, slow movements with frequent smiles and touches.

❑ Language - keep it simple, often backed up with photographs, pictures, body language, gesture and facial expressions.

❑ For any child with autism, learning to communicate about the things that are important to them is the best place to start.

❑ When trying to work with an autistic child get down to their level by sitting or kneeling on the floor, or for a more structured approach use a small table with a chair at the right height.

❑ For young children with autism a key aim is to help them enjoy exploring their own lips, tongue and teeth and the sounds they can make. It is important to make any play with sounds fun.

❑ Encourage children to join in with 'turn taking' play using sounds. This is a way of practising conversation as well as practising speech sounds.

❑ Encourage words - but don't worry if they don't sound quite right to begin with.

❑ The play of children with autism is often taken over by their need for 'sameness'. Play becomes another sort of repetitive activity which can block other people out. Try to encourage variety in the child's play so that new experience and learning is made possible.

❑ Children with autism also need to learn how to play with people. They need to learn that people can be interesting and fun. Again this opens up a whole range of new experiences and opportunities to learn.

❑ Keep a watchful eye to ensure that the child is not teased or bullied.

and catch the ball games.

Appropriate provision

As a spectrum disorder, autism demands a flexible response and in practical terms a range of provision is needed. Many authorities aim for all children with special needs to be taught within their local mainstream schools. This gives the children a chance to become integrated into society with non-disabled peers and offers the possibility of making friends close to home.

Helpful approaches

Early years workers who care for a child with autism should be aware of several helpful approaches.

Visually interesting toys/activities: Children with autistic spectrum disorders tend to prefer toys that involve visuo spatial skills such as shape and colour matching, jigsaw puzzles or constructional materials. Examples include: bubble blowers, torches, shape and colour matching toys, jigsaws, pop-up toys, construction toys, train toys, drawing, colouring and painting, books with flaps, touch and feel books, puzzle books and videos.

Physical activity: It is useful to encourage physical activities that are enjoyable without the need for imagination or understanding and use of language. Physical exercise is reported to diminish inappropriate behaviour and such activities are also helpful for improving motor co-ordination. Many children love 'rough and tumble' play which helps them develop eye contact and social interaction. Examples include: swings, slides, musical toys, water toys, rocking horses, trampolines, climbing frames, ride-on toys, paddling pools, sand pits.

Games to play with other people: Try to engage the children in simple games. Dancing games such as 'The Hokey Cokey' involve others and have consistent rules. Children can pick up and enjoy the routine of these activities. Other examples include: singing and dancing games, pass the parcel, peek-a-boo, 'Round and round the garden', simple picture/lotto games, snap, skittles,

Where to go for help

A first point of contact for parents and carers seeking advice or information is the NAS's Autism Helpline, a written and telephone enquiry service. The phone line is open 10am - 4pm weekdays.
Telephone: 0870 600 8585.

Professionals may be interested in the society's information centre which provides advice and information for students, researchers, teachers and members of the public with an interest in autism (Telephone: 0207 903 3599). The society's publications department offers a wide range of helpful literature.

For more information, write to The National Autistic Society, 393 City Road, London, EC1V 1NG.

For some children with autism mainstream education is both appropriate and desirable. With the support and advice of knowledgeable professionals it can be adapted to meet individual needs. For other children, however, the mainstream environment can be terrifying and confusing with things appearing to happen at random and in unexpected ways. This leads to great distress for the child and disruption for the school.

While excellent, high quality specialist education for children with autism exists in the UK, sadly there are too few places and parents often have to struggle to find the right place for their child. Sometimes their choice is limited or the place they eventually find is many miles from home.

The National Autistic Society (NAS) has been at the leading edge of devising appropriate programmes and runs schools for children whose abilities cover the full range of the autistic spectrum. Day and residential options offer flexible responses to the needs of each child and their family.

Kate Griffin, The National Autistic Society

Children need regular chances, planned and spontaneous, to recognise their own names. Caroline Jones explains how these chances can become a natural part of nursery routine

Name recognition

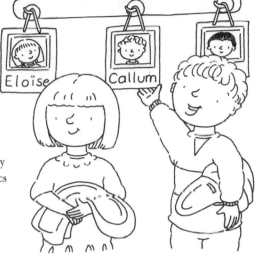

Name recognition opens the door to realising that words have meaning. Once children have mastered the skill of remembering the shape and pattern of their name this can soon be developed to include other familiar words. By regular and careful exposure to the written version of their name children naturally begin to learn that the name is made up from letters of the alphabet. They begin to understand that those letters can be found in other words and to recognise their shape and sounds in other contexts.

A child is more likely to recognise their own name and familiar words by meeting them in useful contexts. One of the most effective ways of introducing names and familiar words is to adopt a 'drip feed' approach. Let children see their name in use in lots of places all the time until they eventually remember it and recognise it without relying on an adult to read it to them. There are a variety of strategies which you can use to make name recognition a natural and enjoyable experience.

Coat pegs

Nurseries often stick pictures alongside coat pegs to help children identify which is theirs. Children soon remember which picture is on their peg. As they see their coat peg so frequently, it is an ideal place to begin. Ask parents for a photograph of their child or take one yourself. Mount it on card and write the child's name under the photograph. (Always use upper, that is capital, and lower case, or small, letters appropriately.) On the back of the card write only the child's name. Punch holes and thread a piece of string through the top of the card. Hang with the picture facing outwards on the child's coat peg so they can achieve immediate success. Then, when the child is ready, remove the picture prompt by turning the card the other way. Let them turn over to check if they need to.

Snack time

Using the same principle, place mats can be made for each child. Alternatively, simply put the same name cards on the tables at drink time and tell the children to sit by their name. Give help to those who need it. While they wait for their drinks they can look at and talk about the characteristics of their name and trace the letter shapes with their fingers.

Registration time

A popular idea is the 'We are here today' board. Make cards, badges or use the coat peg cards again. Children pick out their names as the register is called and hang them on a board, put them in a box or even stick them onto a Velcro board. This should be done in small groups or even pairs at first - it can be difficult for the first child to find their name when there are another 29 on the table. With a smaller group to select from the need for an adult prompt is reduced and the likelihood of success is increased.

Adapting ordinary activities

Children with a poor visual memory or who are visually impaired will need extra support. With adult help, at first, 'writing' their names in the sand, drawing with their finger on the table, painting with water on the slabs outside, can help children remember the shapes and encourage correct letter formation. Name recognition can be incorporated into many commonplace games and routine nursery activities.
- Play 'Match the name' using a home-made domino game or lotto names.
- Using the name cards play 'Find the name' - start with two different names to begin with. Vary it by including another name with the same initial letter. Increase the number of names to play in a group of children. Turn over cards from face down. Ask the child 'Which one is your name?'
- When choosing helpers, identifying whose birthday it is, whose turn it is on the big bike, and so on, hold up the name card

and ask the children to look closely to see if it is them you are referring to.
- Letters can be used to make little jigsaws. Cut each name into individual letters and piece together in the right order.

Labelling children's work

It is important that all the adults in your group, including students and parent helpers, are aware of how to spell every child's name correctly. A master list, taken from the registration form, is invaluable and avoids the situation where the Michaels and Rachaels of this world take home paintings with incorrectly spelt names. All children's work on display or to take home should have the name clearly written in the top left-hand corner, on the front. This is a model for the children and will help them to realise that this is where writing begins, as they become aware that text moves from left to right. If paintings and drawings are named in this way they provide another opportunity for name recognition. As they leave to go home, children can find their own pictures, instead of depending on an adult. If the child has painted over the whole space write the name on a self-adhesive label. Keep a good quality felt-tip or pencil near to where children are working as names written in a hurry with the nearest wax crayon do not set a good example. Children will learn from watching adults clearly printing names.

Caroline Jones

Debbie Denham explains how to make your surroundings and the activities which take place in them underline the message that books are important

Books in the nursery

It is worth spending time on carefully selecting books for children. There are more than 8,000 children's books published every year in the UK and, understandably, it is often difficult to choose from amongst this vast number. It is tempting to select books from cheap bookshops or buy old favourites rather than be adventurous, but children should be exposed to a wide range of good quality books.

Any collection of books for the under-fives should include books which show children and adults from different cultural backgrounds, and those with disabilities, in a positive role; boys and girls and adults in non-traditional roles; and books which help children deal with anxieties and difficult issues.

Examine the books you already have and try to get a clear idea of what you are looking for before buying any new ones. This limits impulse buying and means that gaps in your collection are filled systematically. You can use local libraries and bookshops to view a wide range of the books currently available.

After making your selection you need to think about where you will buy the books from. Library suppliers and specialist children's bookshops are useful sources and may even offer you a discount. Your local Schools Library Service may also be able to help.

Displaying books

Your new books need to be displayed effectively. Young children will not recognise authors or titles but will be drawn to an attractive cover illustration. The best way of showing a book is, therefore, with the front cover facing outwards.

Every early years setting needs a clearly defined book corner with shelves or racks on which books can be displayed. Books should be accessible to children and not mounted high up on walls or kept in cupboards. Carpeted floors and a number of bean bags and cushions will make the corner a comfortable area in which to sit. It can then be used for story times and by individual children who want to look at, read and share books. Try not to restrict displays to one area - window ledges, spare shelving, racks and even stacker boxes can all be used to display books effectively around the classroom. Relevant stories should be incorporated into any displays.

Sharing books

As well as having a set story time each day, encourage children to read and look at books throughout the day. For example, a suitable story could be read to support a craft activity whilst it is taking place rather than waiting for story time. Craft activities can be built around books and puppets and role playing are an ideal way of exploring the stories in books. Let children put on dressing-up clothes to act out their favourite stories. Story time can also be enhanced if staff use appropriate props when reading. Children should be encouraged to read and share books with other children and adults at every opportunity. In this way they will learn to copy storytelling techniques and enjoy looking at pictures with each other.

Caring for books

It is inevitable that some damage will be caused to books which are well used. It is possible to minimise this damage by following a few simple rules:

❏ if you buy books from a library supplier they may be able to reinforce them for you. Although this can be expensive, it will considerably extend the life of the book.

❏ if you cannot get books which have been reinforced you can cover them with clear sticky-backed plastic - particularly useful for paperback picture books which tend to look dog eared very quickly

❏ encourage children to wash their hands before using books

❏ insist children return books to their correct places after use

❏ make sure books are an everyday part of nursery life. Make them easily accessible and children will soon learn to treat them with respect.

Making books

One way to encourage children to use books is to help them make their own. This will help them develop an understanding of the writing process and the creative skills which are needed to produce a book. As well as giving children a sense of achievement, making their own books will engender a pride in the books at nursery. When finished, children's own books could be included amongst the others in the nursery book corner. At a very simple level, it is possible to collect a series of A4 sheets within a folded A3 sheet of card or sugar paper and staple down the edge.

There are a number of books available which contain more sophisticated ideas for making books for and with children. *Making Books: A Step-by-Step Guide to your own Publishing*, published by Macdonald Young Books, includes ideas for children to create their own books and examines concepts such as design, shape, lettering and printing. *Making a Book*, published by Wayland, is aimed at older children and discusses all stages of book production from the initial idea to the final book. Although aimed at older children it does contain some activities which could be adapted for use in the nursery.

Debbie Denham

Communication, Language and Literacy

A good picture book is probably the most useful of all resources available to us - cheap, accessible, fun, something children can use by themselves, in a group at school or at home with their families. But do you value it as much as you should?

Using picture books

The term 'picture book' sometimes causes confusion. While a few picture books use pictures alone, most have both words and pictures. The picture book differs from the illustrated story in that the pictures are just as important as the text in telling the story.

Why they are so important

Early experiences with picture books are essential to the development of literacy. Alphabet books, rhyming texts and poems can all help children to learn their letters and sounds, but literacy means much more than simply being able to read the printed word. Written language is quite different from spoken language. The child needs to have as wide an experience of books as possible so that when he starts to read for himself, he will be coming across familiar forms of language. Choose a variety of books with different language styles - humour, poetic descriptions, dialogue, stories written in clear, everyday language, dual language to give just a few examples.

Don't be afraid of vocabulary that is unfamiliar to the child. It's much easier for a child to make sense of a new word if he comes across it in a picture book, with the context of the story and the pictures to help him. Make a point of looking out for books with a few challenging words, as well as books that deliberately aim to increase vocabulary.

Learning how a story works is also important. Help the children by focussing their attention on certain key aspects of the story.
❏ Ask questions such as, 'What do you think happens next?' or 'If you were Tommy in the story, what would you have done?'

❏ Encourage older children to think about a different possible ending to a story they know well. They could even act it out as part of their creative development.

❏ Talk about the central character - name, appearance and so on - to highlight that this is the person or animal whose fortunes we are going to follow as the story progresses.
Of course, we're not aiming to turn the children into literary critics before they even start school, but you will have done all you can to help them feel more comfortable and familiar with stories in general.

Getting to know books

Becoming comfortable with books includes learning how to handle a book as an object. Little ones need to be shown how to carry a book safely and how to turn the pages. They need to learn how to take a book off the shelf, and how to put it back.

Teach your children the names of the different parts - the pages, the spine, the front cover, the back cover, the gutter (the crease in the middle of the book), the endpapers (the inside of the covers, often beautifully decorated). Show them the title and the names of

the author and illustrator. Talk about the people who have made the book. Older ones can learn about how a book is put together and published - perhaps even make their own.

Story time conversations

Picture books can trigger some wonderful conversations between adult and child. They often start off because the child wants to know more or has misunderstood what he has heard or seen. It's tempting to feel that we shouldn't allow interruptions to the story, but these interruptions can be invaluable. If you respond as fully as possible to questions and comments, you can combine your knowledge with the story and pictures to increase the learning opportunities for the child.

This kind of story time conversation is more useful (and easier to conduct) with a single child or small group than with the whole class. There are also advantages for the child whose language is not well developed. It's often easier to make sense of what he is saying when you are discussing a story you have both heard and pictures you can both see - and understanding the child's meaning is an important part of helping him develop the ability to converse.

If you are working with a small group, make sure the children can see the pictures clearly. Let them look at a picture for as long as they want before turning the page (another reason for having small groups). Perhaps most important of all, be prepared to re-read the book for as long as it holds the children's interest and make it freely available in the book corner. Repetition is essential to the child's learning and if the book raises questions or comments, you may find that these develop from one reading to the next.

Hilary White

As adults, the books and other materials we read have a profound effect on the way we look at life. The same is equally true of children. It is, therefore, vital that you choose children's books with great care, says Mary Townsend

Choosing books
for young children

You need to provide children with a wide variety of books which are enjoyable, stimulating and meaningful to them. Don't be tempted to buy cheap, poor quality books. It's better to have a few good quality ones, and supplement them by borrowing from the library while you build up your supply of books.

Most good bookshops provide a wide selection, but there are specialist educational suppliers such as Letterbox, Community Insight and Roving Books who are particularly aware of equal opportunities issues.

Check your books regularly to make sure that they are suitable and also in good repair. You can't expect children to value books if they are torn and tattered.

You will probably have many of the well-loved traditional stories such as 'The Gingerbread Man', 'Red Riding Hood' and 'The Three Little Pigs' on your bookshelves. It's important to keep these, but because they tend to show stereotypical roles and have a white European emphasis, you need to balance them with books which give the children a wider view of the world. Some books, such as 'The Hunchback of Notre Dame', are not suitable at all because they show people with disabilities in a negative way. The check-list below will help you to choose a good selection of books:

❑ **Are the illustrations good and in a variety of styles?**
Look for good quality illustrations with the relevant picture next to the text. Some should be clear and bold, others can have more detail. Small books or books with detailed illustrations are fine for use with one or two children, but for larger groups you will need large, clear illustrations. You

Why do you need to provide books for children?
- Firstly, because children of all ages love them!
- It's a good sharing time between the child(ren) and adult
- It encourages children to respect books
- It prepares children for reading and writing
- It helps language development
- It extends children's experience of the world they live in
- It helps intellectual development
- It encourages imagination and creativity
- It helps them to come to terms with anxieties and fears

can get big book versions from many publishers now, including old favourites like *The Very Hungry Caterpillar* by Eric Carle (Puffin) and *Not Now, Bernard!* by David McKee (Red Fox).

❑ **Do they reflect the children's own experience and interests?**
Many older books show a middle class white family living in a detached house with a large garden. Look for stories situated in a town, too, where people live in flats or terraced houses, like *Lucy and Tom Go to School* by Shirley Hughes (Puffin). Choose stories which reflect the children's own experiences, like going swimming, shopping, to the playground, to the doctor.

❑ **Do they show people from different cultural and ethnic backgrounds?**
Look for stories which have a black child as the main character, such as *David and the Tooth Fairy* by Wendy Webb (W Webb Books) or *Boxed in* by Ann Sibley O'Brien. Include books which help the children to learn more about different cultures and religions, and ones which include children and adults from different backgrounds as a natural part of

the book, whether fact or fiction.

❑ **Do they show girls and boys, women and men in non-traditional roles?**
Some older books show the little girl in the kitchen helping mum with the cooking, and the boy outside with dad, doing DIY or playing football. You need to look for books where dad is in the caring role or doing the washing up, such as *Jamaica's Find* (Houghton Muffin), or mum going out to work or doing interesting things, like in *Alex's Bed.*

❑ **Do they show people with disabilities in a positive role?**
There is now a growing number of stories in which a child or an adult with a disability plays a leading role, such as *Are We There Yet?* by Clare Beaton (bsmall) and the Lucy and Letang stories.

❑ **Do they include dual language books?**
Many of the well-loved favourites, like *Where's Spot?* by Eric Hill (Puffin) and *Peace at Last* by Jill Murphy (Macmillan), are available in two languages. It's important that children see and hear different languages, so that they accept this as a normal part of life, instead of something to be ridiculed. For bilingual children, it's especially important that they experience books which they can relate to.

❑ **Do they include information books, song and rhyme books, funny books, poetry, books without words, books they have made themselves?**
You need to aim for as wide a variety of books as possible, both for children to use by themselves and for you to share with them. Don't forget that children love books they have helped to make – it may be a scrap book with photographs of an outing with captions you or they have

written or a story they have produced with a word processor and illustrated.

❏ Are they appropriate for the age of the children?

Babies need tough books – board, cloth or plastic – to use on their own, but they will enjoy proper books with an adult. Pictures should be simple, brightly coloured and of things they will recognise.

By the age of two, children will enjoy simple stories, nursery rhymes, and novelty books. Stories should be about families' everyday experiences, with simple text and uncluttered pictures.

By three years old children will be handling books well if they have been taught properly. They will be interested in a wider range of stories which will still be quite short but are becoming more complex. They will enjoy traditional tales like 'The Gingerbread Man' and 'The Little Red Hen', which have repetitive lines for them to join in with, books about special events like birthdays, books about everyday events, and songs and rhymes.

Between four and eight children are enjoying increasingly complex stories on many different themes, both fiction and information. Books will often be used as part of a theme or topic. They will enjoy fantasy and funny stories. From about the age of four, children will be beginning to learn to read, and as this skill progresses they will enjoy reading by themselves, but they will still enjoy listening to an adult reading to them. Seven- and eight-year-olds will enjoy a book with chapters which you can read a little of each day.

Encouraging children to use the books

We must show children that we enjoy and value books. If we give children experience of books from an early age it will help them to develop a positive attitude to books and reading. This means that you should be sharing books with children on a daily basis, both in formal story times and informally, one to one in the book corner when the opportunity arises. Children should also have free access to books during play sessions.

Look at the book corner in your setting. Is it inviting and comfortable? Are the books in good condition and displayed attractively? Can the children reach them easily? If you think it needs improving, give it a facelift.

Telling tales

You should aim to have a story and singing session every day. The length of the session will depend on the age of the child - for two-year-olds ten minutes is as long as they will manage to sit still, and you would need to divide this into a very short story followed by some singing and finger rhymes. For three- and four-year-olds, 20 minutes is plenty. It's better to make it a special time each day, so that the children get used to it – perhaps in the middle or at the end of the session, or straight after mealtimes when you want the children to have a rest.

You don't always need to have a book for storytelling. Try telling stories you know without a book or, if you can, make up your own. You can use props or visual aids to help you – for instance, objects included in the story, toys, puppets, hats, picture cards on a display board, or musical instruments. These props will be invaluable when telling a story to a child with a sensory impairment.

Involve the children in the story as much as you can. How you organise this will depend on the story and the age of the children – you might want to tell the whole story through and then let the children comment, or let them join in as you go. Try not to lose the continuity of the story with too much interruption.

Songs and rhymes

Singing and rhymes have all the benefits that stories have for children and more – the rhythm and pattern of songs, rhymes and poetry is particularly beneficial for language development, especially for children whose first language is not English. There is also a greater mutual involvement of the adult and the children – when you are all singing together there is a lot of eye contact and attention. Using actions increases the enjoyment and concentration for younger children and those who have limited language, because they can do the actions

even if they don't know, or are unable to say, all the words.

There are some good song, rhyme and poetry books available, so if you can, have a selection of these for all of the staff to use. Another lovely idea is to make a collection of your own favourites. You can write or word-process these and collect them into a folder. Illustrate them yourself or look for postcards and pictures to illustrate them. If you protect them with plastic pockets, the children can use them, too.

You can use books and stories in a variety of ways:
- ❏ as a starting point for a topic
- ❏ as a starting point for music, drama or role play
- ❏ to enhance an interest table
- ❏ as a learning tool for counting, colour, alphabet and so on
- ❏ as a means of finding information

All the time you are developing children's pre-reading and pre-writing skills through the use of books, stories and rhymes. Very young children will be unaware of the difference between pictures and print, but they will gradually become aware that the print is associated with the words you are saying.

You can help them to understand this by following the words with your finger as you say them. You can also use other opportunities like reading labels on food, road names, words on lorries and buses. By writing what children have told you about their pictures or models you will reinforce the link between reading and writing. If you make sure they have access to writing materials, they will begin to do this for themselves, using 'play' writing.

Once children start school they will begin to create their own stories and accounts – at first these may be dictated to the teacher and copied, but they will quickly begin to write for themselves, especially if they have been given the right experiences in the early years setting.

Mary Townsend

A wide variety of books are now available in big book format. These books were designed for schools but are ideal for use in early years settings. By planning carefully how you use them, you can also play a key role in preparing children for the Literacy Hour

Choosing and using big books

A big book is used by a member of staff in the same way that most story books would be used by an individual reading with one child. The major differences are size and the number of children actively involved in reading. The size of the text allows all the children to follow the writing and be active participants in reading and working in a group helps to develop increasing fluency, confidence and independence. Shared reading activities promote the skills that provide the bridge between reading to children and the children reading on their own.

Think about your aims

As when choosing any piece of literature for use with children you will need to think carefully about exactly what it is you wish to achieve by using the text. In using big books you are modelling and demonstrating good reading habits. You should be using your voice to read with expression, allowing the children to identify characters and how they might speak. It is important to show how punctuation affects the reading of the text. There's no need to use technical vocabulary - just reading it in a variety of ways should be enough.

A big book can be used with a small or large group, but the real beauty of it is that all children can see the words and pictures clearly and so can join in at their own level when they feel able. Just sharing the book and enjoying the reading are the most important things at this stage.

Useful techniques

In the early years setting you should be helping children become familiar with the orientation of text, correct handling of the book, and the use of picture clues to talk about the context of the story.

To develop children's understanding of the links between the spoken and written word try using a finger pointer on a stick; the

children can follow the words easily as they are pointed to. They will, as they become more confident with the text, enjoy taking turns to use the pointer themselves, making the direct link between the written and spoken word obvious. The finger pointer also helps prevent you masking words and illustrations with your arm.

As the children become familiar with the routine of reading a big book together, over time they will begin to identify common words and phrases in the text. They will start to recognise letters of the alphabet and

Useful pointers

Ask yourself the following questions when you're choosing a big book:

■ Is it appropriate to your current theme? (for example, 'The Farm')
■ Can it be used in a variety of ways? Can a range of activities be planned from it?
■ Does it provide good examples of rhyme or patterned language?
■ Is it a traditional tale or a story that the children may have encountered before, giving them confidence with the text?
■ Is it well illustrated, with good use of picture cues that will help the children predict what will happen next?
■ Is the writing clear, demonstrating a variety of punctuation and styles? For example, are some words emphasised in bold or colour?
■ Are there examples of speech so that the children can join in the story?

enjoy spotting rhymes and patterns in language. In Reception classes it is normal to use the same text daily for a whole week. This may be too much for pre-school groups but revisiting the book two or three times in a week will provide excellent opportunities for language development, especially if activities linked to the book have been incorporated into your planning.

The learning objectives are not unique to the Literacy Hour; you will recognise many aspects of them from the Early Learning Goals. The Reception class objectives were developed in conjunction with the ELGs and they support each other.

It is important to think about how much use the big book will get. There are big books which contain compilations of nursery rhymes or poems as well as non-fiction books that cover a range of themes. These books can be returned to time and time again and each time a new focus developed.

A lot of favourite books are now available in big book format. If you can afford it, it is a good idea to buy not only the big book but multiple copies (four or five) of the traditionally sized book as well. The children will love to read along with you or alongside their friends, or to dolls and teddies. This provides them with truly interactive experiences of books during a circle or story time. If funds are limited, the compilation type books are a better buy, but remember that it is better to have one or two high quality, versatile texts than ten cheap ones that don't deliver your objectives and are not attractive to the children.

Make your own!

One alternative, of course, is to make your own! These could be based upon a visit or activities involving children in the group. Using the children's illustrations or photographs of the children make them even more personal. The children will get a great deal of satisfaction from identifying themselves and recognising their names and you are able to develop all the major aspects of literacy mentioned, as well as building up a collection of books that the children will really identify with and enjoy reading.

It is not advisable to try to enlarge or copy whole books to turn them into big books. The results are not attractive and you may infringe copyright laws.

Activities using big books

These are just a few of the activities that could be carried out when using a big book as a focus for story or circle time:

☐ Find words that start with the same letter as a child's name.

☐ Match words from a key word card to words in the text.

☐ Predict what will happen on the next page.

☐ Change the end of the story to make it happy, sad, and so on.

☐ Cover over words in the text with Blu-tack and card so that the children can guess what will fit.

☐ Skip a page - does it affect the story?

☐ Read the story in a range of different voices.

☐ Retell the story with the children using different words.

☐ Make a story tape using the children's voices for speaking parts.

☐ Develop vocabulary by asking the children to identify objects in the illustrations.

☐ Introduce mathematical terms by asking about quantity, size or position of objects.

☐ Use open-ended questions to stimulate discussion about the book.

☐ Make sure that you leave the book on display where the children can look at it and use the finger pointer freely - they will enjoy playing teacher!

☐ Talk about the use of the front cover illustrations. What do they think the book is about?

☐ Encourage the children to recognise page numbers, the title, and so on.

☐ Write down the character names and use them in role-play areas.

It is better to focus on one or two activities at a time so that the children become familiar

What is the Literacy Hour?

Literacy is the new jargon for what we used to call reading and writing.
The National Literacy Strategy and its forerunner, the National Literacy Project, were set up to raise literacy standards across the country. The strategy is based around a clearly defined framework which sets out teaching objectives for pupils from Reception age to Year 6 (five to eleven years of age). Everyone involved in the scheme must stick closely to these objectives. They are organised into termly packages of work with a specific range of fiction, non fiction and poetry texts to be studied. The objectives are divided into three sections - Word level work, Sentence level work and Text level work. Most teaching is based around a specific book or 'text' that delivers the objectives or teaching points. These books are generally big books or an enlarged section of a text.

■ **Word level work** consists of phonics, spelling and vocabulary, also handwriting.

■ **Sentence level work** is the study of grammar, punctuation and sentence construction.

■ **Text level work** is based on comprehension and composition skills across a wide range of literature styles

These three strands are organised in a hierarchical fashion from year group to year group and the framework identifies specifically what is expected to be achieved by the average child at the end of a year. There is some room for revision and back tracking in the early stages, but the emphasis throughout is on high expectations and each year group is expected to achieve its objectives.

The strategy is based on the following key principals:

■ High expectations of teachers, children, curriculum planning and assessment.

■ A dedicated Literacy Hour each day.

■ Developing positive attitudes and confidence.

■ Giving children a range of strategies with which to tackle language activities.

■ An emphasis upon speaking and listening skills from a very early stage.

■ Interactive and ambitious activities that stimulate the children's interest in learning.

The Literacy Hour is divided into four distinct teaching times. The activities are planned over a series of weeks and the teacher is expected to use a wide range of teaching techniques

Structure of the Literacy Hour at Key Stage 1

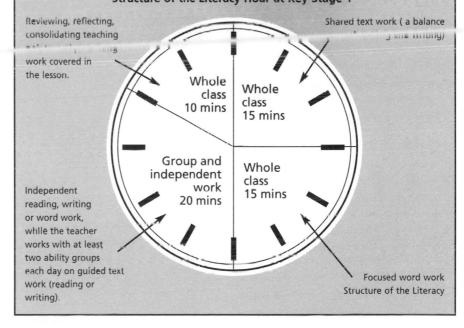

Reviewing, reflecting, consolidating teaching points and planning work covered in the lesson.

Shared text work (a balance of reading and writing)

Whole class 10 mins

Whole class 15 mins

Group and independent work 20 mins

Whole class 15 mins

Independent reading, writing or word work, while the teacher works with at least two ability groups each day on guided text work (reading or writing).

Focused word work
Structure of the Literacy

with the organisation of the session and are not confused by change. Gradually introduce new ideas and give all of the children the opportunity to join in the session, perhaps using a puppet to demonstrate what it is you would like the

children to do. For example, using the pointer to show everyone a word that starts with the same letter as your name.

Shirley Davison

Once learned, information skills will be used by children throughout their life, so the sooner they begin to learn them the better, argues Debbie Denham

Information **skills**

Information skills are the competencies we all need to help us to find and use information effectively. We particularly need these skills in today's society because of the increasing volume of information available from an expanding number of sources. Some people are even calling it an information explosion.

Children today need to grow up with skills which will allow them to locate, retrieve and use information effectively. As more and more families have access to computers, CD ROMs and the Internet, there is an even more bewildering array of sources of information to negotiate. Children need strategies to help them find their way through this vast amount of information.

In schools, the National Curriculum has placed an increasing emphasis on resource based learning, requiring children to find information themselves. In later life, for work and leisure purposes, we also need to be able to access and use information effectively.

What are information skills?

Information skills are distinct and all involve the handling of information.

They include:
- acquiring information
- retrieving information
- organising information
- interpreting information
- communicating information

It is possible to introduce children to the concept of looking for, selecting and using information from a wide variety of sources from an early age.

Introducing information skills

There are several ways to introduce information skills to very young children even before they can read:

- Children need to understand how a library works. Take them to a local library and show them the different categories of books – the picture books, fiction and non-fiction.
- You can introduce them to different ways of classifying books by sorting other everyday items. Choose a variety of small items and encourage children to think about the different ways in which we can classify them – by size, shape, colour, type.
- Show children how information in books is grouped into chapters relating to different subjects.
- Introduce children to the concept of how books work. Let them see you looking up subjects in the index. Don't always read the book from cover to cover but dip in and out of it looking up appropriate. Use contents pages and show them how to look for page numbers.

- Buy a good quality first encyclopaedia and use it, where appropriate, when children ask a question about something they have seen or heard.
- The best way to teach information skills is through:
  - a structured programme of activities
  - a series of developmental and incremental activities
  - reinforcement of previously learned skills
  - integration into the learning process - learning skills as they are required and as part of the curriculum

Information books for the younger child

A number of publishers realised the importance of information books at the end of the eighties, so there is an increasing number of high quality non-fiction books now available for very young children. It is vital that children are introduced to these at an early age.

The distinction between fact and fiction is becoming blurred. For example history novels may well be read to gain facts and high quality non-fiction can engage the emotions just as fiction can. Although there are an increasing number of non-fiction books with a narrative style the author's major intent is to pass on information.

There are some important characteristics of information books:
- the book can be a starting point for other methods of learning.

- an important element in reading these books is not only in the information gained but in the thought processes involved in understanding the information and then in using it.

- information books range from quick reference to descriptive or discursive.

- photo books are now very common and enable the child to pick out objects/people and therefore help to structure their language development.

- publishers are increasingly aware of the need to plan pictorial information as well as textual. They use high quality graphics to make the information easily accessible.

Choosing information books

As with all books for children it is important that information books are carefully selected by using some key criteria:

Content

Authority of author - are they well qualified to write about the subject?
Accuracy - the material should be up-to-date, particularly in areas of science, politics, current affairs, etc. Check that the book isn't a reprint in a new cover.
Language - this should be appropriate to the age group, easily understood, readable and stimulating.
Style - the text should be written in a style to stimulate children's interest and encourage them to delve further into the subject. It should be simple but not simplistic.
Subject matter - this and the text should be appropriate to the age group, so should the style of presentation.
Use of the book - are children encouraged to read further? The layout of the book should help children to find the information they want with good retrieval mechanisms:
• contents list
• accurate index
• up-to-date and appropriate bibliography
• glossary
Bias - a balanced viewpoint should be presented, wherever possible, or the text should overtly state the author's position. Racist or sexist bias should be avoided.

Countries, cultures and people should not be described in a condescending or misleading way.

Production

Appearance - the book needs an attractive, interesting cover. It should be produced in a format suitable for the subject, in a durable binding.
Print - clear, easy to read, well spaced, with a good contrast between print and paper, for ease of reading.

What to look out for

When you're choosing new information books for young children, look out for:
- bright, colourful pictures
- large, clear text
- photographs which do not look dated
- a story format which is often easier for young children to understand
- information presented in small manageable chunks
- an index and contents page, where appropriate
- the date of publication - the information needs to be accurate

Debbie Denham

'Information books in the school library, public library and the home are providers of knowledge. Knowledge for school purposes for personal interest or even knowledge for its own sake, is necessary for the intellectual, social and emotional development of all children.'

Titles to try

Simple Maths series by A & C Black - easy-to-understand basic maths activities with some useful notes for parents and teachers at the back.

Look at Nature series by Franklin Watts - an interesting approach to the human and animal worlds. Each title selects a different characteristic, for example *Tongues and Tasting* or *Paws and Claws* and examines different animals' attributes.

Dorling Kindersley has a vast range of books for young readers and learners. Their trade mark is bright clear photographs against a plain white background. Try:

Mighty Machines – an in-depth look at a variety of large machines which would particularly appeal to young boys!

The Children's Picture Dictionary (ISBN 0 513 5269 1) - a useful first reference book.

Popposites (designed by Jung-Huyn Yoon ISBN 0 7513 5418 X) – a fun pop-up book introducing the concept of opposites.

What's Inside series - an early introduction to the workings of everyday machines.

See How they Grow series - see the baby animals grow from birth to adulthood in simple photographs with a story-like text.

Story time is supposed to be a special time - it can also be a stressful time for you for the simple reason that many young children find it impossible to sit still! We offer some practical advice on how to establish a good approach

Organising story time

You can waste a lot of time just getting children ready for story time - sitting them down together quietly and co-operatively - so it's a good idea to establish a routine and set down rules so that they know what is expected of them:

- where to sit (on the carpet, in the book corner) and
- how to sit (crossed legs, hands in lap, no fidgeting, no distracting others, no talking, looking at you).

Help children to settle down by doing action or finger rhymes that get them involved and focused and then have a calm conclusion.

I wriggle my fingers, I wriggle my toes
I wriggle my shoulders, I wriggle my nose
And now I'm as still as still can be
There are no wriggles left in me!

Point to the ceiling
Point to the floor
Point to the window
Point to the door
Clap your hands together
Count one, two, three
Now everybody look at me!

If the children are very noisy, resist the temptation to shout - the louder you shout the louder they will get! Just quietly start to do the actions and by the time you reach the end you should find that everyone is joining in and you have their attention. If you build this technique into your routine, they will soon recognise the signals and come to know what to do.

Story time does not have to be at the same time every day. A popular time is just before home time or after a mid-morning drink when children are already sitting quietly. It is also a good device after a session of active play or when children are becoming restless and you need an opportunity to bring them together and calm them down.

Don't expect too much of them at first. They will only be able to sit still for short time spans - say 15 minutes at the most, but you should gradually be able to introduce longer stories.

Setting the scene

Where and how you sit is up to you as long as the children can see your face and the pictures in the book - eye contact is vital. Try to sit as close to the children as you can. If you have a large group you will find it easier to sit on a low chair with children gathered at your feet. With a small group you could sit around a table, if there are only three or four children you can sit beside them on the bean bags! Children should have the chance to experience storytime in all of these situations. Make the environment as comfortable and attractive as possible - soft cushions, pot plants and toys to cuddle all add to the atmosphere.

You could set the scene by playing appropriate music, either related to the mood or content of the story or simply a quiet relaxing piece of music to give a calm introduction. Another idea is to have a story box - a special wooden box or wicker basket which you keep in the story area - containing items from the story which you can bring out at the appropriate points or present at the beginning to encourage prediction.

Reading the story

During story time you are presenting yourself as a reader and providing a role model for the children. Try to convey your enthusiasm for the story through good use of intonation, facial expression and gestures. Try not to be distracted by children who interrupt or fidget. Instead, draw these children into the story in a positive way by asking them to turn pages for you or to produce visual aids like soft toy or Fuzzy Felt characters at the appropriate moment.

Help all of them to be active listeners by encouraging them to join in with repeated phrases and alliteration, and to supply the rhyming words when you pause appropriately. This heightens the children's awareness of sounds which will help them when they start to learn to read.

Hold the book so that all the children are able to see the pages - it helps if you can perfect the art of reading upside down! Point to the words as you read them to show that print carries meaning and goes from left to right. If there are speech bubbles, ask the children what they think the person is saying. Involve them at appropriate points to teach them that you will stop to let them join in but not when they interrupt.

- What do they think is going to happen next?
- What do they think he/she is feeling?
- Have they ever done ...?
- Would they like to do ...?

Whenever you come to a new or unusual word, ask them if they know what it means.

Pictures can excite further comment about the characters and the setting, they encourage detailed observation, extend the children's thought and encourage them to search for clues when enjoying books for themselves.

Big books make it even easier to share all the features of the text with the children. Talk about the title, author and illustrator, where you are going to start reading and the direction of print. Children can also begin to associate repeated phrases with the corresponding print.

Finally, ring the changes by having a variety of venues for story, not forgetting outside, by having different size groups and by inviting other adults, such as parents, to come in and read their favourite stories.

The blackboard story is one of the most successful strategies we have used to develop language and literacy skills, says Sue Hedley. Children can become authors at three!

Making a **blackboard** story

Children come to nursery from a wide and varied background with many different experiences and knowledge of story telling. I have found that although most children do have access to books and stories, television and videos are the main source of entertainment for children in story/cartoon form. These may have a place and some value, but they do not involve children in an active learning process, encouraging them to use and develop their own thoughts and ideas in an interactive way. In our nursery we have developed the blackboard story, where children create their own story and are quickly becoming authors at three!!

The Communication, Language and Literacy ELGs say that children should 'make up their own stories', 'use language to imagine and recreate roles and experiences' and 'use talk to organise, sequence and clarify thinking, ideas, feelings and events'.

Setting: Group of 13 children, aged three to four, in a quiet room.

Time: 15 minutes. Children sit in a semi-circle facing large blackboard propped against the wall.

Resources: Large blackboard, chalks and board rubber.

Getting started: Discuss 'what is a story?' A story has pictures and words. Sometimes we can read a story just by looking at the pictures.

Opening statement: It is very important that the opening statement captures the children's interest immediately. The theme of the story can often be related to a child's individual interest such as spaceships, dinosaurs or monsters! 'Today we are going to make a story for small group time. Can you help?'

Teacher: 'Once upon a time there was a giant.'

Children: 'A giant, a big giant'.

Teacher: 'What was the giant called?'

Children: 'Jack.'

Teacher: 'What did Jack do?'

Children: 'He was sad.'

Teacher: Repeats 'He was sad.' Teacher draws. (large) 'Why was he sad?'

Children: 'Because he's lost his money.' Teacher draws money

Teacher: 'How much money did he lose?'

Children: 'Twenty pounds.' Teacher draws

Teacher: ...m... What could Jack do now?'

Children: 'His wife came to the house.'

Teacher: 'What was her name?'

Christine Gilmartin shares her blackboard story, 'Jack'

continued overleaf

The blackboard story is one of the most successful strategies we have used to develop language and literacy skills. The focus is child initiated communication and how children can dictate stories in a group and individually with a responsive adult. The experience highly motivates the children and is often consolidated in their role play, painting and drawings. When you have finished, read back the finished story, giving children the chance to repeat some parts or make their own changes at the end, drawing on the blackboard, taking turns, questioning and developing these skills. To follow up this experience during work time the following day, have the blackboard available so that children can recreate their experience of story making.

When the story is finished perhaps the children could draw the pictures to go with the story. It can then be typed out, a sentence to a page, pictures stuck on and made into a book. The book can then be kept in the book corner for the children to revisit.

Children: 'Janine.' (A mum helping in nursery that day!)

Teacher: 'Janine said, "Why are you sad Jack?"'

Children: All shout, 'because I've lost my money!'

Teacher: 'Janine says, "I'll help you look for it Jack. Don't cry."'

Teacher questions: 'Where do you think she could look?'

Children: 'Downstairs.'

Teacher: 'Jack went downstairs with Janine.' 'Was the money there?'

Children: 'No'.

Teacher: 'Where else could they look?'

Children: 'Outside at the beach.'

Teacher: 'Janine and Jack opened the big front door.' 'What number will we make the door?'

Children: '36'

Teacher: 'They then walked down to the beach.' 'What did they take to the beach?'

Children: 'Sandwiches, spade, bucket, pop, towel.'

Teacher: 'They looked very hard for Jack's money. Was it there?'

Children: 'YES!!! They found it in the sand!'

Teacher: 'What happened next? Was Jack still sad?'

Children: 'Jack was happy. He smiled. He's found his money in the sand.'

Teacher: 'When had he lost it?'

Children: 'When he was making a castle!'

THE END

Each story is unique just as each child is. The stories come from the children and their own thoughts and ideas. Children of three and four are becoming creative story writers. Developing characters, the setting, the plot, they express feelings and emotions - they decide what made Jack sad because he lost his money. Children are problem-solving - Jack had to find his money! They are learning the format of a story: a beginning, middle and end. And never forget the story because they have been the authors!

Sue Hedley

Starting points

Here are some ideas for other stories - but do make up your own. There may be something happening in the life of your nursery which you might want to use.

1 Today is Emma's birthday. She's excited because she is going to have a . . . . .

2 Once upon a time there was a boy/girl called . . . . . who had to go to hospital because she/he had . . . . .

3 Tom woke up and stretched. Today was a very special day. He was going to . . . .

4 Once upon a time there was a scary monster called . . . . . He lived in . . . . .

5 Once upon a time there was a lion called Jake but he was very sad because. . .

Most children love stories. Almost all children enjoy music. Putting the two together can be a fun way of livening up a familiar story; it might also entice any children in your group who are not yet gripped by the book bug, says Anne Hunter

Putting stories to music

Much has been said about the importance of rhythm and rhyme in the learning processes of early language and literacy. The first literature took the form of poetry, chanted or sung, which was passed down orally through the ages.

Children do seem to develop their love and knowledge of language (or oracy skills) by becoming familiar with rhyme and by being aware of the other musical qualities of speech. These include rhythm, pitch (high/low) and dynamics (loud/soft). If we acknowledge this link, then perhaps we could also use music in the broader sense to extend our children's experiences of books and storytelling.

Valuable links

Books can seem more accessible when children become part of the story by adding sound effects, joining in chants or even making the story into a song. The bonus for you is that as well as Communication, Language and Literacy you will also be covering most of the other areas of learning as well. While the children are all joining in with the vocal sound effects, and later when they are taking turns to play their instruments, they will be developing essential co-operation skills. The book I have chosen also encourages familiarity with numbers up to ten, while inviting discussion of the different sizes of the toys. The links with Creative Development are obvious - and if you decide to have a go at acting out the song (children love the 'roll over' bit), then you've got some Physical Development as well!

Ten in the bed

I hope to show how the experience of reading *Ten in the Bed* by Penny Dale (Walker Books, ISBN 0-7445-0797-9) can be enhanced by the use of vocal and instrumental sound effects. You don't have to try it all at once; you could just pick out one activity which seems appropriate for your group. Alternatively, you could spread the activities out over a week or two (perhaps ten minutes a day), ending in a small performance. A group of ten children would be ideal, particularly for the instrumental section, if this is possible.

First, introduce the story in the usual way. Invite the children to join in the sound effects vocally (for example, Nelly fell out - CRASH!). They will probably do this anyway after a couple of hearings! Think of the different sizes of the animals; Nelly will certainly require big voices (use your own limits here!), however, Mouse will need a quiet, whispered 'Dink'. This gives the children the chance to experiment with dynamics, one of the key components of music making. If this works well you could give the children a sound each to say, pointing to them when it is their turn. It is only fair to let everyone join in on the word 'Crash!' Don't forget to choose somebody to say the part of the Little One - 'I'm cold, I miss you!' If you have some corresponding cuddly toys around, then why not let them join in as well!

Sing the story

When the children are comfortable with this then try singing the story instead of reading it (use the familiar tune, 'There were ten in the bed . . .'). This way the children will soon be participating in the whole book! Keep making the sound effects vocally - give lots of praise if the children remember what sound is coming next.

Later, choose nine different musical instruments (home-made ones are fine - see overleaf) and demonstrate yourself what each one sounds like. Try to have as varied a selection as your resources allow. Sit in a circle and arrange the instruments in the middle on a small beanbag or blanket (preferably out of arm's reach!).

Now read the story again. This time, when you reach a sound effect word, ask a different child to choose an instrument to match that sound. Give them lots of encouragement if they feel nervous about doing this; demonstrate the instruments again if necessary. Suggest that large toys would probably make a loud noise, like a drum or a cymbal, whereas small toys would sound a lot quieter, perhaps using a triangle, Indian bells or claves.

Taking turns to play

Now comes the really hard part: can the children sit with their chosen instruments in front of them (having been given the chance to explore and 'practise' for a minute) while you read the story again from beginning to end? They need to watch you, the 'conductor', very carefully, waiting for you to point to them when it is their turn to play. Each child will need to remember which sound his or her instrument represents. This will probably take some time; it requires great self-discipline to be given a musical instrument and *not* play it! Use the policeman's 'stop' sign - outstretched arm with flat hand, palm to the front - to let the children know when to stop playing. As you know, some children get carried away by the fun of making a noise! At the end, when all the toys jump back into bed, see if the children can again respond with their instruments when they hear the correct sound-word.

Finally, see if you can give a full musical performance of 'Ten in the Bed' - with everybody singing the song and playing the sound effects. Use some movement if you like - with a larger group you could have some children acting out the story while the others sing and play instruments. You don't need an audience, but if you can grab a few people to show their appreciation of your wonderful children, so much the better!

Anne Hunter

If you and the children enjoyed this activity, other favourite books that could be treated similarly might be:
Peace at Last - Jill Murphy
Mr Gumpy's Outing - John Burningham
We're Going on a Bear Hunt - Michael Rosen and Helen Oxenburg

Accompanying the song

Here are a few ideas for how to make your own musical instruments to accompany the song.

Making a tambourine

You will need: a paper plate; string or wool; pasta tubes, beads or milk bottle tops.

- Make four holes in your plate, as shown.
- Tape one end of a piece of string to the back of the plate and thread it through to the front.
- Now thread on some pasta, just enough to fit between two holes.
- Thread the other end through to the back and tape down (not so tightly that the pasta won't jangle).
- Trim any excess string.
- Repeat with the other two holes.

Your tambourine is ready to shake (gently!) You could decorate it with crayons, pens and stickers.

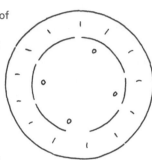

Making a scraper

You will need: a small plastic bottle with ridges (mineral water bottles are great for this); a short length of dowling or wooden spoon; coloured sand or different coloured dry pulses, stickers (optional)

- Fill the bottle with layers of coloured sand or different pulses such as lentils, barley, rice. This strengthens the bottle as well as making it look more attractive. You could also stick bright stickers around the bottle.
- Use the dowling or wooden spoon to scrape your scraper! (Make sure whatever you use has flat or rounded ends, for safety.)

Show the children how to use the stick in a downwards direction, making one scrape at a time.

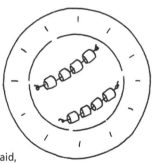

When to play them

Before every verse, scrape the scraper once for every person in the bed, counting out loud at the same time. Each time one person falls out, give a good shake on the tambourine, in other words, give ten scrapes on the scraper, counting as you go, then sing:
'There were ten in the bed and the little one said,

'Roll over! Roll over!'

So they all rolled over and one fell out. SHAKE!

Give nine scrapes, then ...

'There were nine in the bed and the little one said,

'Roll over! Roll over!'

So they all rolled over and one fell out. SHAKE!

Give eight scrapes, and so on

Continue until there is one left (and one scrape)

Then end together vocally with an emphatic 'Good night!'

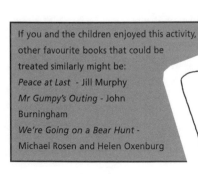

When babies begin to talk, they love to repeat sounds and noises over and over again. They enjoy the sounds of language. A love of sounds and rhymes is born through this activity. Rachel Sparks Linfield and Rosemary Mead give you some starting points

Learning to rhyme

Being able to detect and to make rhyming sounds and words are valuable skills that aid the development of reading. These activities and games will help children to identify rhyming words. As children enjoy joining in these rhyming activities they will be encouraged to listen, to distinguish sounds and to become more ready to learn, and to enjoy, reading.

In the early stages of picking out rhyming words, many children will say words rhyme because they begin with the same sound. For example, when hearing 'bag', 'Ben' and 'hen' some children would say 'Ben' and 'bag' rhyme because they both begin with a 'b'. Therefore, it is vital that the children have had ample opportunity to hear rhyming stories, say nursery and counting rhymes and generally enjoy listening to a wide range of rhyming words before they embark on selecting rhyming words.

Rhyming couplets

Recite with the children rhymes which have rhyming couplets such as 'Humpty Dumpty'. At first, try to avoid ones such as 'Baa Baa Black Sheep' which can cause confusion in that 'dame' is made to rhyme with 'lane'. Encourage the children to mime to the rhymes. When children know the rhymes well, recite one with a changed word that does not fit for rhyming. For example, 'Jack and Jill went up the stairs'.
Ask children to identify the changed word. Talk about why the word does not fit. What is the real word? Can the children suggest any other words that would also rhyme?

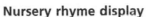

Nursery rhyme display

Put out, on a table, a selection of nursery rhyme books and puppets of nursery rhyme characters made from card stuck on to lolly sticks (see diagram). Invite children to recite nursery rhymes and to turn them into plays with the puppets.

Books

Make a collection of good quality picture books with rhyming text such as:

Each Peach Pear Plum by Janet and Allan Ahlberg (Picture Lions)

Bright Eyes Brown Skin by Cheryl Hudson and Bernadette Ford (Sundance)

It's the Bear! by Jez Alborough (Walker Books)

Where's My Teddy? by Jez Alborough (Walker Books)

This is the Bear and the Picnic Lunch by Sarah Hayes and Helen Craig (Walker Books)

A Fox Got My Socks by Helen Offen (Red Fox)

The Sheep Gave a Leap by Helen Offen (Red Fox)

Read one of the books chosen by a child to the group. Later in the week, re-read the book but this time pause towards the end of some lines to let children supply the rhyming word. As the books become more familiar, children will enjoy looking at the books on their own and reciting the text.

Rhyming table

Make a 'rhyming table' of objects and pictures that rhyme. Invite children to bring things from home that might rhyme with the chosen 'word for the week'.

Your own big book

Make a big book of things that rhyme. At the top of each page write 'All these words rhyme with ... (chosen word)'. Ask children to suggest words and write these on the page. Invite children to draw pictures to illustrate the words.

Number rhyme

As a group, find words to rhyme with each number to ten to make a rhyming number frieze. Write each number on a piece of paper and ask children to draw that number of the suggested rhyming word. (Try 'hive' or 'dive' for five and 'line' for nine).

Rhyming pairs

Make pairs of cards with pictures of things that rhyme such as socks and box, man and van, cat and hat, house and mouse. Use these cards for sorting and play games such as snap and pelmanism where cards are laid out face down, two are turned over and kept if they rhyme. Play continues until all rhyming pairs have been claimed. Cards can also be used in threes with children asked to identify the picture that does not rhyme.

I spy

Play 'I spy with my little eye something which rhymes with ...'

Sticky fish

Make a magnetic fishing game in which children 'fish' for pairs of pictures which rhyme.

Rachel Sparks Linfield and Rosemary Mead

Long before they can read and write independently, children respond to poetry. Sian Hughes shows you how to have some fun with a popular playground chant

Rhythm and rhyme

If you or parents don't want to use the word 'knickers', 'trousers' will work just as well - it just won't bring forth the same laughter!

Good reading is creative. A good reader thinks ahead, predicts, guesses, wonders, looks back, makes bits up. Good readers are also accurate. Try reading a child a favourite story in the wrong order, or missing out a page. Not all children, however, naturally fall into these habits of interaction and accuracy. Their 'reading' needs to be challenged, woken up and teased into life: this can be done through poetry before they can read or write a single word.

On a long train journey I heard a young woman singing to her toddler. He asked for 'Baa Baa Black Sheep' 20 times in a row until she sang 'Baa Baa black sheep, have you any water?' then 'wellingtons?' then 'windows?' - stringing out the Ws until the child was hopping with anticipation. What a brilliant idea!

I've tried it since with this poem, one of the first 'rude' chants I learned in a playground, aged four, and a big hit with every young group I have taught. Start with the 'right' version:

Mrs White
had a fright
in the middle of the night.

Mrs Red
went to bed
with a turban on her head.

Mrs Brown
went to town
with her knickers hanging down

Mrs Green
saw the scene
put it in a magazine.

Try sorting illustration materials into sets of the appropriate colours, then making a set of illustrations on coloured paper. These make a good class book when put together in a concertina, or a frieze display. (There's

a beautifully illustrated version of all the verses in *Tail Feathers from Mother Goose* (Walker Books) but some of the best illustration work comes from children who learn the poem before they see the pictures.)

Small groups of children can perform each section to the others. Most will soon know it all by heart, but saying it aloud to the class is much harder, and for some, a small section at a time is as much as you can expect.

Make up verses of your own, using single-syllable colours, and sticking to the rhythm:

Mrs Blue
made some stew
with meat and peas and carrots too

Change the last line - *She couldn't think what else to do* or *Then she flushed it down the loo.* Get them to choose the one they like best.

Now the fun starts. When the children ask for the poem, get it hopelessly wrong. *Mrs White had a fright at seven o'clock on Wednesday morning.* What's the matter? Why is it wrong? You need quite a sophisticated vocabulary to explain this, but if they try to, you can introduce words they need, like 'rhyme'.

Slip in smaller 'mistakes'. Some are easy to spot, because they defeat the rhyme - *Mrs Red went to bed with a turban on her nose,* for example. Then you can make it more difficult - *Mrs Red went to bed with a tea towel on her head.* Or a teapot. If your mistakes start with the right sound it's harder to spot.

You can 'spoil' the poem completely, running over rhythm as well as rhyme - *Mrs Brown went to town with her knickers and her socks on of course because she's not silly.* Mrs Brown can do any number of things in the right rhythm of course, with or without the proper rhyme: she can go to town *on the number 15 bus,* or *to buy a new hat in the sales,* or *to buy a purple dressing gown,* or *dress up as a circus clown,* or *with her face fixed in a frown.*

Muddle up the beginnings and endings of verses and get the children to put them back in the right order. This relies entirely on sounds, not stories, so is good training for aural accuracy - if *Mrs Brown went to town with a turban on her head,* or *Mrs White had a fright with her knickers hanging down,* or *Mrs Red went to bed in the middle of the night.*

If you really cannot stand the poem, try doing the same with Michael Rosen's 'Down Behind the Dustbin'. (You'll find it in the anthology *The Ring of Words,* Faber and Faber 1998, now out in paperback.) It too can be added to endlessly, and has a regularity that is useful for 'getting it wrong'.

Sian Hughes

Communication, Language and Literacy

Lullabies are probably the first poems many children hear. They play an important part in language development and family culture. They're too good to save for bedtime, says Sian Hughes

The **language** of lullabies

Lullabies, like counting rhymes and skipping songs, seem to exist in every culture. Everywhere in the world children are rocked and sung to sleep. It is probably the first poetry we ever hear. When a child arrives at pre-school or nursery they are probably already familiar with a number of these songs. Hand them a toy and ask them to help send it off to sleep, and see how many of them start singing.

A song of their own

When I worked on a family literacy project in Manchester, I met a group of mothers and children, who taught me a lullaby sung in Somalia. All the mothers sang a version of the song, but each of them had a slightly different way of singing it. A translation cannot replace the original, but this is the English text of Safia's song for her son Abdi:

Abdi, don't ever be without
a caring mother.
You and your brothers
live in goodness
Don't ever be without
many brothers and sisters.
My body burns when you cry.

Abdi, you are a raised flag.
You and your father are excellent.
Your grandfather is good.

(Translated by Muna Jama, in *Our Experience* Gatehouse Books, Manchester 1996.)

Even in the same family each child had a song they thought of as entirely their own, because their own name was used in it.

Ask your children if they can remember the words of any favourite songs sung in their families at bedtime, either to themselves or baby brothers and sisters. See if anyone has heard of 'Rock-a-bye baby'.

Rock-a-bye baby

Small groups of nursery children will be content to sing this song over and over many times, knowing that their 'own' verse is coming soon - simply replace 'baby' with a child's name.

Longer or shorter names are not really a problem - think of how many ways you have sung the line with a name in 'Happy birthday' this year.

Try to find a large format landscape picture with trees in it, then cut out a picture of a child in a cradle. The child whose turn it is to have their name sung can move the picture of the cradle to wherever they would like to be in the picture. Each time they can describe where they have put themselves in the picture. This can be a useful source of new vocabulary as well as providing practice in using positional words such as 'on', 'under' and 'next to'. The main problem with games like this is that the adults are bored of them long before the children!

Hush little baby

A more challenging song to learn is 'Hush little baby'. The tune is wonderfully simple, and within the range of even very young voices. You can remind the singers of the next object they are to 'buy' for the baby to persuade it to go to sleep, with a series of pictures. Some children will be able to arrange the pictures in order for themselves.

The sequencing of a song like this, which uses rhyme as its logic, is always immensely appealing to children, and those who work out the 'secret' of how you know what is next, are generally very pleased with themselves.

There are probably as many versions of this one as there are of the Somali favourite, but this is a relatively simple one that works the required magic of linking the objects by rhymes all the way to 'You'll still be the sweetest little baby in town' when the singing slows right down.

Of course, it doesn't have to be Daddy who does all the buying. There are as many versions with Mummy I'm sure. Sing whichever one the children are comfortable with.

Sian Hughes

Children need time and opportunities to explore their own ideas and experiment with written forms. Sue Hedley traces the stages in the development of writing from drawing, through scribble to letter formation

How writing emerges

For anything to emerge, grow and develop it has to be nurtured. Emergent writing is a process of growth and development from within the child with specific identifiable stages recognised through validated research.

Harriet Inedell (1898) wrote: 'Scribbling is to writing what babbling is to talking. As a babbling child thinks he talks, so the scribbling child thinks he writes. One is as natural to him, as universal, as much a part of his growth as the other. He needs no urging to practise either.'

Why emergent writing is important

First it is coming from and delivered by the child. They are communicating their understanding and their experiences.

Secondly, because emergent writing comes from the child's own thoughts and ideas, there is no right or wrong. Children can't fail. If we recognise this and believe in the child's own emerging skills and abilities we are saying that we have trust in their ability. If children have ownership and trust in themselves they gain confidence and a desire to do more. This leads to interest and motivation and, most of all, a feeling of success. I can do it, I am capable! I am worthwhile! If children experience this feeling of pleasure and success it gives them a positive attitude towards learning and a foundation for learning for life.

In 1998 an APU (Assessment and Performance Unit) survey of language performance revealed that not less than two out of ten pupils developed negative attitudes about writing by the time they were eleven. The report states that these attitudes are established primarily when children are first being taught to read and write because demands are placed on them to produce neat, correctly spelt writing. These children

feel discouraged because the most important things of all, the content and the process of the writing, have not been the criteria in judgement. These premature attempts to teach writing can have a life-long effect. Once they experience failure and the 'I can never do it good enough' syndrome, children can quickly become frustrated, angry, disinterested and lose motivation. Most important of all, it has a profound effect on the child's self-esteem which often continues into adulthood.

There is no short cut! We must value, encourage and develop this unique process through observation and making the most of appropriate opportunities and activities. With very young children it's not the end product that matters. We must look for the meaning of the child's writing at the earliest of mark making. For example, 'Tell me about your writing' to install a positive attitude and genuine interest.

The adult role

The supportive role of the adult is of paramount importance when encouraging children to write. We must encourage children to write 'in their own way'. Children whose writing is supported at every step tend to have a lot to communicate and become enthusiastic writers. Children who must master letter formation, spelling and grammar before they are allowed to write their own compositions will often view the writing process as tedious and unrewarding. To support children's writing, it is important to understand how writing evolves from drawing and scribbling to letter-like forms,

> What do we mean by the term emergent writer? Nigel Hall states 'emergence is a gradual process, it takes place over time. That development takes place within the child. That for something to emerge there has to be something there in the first place.' The term emergent has also been paralleled with the term 'natural' - provided by nature; in born.

invented spelling and, finally, conventional forms.

Drawing

While most pre-school children can distinguish between pictures and writing it is not yet clear to them that adults read the print in a storybook. Probably because they derive meaning from storybook illustrations, children's early writing is comprised mainly of pictures. In this form of writing, children create picture stories using the same techniques our ancestors used when they drew scenes on cave walls. While most pre-schoolers write about everyday happenings, viewing their drawing as a form of written communication expands our appreciation of their ability to express their ideas. For example, one child wrote a story by drawing four people of various sizes. 'This is about my family. Me, Josh, mam and dad going to the beach,' he said.

Scribbling

Young children who scribble will generate several lines of writing that are wavey or letter-like in appearance. As they scribble they are conscious of writing something for others to read. While the dictionary defines scribbling as hurried, careless, meaningless marks, for young children scribbling is a meaningful form of communication. Young children need every opportunity to practise and explore the scribbling stage supported by an enthusiastic adult.

Letter-like forms

As young children explore writing and create stories, they invent forms that have many of the characteristics of letters but are not conventional letters. They may also incorporate some familiar symbols, perhaps a series of circles or lines. Children often use these letter-like forms in their dramatic play, for example, Scott's plan of how to get to the pirate cave. It consisted of numerous circles and tunnel shapes joined together with the odd 'S' from his name. These were systematically placed around the border of the paper. 'There! Everyone will know how to get there now,' he said.

Invented spelling

As they become familiar with the letters in their name and other important letters, children will begin to use them in their writing. At first, children will often write a string of unrelated letters. However, eventually they will begin to isolate a sound or two in a word and use letters and numbers to signify the sounds. For example, when my children decided they needed a puppet theatre, Rachel said she needed a big

piece of card to write on. After carefully considering the sounds she came back and said, 'Look, it says puppet theatre.'

Rachel had the confidence and motivation. She knew she was in a safe, supportive environment to try out her ideas. It told me so much about her stage of development and her understanding of written communication. Rachel went on to make a book about the characters of the puppets with pages covered in emergent writing!

Conventional forms

As children's writing abilities emerge gradually over their first six years, most children are not highly involved in conventional spelling. However, they are interested in the correct spelling of their own names! How many times have you been told off for not spelling a name correctly? This is because it has full meaning and ownership to the child - it is of great interest to them because it belongs to them.

So, how do you sustain and develop this interest?

Nigel Hall, in his book, *The Emergence of Literacy* (Hodder & Stoughton, ISBN 0 340 402 16 4) poses three questions:

❑ Do young children have a commitment to writing?

❑ Do children know when and why people write?

❑ Do children know how people write?

These are three thought-provoking questions to ask yourself when you are planning your environment and your curriculum and when thinking about your role. Young children are influenced by people who are significant in their lives and adults in any early years setting present powerful role models.

Do children see you:
❑ writing messages about the current day
❑ writing notices for parents
❑ filling in forms
❑ writing observations
❑ scribbling children's words and stories
Who writes the labels? The adult, the child - or both?

Do children have access to writing materials in all areas?

Is the print in the classroom the children's own writing (whatever stage it might be)? Or is it always that of the adult? Children need to know that their efforts are important if we want them to develop a positive attitude to writing.

We must evaluate our practice, we must think long and hard about our beliefs about how children learn. The evidence is there, researched and validated.

We must offer an environment rich in language print, shared with and by the children. We must provide meaningful opportunities in the curriculum.

Encourage children to write in their own special way - and accept that it will not look like adults writing! Give children a purpose for writing, observe their interests and find ways to extend writing in all areas of their play.

If we do this, children will reach the goals and much much more because they will also have faith, trust and confidence in their own ability. They will have experienced success not failure, which will enable them to engage with the world and become confident communicators.

Sue Hedley

The development of writing

1. Drawing

2. Scribbling
    - random
    - controlled

3. Letter-like forms

4. Letters
    - random
    - patterned

5. Invented spelling

6. Conventional writing ages

Ages 2 – 3yrs

Ages 8 – 9yrs

1998 High/Scope Educational Research Foundation

To the untrained eye a child may look as if they are scribbling when really they are engaged in a valuable part of the process of learning to write. You need to encourage this and provide as many opportunities as you can for children to experiment

How to **encourage**
emergent writing

Children need to have time and opportunity to explore their own ideas about writing and experiment with written forms. This stage will last beyond the nursery years - children will still be developing their understanding of writing when they are seven years old.

When young children come to nursery they have already taken major steps towards the mastery of spoken language. Without any formal instruction children's ability to speak fluently emerges gradually as they unconsciously construct their own language rules, test them out and refine them. The ability to speak correctly grows as children observe, listen and interact with their environment. Eventually, and naturally, children learn to talk - without drills or vocabulary quizzes.

Research evidence (Marie Clay, 1975, Nigel Hall, 1987, Elizabeth Sulzby 1986 &1987, June Barnhart, 1990) indicates that young children can become fluent writers through a similar process. Given the chance to observe and experience written language all around them they invent their own strategies, rules and systems of decoding written language. And they produce their own writing - emergent writing. Your role should be to support this natural process.

Planning the environment

You must structure the environment so that it is rich in possibilities for using and enjoying written language. The environment should provide opportunities for experiences with written language suitable for children with widely varying interests, abilities and cultures, especially those children using English as their second language.

In a rich print environment, written language is everywhere, for example through labelling.

Labelling

Labelling on shelves, materials and resources - beginning with the real object for the very young child, progressing to picture symbol, and then written form. As children develop and progress, they can write their own emergent labels around the setting. Always involve the children when you are labelling the environment. That way you are reinforcing that the object, picture symbol or words are communicating a meaning. For example, a picture of the felt-tip pens means this is where the pens stay! We often do these jobs ourselves when the children have gone home! I look upon it as a valuable learning experience which helps children gain ownership and understanding of their environment. For example, asking children 'What do you think we could do to tell everyone that the dressing-up clothes stay here?' Children often come up with brilliant ideas that are better than...

Children whose first language is not English can be supported by having experience of matching the object with the picture and asking one of the parents to come in and write a supporting label in their home language.

Another key strategy to structure the environment is to provide a wide variety of drawing and writing materials in each area. For example, a well-equipped art area offers children all kinds of writing materials throughout the day:

- ❑ paper in various sizes
- ❑ paper in various colours and shapes
- ❑ various sized brushes, thick and thin
- ❑ marking pens
- ❑ crayons
- ❑ coloured pencils
- ❑ coloured chalk which can be used inside and during outside time for writing experiences.

Another popular set-up is the writing area/office area which includes resources such as:

- ❑ notepads
- ❑ forms to fill in
- ❑ unused diaries
- ❑ old calendars
- ❑ invitations
- ❑ post cards
- ❑ folders
- ❑ envelopes
- ❑ clip boards
- ❑ a class list with names on
- ❑ imitation cheques
- ❑ stickers
- ❑ Argos forms
- ❑ stamps
- ❑ pens, pencils, felt-tips, chalks
- ❑ chalk boards and rubber
- ❑ old birthday and Christmas cards

I have seen children concentrating very hard writing on Christmas cards, especially after Christmas!

Prop boxes

Because children's interests change daily another valuable strategy to encourage children's writing is to develop prop boxes for different areas. For example, in the role-play area you might want a cafe prop box, which will include a menu, a note pad with a chain pen for children to write down the customers' orders. Chain pens always fascinate children and they love to write with them - so you'll need more than one! Also a receipt book for the bill. The beauty of a prop box is it can be moved round the nursery which enables children to have a mobile cafe.

The large block area, for example, can include a fire station box where all the appropriate writing materials are ready - the clip board with a pen to write down the addresses of the fire. Children often like to draw a map of how they might get there especially if the fire is in the home area, they can draw a simple plan of the nursery.

When collecting items for your prop boxes, remember to look for things which will avoid gender strenghtening and promote an awareness of different cultures. You could have a festivals box at different times of the year such as Christmas, Diwali and Chinese New Year.

Role play

Last term, my children were interested in weddings, so we decided to develop a wedding prop box which was placed in the home area. This consisted of dresses, veils, posies, hats, camera, wedding magazines, pencils, pens and paper on which they wrote out what they needed for a wedding and an invitation list in emergent writing of who was coming to the wedding. We bought some invitation cards which the children wrote out and sent and which, to the children's delight, arrived back at the nursery.

If you watch for the children's interests, you can make a prop box for anything. I have developed:

Prop boxes
Different coloured stacker boxes are ideal for prop boxes.

Wedding box
Resources:
2 dresses
waistcoat for groom/bow tie
2 bouquets of flowers
2 button holes
2 cameras
2 veils
2 pairs of shoes
wedding music
2 invitation cards
wedding lists made by the children suitcase/labels for honeymoon rings (home made in technology from silver paper and cardboard).

□ a pirates' box with writing materials to draw treasure maps;

□ a wedding box to make lists, cards and invitations;

□ a witches' box with writing materials to write their spells and potions down;

□ a builders' box with order books, bills and receipts;

Builder's box
overalls
2 trowels
bricks
blocks - (different sizes)
spirit level
2 clipboards to draw plans
paper
safety glasses
set of old plans from a planning department
hard hats
forms for estimates
letterheaded bill with nursery/school name on
pencils
pens
ideally a visit to a building site!!!

When collecting items for your prop boxes, remember to look for things which will avoid gender stereotyping and promote an awareness of different cultures. You could have a festivals box at different times of the year such as Christmas, Diwali and Chinese New Year.

□ plus all the well-known traditional theme boxes for the hospital, hairdressers, McDonald's, fish and chip shop, transport, cabin crew, station, cafe, garage and travel agents.

If the children are taken on a visit, they will be able to see people writing and begin to understand why they write. I have come away from visits with arms laden with support material to take back to nursery for example, travel shop forms to fill in brochures to look through, suitcase tags/labels - children can even make their own passports. These are all activities which will encourage and develop writing.

Computers

Another key strategy is the use of computers. Computers equipped with age appropriate software offer satisfying child friendly writing tools. While many programs use letters and numbers incidentally, pre-school word-processing programs allow children to produce enlarged print and in some cases, to hear what they have written. Children's drawing programs also support children's emergent writing by allowing them to use the mouse to draw and make scribbles and marks to accompany their drawing.

Computers let children produce text without having to hold and guide a pencil. They make it easy for adults to see how well young children can express themselves in writing!

Small group time and emergent writing

One successful activity which I have used to encourage emergent writing is developing a child's own picture diary. A picture diary is a small unlined book which the children use once a week at small group time to draw a picture about anything they like or about something they have liked doing in the nursery. These pictures are dated from September - July so that the child, parent and teacher can see the developmental progress shared with the child's new Reception teacher.

Making picture diaries

Although every child in the nursery had a picture diary book (all 52 of them!), we worked with a group of six to eight children each small group time. We handed out eight small unlined books (easier for children to handle and take up less space on the table). The children sat around the table, one child (the special helper) gave the books out. A piece of unlined paper was stuck on the front of the books so the children could draw themselves or a picture to give them ownership of the book so they could

recognise and 'read' the cover. By the end of the year everybody could read everybody else's too!

We also had eight pots of different coloured felt-tip pens and eight pencils. The children could choose what to draw/write with. To introduce the session the children would sit in a circle on the carpet and plan what they were going to draw or write about. This really encouraged the children to think about what they were going to do. The adult would ask each child, 'What are you going to draw about today?' and discuss it with the child. This emphasised how the adult was genuinely interested in their thoughts and ideas and how valued their efforts were! Those children who didn't have any ideas were encouraged by the adult and other children about what they could draw about. For example, 'I saw you playing with Jonathan in the block area today. Would you like to tell us about that in your drawing?' Children then went to the table where they were given their picture diary book. I always put the date and day on while the children were watching - role modelling again a purpose for writing.

After the child had drawn their picture the child would dictate to the adult what their picture was about. For what can be more meaningful than the child's own words?

When you write down a child's dictation, you know you are capturing the child's interests described in his or her own vocabulary and speech patterns. When you read the dictation back to the child, you are demonstrating the connection between speech and writing.

When taking dictation, it is important to write down exactly what the child says even though it may not be grammatically correct. The important thing is to encourage and support the use of written language at their stage of development. This activity caters for all ages and stages and it is a failure free, enjoyable and extremely meaningful to the child.

Home/school journal

Developing from the picture diary another popular strategy is the home/school journal which starts in Reception for four- to five-year-olds. The books are organised the same as the picture diary to practise continuity of meaning. Each child would draw and write their name in their own special way, again to have ownership. This was taken from home to school. The child would take the book home and draw and write about anything they would like to share with us. Parents knew it had to be the child's own ideas and writing because they had attended the literacy workshop in the nursery. The book would come back to school and the adult would read it with the child and share it with the group at sharing time. The adult would then write back to the child commenting, acknowledging and sharing genuine interest in what the child had to communicate.

Children love to hear stories about what the teacher does so often I would write about what I liked to do or what my favourite food was then finish with a question such as: 'Can you tell me what your favourite food is?' This is not only a way of providing an excellent opportunity to develop emergent writing but also to help build authentic relationships with both children and parents as partners in education.

Sue Hedley

Mark making

Materials

Flat smooth table big enough to take a pair or small group

Open shelving or racks. Small quantities of a selection of mark makers, including felt pens, pencils and pencil crayons

A selection of different types of paper in a variety of sizes

A number of envelopes of different sizes and types

Two or three page books ready made up

A variety of printed/written material, for example, a calendar, a class list, an address book, an alphabet

A notice board

A hole punch, sticky tape, paper clips, scissors, pencil sharpener, stapler, eraser, ruler, school address stamp, date stamp, clipboard

Unused diaries, forms, files, desk tidy, letter rack.

Organisation

This is an activity which is best placed at the hub of things so that it can be used when 'writing' needs to be done in connection with other activities

Small quantities of things replenished regularly are best

Other materials can be added, such as a telephone, for office play

Materials should be stored on the table in a large desk tidy/letter rack so that they are easily accessible

All materials should be available all the time so that children can move from exploring the materials, often a very resource demanding period, to using them

Mark making materials may need to go in many other areas for example, block area, role-play area

Activities you will see	Examples of learning
Children drawing pictures	Development of representational and aesthetic skills
Children creating picture stories	Development of narrative skill and the use of context (picture) clues in reading
Children exploring invented writing	Development of the concept of symbolic representation
Children writing their own name	Learning of letter forms
Children writing letters to other people	Development of the concept of writing as communication
Children writing lists, messages, notices, invitations	Learning the uses and value of writing
Children making greeting cards	Designing and making
Children making and writing their own books	How books and stories work, the knowledge that books have authors and illustrators, a sense of audience
Children practising calligraphy	Fine motor skills
Children exploring the properties of different mark makers	Exploring, experimenting
Adults writing	Conventions of writing
Adults writing with and for children	The value of writing
Children behaving as writers in role-play situations	The relevance of writing

Communication, Language and Literacy

Practitioners are being encouraged to divide their settings into areas, where the children are encouraged to visit freely throughout the session. This is called child-initiated learning. Alison Grant tells you how to go about creating a graphics area to enable children to develop their pre-writing skills

How to set up a graphics area

The *Curriculum Guidance for the Foundation Stage* states that practitioners should 'provide opportunities for children to see adults writing and for children to experiment with writing for themselves for example through making marks, personal symbols (emergent writing) and conventional script'.

The Early Learning Goal for this is:

■ Attempt writing for different purposes, using features such as lists, stories and instructions.

How to create a graphics area

All you need is an area in your room with tables and chairs and storage space. Storage space should be accessible to the children so that they can obtain the equipment as and when they want it. Equipment should be labelled in both picture and written form so that the children know where the equipment belongs.

Using the graphics area

Allow the children free access to the area and if you have planned a special writing activity (such as writing Mother's Day cards) sit in this area as well. As the children move around the setting and engage in other activities they may need to write something, for example a shopping list for role play or a label for their construction model. If everything is available in the graphics area they will know where to go and get it. Adults should encourage this as it develops writing for a purpose and is more meaningful to the children than copying a worksheet.

Although you have set up a specific

writing area, children should see that writing can go on in all areas so, for example, keep a clipboard and paper in the construction area and make resources available to write outside.

Planning for the graphics area

When introducing the graphics area you will need to show the children how the equipment is used safely and appropriately and where it belongs at tidy-up time.

Have part of your short-term planning devoted to the graphics area so that you think carefully about what you want the children to learn and the skills you want them to develop.

A lot of child-initiated learning will take place in the graphics area that you will be unable to plan for, but you must be aware of this and try to

encourage further learning.

Planning should include allowing the children to:

■ Become independent

■ Find and use resources for themselves

■ Write for a purpose

■ Be given time to develop ideas

Learning is not isolated so constant access must be available to extend writing into all areas of the room and the curriculum.

Monitoring

Make sure that you monitor who uses the graphics area so that you can encourage *all* the children to use it. Monitoring should be done by regular observations. You could also have a sheet of names which are regularly marked by the child or an adult when

Chapter 4

Unit C16: Observe and assess the development and behaviour of children

About this unit

Child observation is a vital part of your work with young children, to enable you to plan effectively to meet their needs. As it is so important, we have encouraged you to use it throughout the other units as part of your evidence, and to help you to gain a thorough understanding of children's stages of development and individual needs.

There are different ways of recording child observation which you need to show that you can do. The guidelines in this chapter will show you examples of the different methods you can use. Try to observe as many different ages as possible, and a good range of areas of development and behaviour, so that you build up a good picture of the different stages of development. It would also be helpful to observe children with additional needs if you get the opportunity.

This chapter links in with M7, 'Plan, implement and evaluate learning activities and experiences', especially Element 2, in which you are required to develop individual learning programmes for children. Child observation is an essential part of this element, because you need to identify the child's individual needs before you can plan an appropriate programme.

Values

The values for both of the elements of this unit focus on the welfare of the child, working in partnership with parents and families, children's learning and development, working with other practitioners and the reflective practitioner. It's good practice to involve parents in assessing their child's development and behaviour. They are the child's first carers and educators, and know their children better than anyone, so it makes sense to consult them when you are making judgements about their children. Many settings ask parents to fill in an informal record about their children's likes and dislikes, the skills they have achieved and so on, when they start attending. Check whether your setting does this. You may also have a daily diary where both you and the parents record important events in the child's day. These are all important aspects of your assessment of the child's needs.

You may from time to time be asked to carry out observations on behalf of a specialist such as an educational psychologist, and be asked to report on your findings at a case conference, so it's essential that you are competent in child observation. It's also good for you as a reflective practitioner, because it helps you to keep reviewing your practice and improving on it, so that you are providing the best experiences you can for the children in your care.

More and more children with special needs are being integrated into early years settings. It will be particularly important to observe these children, because many will need an individual education plan based on sound judgements about their abilities and needs. The article on assessing special educational needs on pages 171 - 176 will give you helpful guidance about how to identify needs and write an individual education plan.

Getting started

In this unit you need to show how you:

◆ Observe children's behaviour and performance

◆ Use observation results to inform the child's future care and education.

We are going to look at both elements together, because for every observation you carry out you need to evaluate the child's needs and use your results to inform your plans for the child's care and education.

Check your list of child observations which you have collected in other units, and see whether they cover the range and PCs for each element. With any luck, you may have already achieved everything you need to! If there are gaps, plan how you will fill them. If you have not completed many units yet, it will be better to leave this unit until later, when you have more child observations to use as evidence.

Knowledge evidence

Hopefully, your evaluations of the observations you have carried out will provide most of the knowledge evidence you need. Do check the underpinning knowledge as you write your evaluations.

Element C16.1 Observe children's behaviour and performance

Element C16.2 Use observation results to inform the children's future care and education

Key issues

You need to be clear about why you need to observe children, and be able to explain that to parents, and to colleagues if necessary. You also need to be aware that there is no point in carrying out observations unless you use them to plan appropriate activities and experiences to help the child to develop further, or to agree a strategy for resolving a particular difficulty. All children are individuals who learn at their own pace and in their own way. Through observing them carefully, you can plan for their individual needs.

Your setting may carry out baseline assessment to find out what children already know and can do when they start attending the setting, and also monitor, assess and record children's development on a regular and ongoing basis. You need to be familiar with your setting's policy and procedure on assessment, so check what this is if you don't know already.

Before starting an observation, you must check with your supervisor whether you need to ask the parents' permission. Some early years settings explain to parents that their child will be observed from time to time throughout the year, and ask them to sign a 'blanket' permission which covers observations carried out by students and candidates as well as the normal day-to-day recording, such as daily diaries and developmental records. Also, remember to check with colleagues that it is a convenient time for you to do an observation.

When carrying out your observation, you need to be as unobtrusive as possible, so that the child(ren) don't notice - easier said than done! Sit back a little from the activity but where you can easily see and hear what's going on. Try not to make it obvious that you're watching. It's best to focus on one or two particular areas of development or behaviour, so that you have a clear aim. Only write what you see and hear, don't make judgements during the observation. If you want to report on language, use a tape recorder. (This is also a good way of observing how effectively you are using language.) Use the format given in Chapter 1 to give the details of who you are observing and why. Don't forget to evaluate what you have observed, and make recommendations about what you need to plan for the child as a result.

Which evidence?

Your assessor will not need to observe you carrying out observation of children. It's more appropriate for your supervisor or colleagues to authenticate your *child observations* by signing them and making a comment to confirm that they are accurate. Better still, they can write a *witness testimony* to say how competent you are at observing children's needs and planning appropriate activities to meet those needs.

> **Remember!**
>
> If you already carry out assessments, use daily diaries or developmental check-lists as part of your daily work, you can use them as evidence, but you must remove any surnames and get permission before including them.

You need to show that you can use different techniques of observation which are most appropriate for the area of development or behaviour you are observing and the number of children involved. The article on pages 153-158 gives you some guidance on *how* to observe children and *why* we observe. It gives two methods of observation - observational jottings which are sometimes called 'snapshots', and focused observations, which are much more detailed and more likely to be focused on a particular area of development or aspect of behaviour.

Observations may be *free description*, where you write what you see in as much detail as possible, or they may be more structured. Here are some suggestions for other types of observations you may find useful:

Structured observation where you may be using a pre-recorded format.

Examples of this are:

◆ a *daily diary* which parents are able to see and discuss at the end of the day, and also contribute to

◆ a *developmental check-list* on which you tick off what skills a child has learned - your setting's developmental records of the children may be in this format

◆ a *time sample*, where you do a 'snapshot' observation of the child's activity for, say, one minute at regular intervals during the day, perhaps every half hour, to give a picture of the child over a period of time. You could use this method where you have a concern about whether the child is able to interact and join in with other children and adults

◆ an *event sample* can be used where a child is perhaps displaying negative behaviour. You observe each time the negative behaviour happens, to see if there is anything specific causing it. You will then need to consult with colleagues and parents about the best way to avoid the situation or deal with it, so that you all use the same strategy to help the child overcome the difficulty.

Pre-coded formats make it quicker and easier when you don't have time to sit and write copious notes. One example of this is the 'target child' format described in the recommended book on child observation (see page 24). A format similar to this is shown below.

You can make your own codes up for activities, to suit the situation, but remember to include the code. This format enables you to write in shorthand form. If you're busy, it's sometimes easier than free description.

You will find that it is not easy to write a detailed observation while watching a child in a busy nursery, and inevitably it will be scribbled down in a hurry. Don't leave it for ages before you write it up neatly, or you will have forgotten the details that you didn't manage to get down.

Write it up the same day if possible, or as soon as possible afterwards. Evaluate it carefully:

◆ What did you learn about the child's skills and ability, stage of development, behaviour?

◆ What are the child's needs?

◆ Do you need to consult with colleagues and parents, or other professionals?

◆ How will you plan the child's future care and education as a result of what you have observed?

Over a period of time, try to observe the whole range of child development and behaviour, both of individuals and of groups of children. If you have carried out observations for each unit, you may already have enough evidence. You can simply cross reference to the appropriate pages in your portfolio.

Check which knowledge evidence you have covered through your observations and evaluations, and if there are any gaps, write a short account to ensure that you have enough evidence.

If you haven't read the articles on child observation which follow, do read them. You will also find some useful information on assessment and record keeping.

Time	Activity	Language	Social
10.00	SP TC using spade to fill bucket Two other children using other sand equipment OC tries to take spade TC tips bucket over, taps bottom and removes bucket	TC 'I'm making a sandcastle' A 'How are you going to do that?' TC 'Look - fill it and tip it out' A 'That's very good, let's see' OC 'I makin' one' TC 'No, that's mine' A 'Here's another one for you, D' TC 'Done it!' A 'What a lovely sandcastle, well done!'	G
10.10	BC TC sitting on carpet reading a book	Pretending to read story - inaudible	S

Codes:

TC	target child	C	construction	WP	water play	S	solitary
OC	other child	SP	sand play	BC	book corner	P	pair
A	adult	Art	creative	PE	physical	G	group

During their first five years, children develop so rapidly that changes take place on a daily basis. If you are going to find out about children as individuals you must observe them regularly. Margaret Edgington provides an insight into what to do and why

Observing young children

Observation has long been seen as a vital element in early years work. Most training courses require students to make written observations in their placements, but once they're qualified and start work, some staff unfortunately seem to feel they do not need to continue. Others say they haven't got time because they are too busy responding to the children, or they feel guilty if they are 'just observing'. Some keep their observations in their heads. I want to show that written observations are essential to enable early years staff to make valid assessments and to match their curriculum to the children's varying needs.

What is observation?

Observation is the first stage in the record-keeping process and requires early years staff to watch and listen carefully and note down as accurately as possible what they see and hear. Observations should provide factual, descriptive information about children's experiences which can be analysed - evidence which can be used by staff to make judgements or assessments of children's learning.

Parents have a right to expect that your assessments are based on factual evidence and are not simply your impressions of their child. This is why recording is so important - what is kept in our heads gets distorted and in time is forgotten. The record-keeping process, illustrated below, involves staff in gathering observational evidence, making some assessments based on this evidence and then (when relevant) planning the next steps for the child and/or planning further observations to gain more evidence.

In this example, factual evidence of a child's activity has been recorded, then analysed and a number of relevant statements of assessment are made. As you get to know different children, you are able to focus on aspects of the child's experience which are significant in their development - you do not have to write down everything they do,

instead you need to concentrate on recording *new* interests, behaviour, relationships, feelings, language, and so on. When analysing observations, you need to focus on making assessment statements which represent significant new learning for the child concerned. The points for planning can be brought to the attention of the whole team in weekly planning sessions.

Written observations may be supplemented by other forms of evidence (which need to be dated and to include notes explaining what happened) for example, photographs of experiences the child has been involved with, examples of drawings, writing, paintings, models, and tape recordings to capture language.

Why is observation essential?

The example below helps us to see that observation is central to early years work because it enables adults to:

❑ focus on children as individuals, highlighting their stage of development, interests and needs

❑ see into each child's personal experience of the setting (the curriculum they personally receive)

Observation:
12.5.98   C (age 4yrs 4 mths) alone in the home corner holding telephone receiver to ear. As she listened she wrote on the telephone message pad:
clloocc744ccllooll
Said 'okay see you later' and replaced receiver.
Assessment:
Communication, Language and Literacy: knows one of purposes of writing - that you can record messages taken from telephone. Can form some letters and numbers correctly.
Personal, Social and Emotional Development: confident to initiate own learning.
Planning
Observe her writing independently - talk to her about what she has written to see if she knows the difference between letters and numbers and the names of the letters/numbers she has written. Add telephone directory to home corner.

- offer evidence to parents and colleagues for assessments made
- plan relevant, meaningful experiences to give children access to the curriculum.

Observation can also raise questions about children's learning, about the quality of the provision made, and about the quality of adult interaction, and can therefore challenge assumptions. If, for example, your carefully planned activity generates little interest and those who do take part say things like 'Can I go now?' or 'Have I finished yet?' you are getting a clear message that you have not met the children's needs! Similarly, if you walk over to a small group engaged with water play, ask a question and they all walk away, you know you have cut across the children's purposes.

Young children give us clear messages through their behaviour, their body language, facial expressions and through language - if we are prepared to see and hear them. Sensitive early years workers who are skilled observers are able to tune into the variety of messages children give and adapt their approach accordingly.

Observation can also aid communication between parents and colleagues. Sharing an observation with a parent, rather than an assessment or judgement, can enable the parent to take part in the analysis process, and often parents can offer information about the child at home which broadens the staff member's view and changes his/her judgement. Similarly, Reception class teachers, carrying out baseline assessment with children they barely know, can add to their own inevitably limited evidence base by referring to observations of the children in their nursery or pre-school setting.

Remember that what works in one setting may not work in another. Some observation is better than none at all! It is important to be realistic about what can be achieved and not to give up if it seems difficult at first.

How can you be objective?

All early years workers bring certain expectations or even assumptions to their work with children, which relate to the values and beliefs they have acquired from their own personal and professional life experience. These expectations affect the way they observe and the way they interpret their observations, and may be concerned with:

- how they view children - both children in general and specific individuals
- how the setting they work in affects their view of children, for example Reception class staff might expect different things from children than nursery class colleagues
- which aspects of learning they give priority to, how they see children as learners, and how they organise the learning environment
- how stereotypical views of gender, social class and culture affect their view of boys and girls and children from different social and cultural backgrounds
- whether adults believe children with special needs can be included in mainstream provision
- how the role of the adult is viewed, for example whether they can share power with children and parents.

Teamwork between staff members, and between staff and parents, is essential to challenge limited assumptions and raise expectations of all children. All staff need to be aware of how their own expectations can limit their ability as an observer and narrow their view of some children. For example, a child who is developmentally immature and is finding it difficult to relate positively to the other children, may only be noticed by staff when she is aggressive to others. She may be seen quite negatively by adults because her behaviour is difficult to handle, because they expect girls to behave differently, and because they have low expectations of her family. They expect her to be a problem, so they only see her when she is presenting challenging behaviour. They need to be aware of the expectations which are leading to this negative view and take steps to observe her when she is not being aggressive. They need to consider the causes of her aggression (for example, does she have the language strategies to enable her to negotiate her way out of a dispute?) and plan to support her personal, social and emotional development.

To avoid potential bias, it is essential to record observations as objectively as possible and not allow assumptions or judgements to intrude. Compare the difference between these pairs of statements:

1 R shared the phone appropriately.

2 R passed the telephone to A and waited, watching A as he talked.

1 S has good manipulative skills.

2 S threaded the darning needle with embroidery cotton and sewed three large stitches in the Binka fabric (see example)

We then come full circle to the end of session meetings when staff report back their observations on children's responses to planned topic work as well as their self-chosen play.

The first statement in each pair is a subjective judgement. Words like 'appropriately' and 'good' are open to different interpretations, whilst the second statements capture much more precisely what the child actually did. The first statements offer the impression of one person, the second provide evidence of what the children were doing. It is the second kind of statement which should be recorded when observations are made.

The aim is to record the fullest possible description of what happened, including accurate examples of language. However, it is never possible for one person to capture everything. It is a useful exercise for staff to observe the same event in pairs and then compare what they have written. If they focus on the differences between their observations they should be able to highlight what they personally tend to notice (for example, do they focus more on physical aspects rather than social? Is one able to capture more accurate language than the other?) and whether they are using any judgemental language. They should be able to see that the more accurate and detailed the observation the more useful it is for analysis and assessment purposes.

PSED	Personal, Social and Emotional Development
L&L	Communication, Language and Literacy
M	Mathematical Development
KUW	Knowledge and Understanding of the World (add S for science; T for technology; H for early history and G for early geography)
P	Physical Development
C	Creative Development (add A for art, M for music, R for role play/drama).

Each area of learning has a separate section in the child's record so observational evidence can be easily added - where an observation shows evidence in more than one area of learning the observation could be copied or a cross-referencing note could be made, for example, see L&L 4.3.98.

Focused observations are recorded less frequently (every six to twelve weeks depending on the number of staff and children), but are essential to gain a full view of children's learning and to ensure that all children are observed regularly. Staff select a child they wish to focus on (some teams select two to four children per week) and plan time to observe the child for between five and fifteen minutes.

Focused observations should be an open record of what the child does and says during the time of the observation. Generally the staff member observing should not be involved with child. Many teams use a prepared sheet for focused observations (see example on following pages) filling in the contextual information before they begin to write. Focused observation requires adults to write fast and look at the same time. Most adults capture the main points (especially accurate language) in note form and write the observation up in more detail soon afterwards.

The staff member would analyse this observation, record significant assessments and indicate ways forward for the child which they would share with the rest of their team and with parents. Some staff focus on a

---

Example of an observational jotting:

Date: 3.4.98

John climbed to the top rung of the climbing frame and said, "Look! I'm higher than you. I'm looking down". Climbs confidently.   P

Uses positional language and language of comparison   M
(Higher down, higher than.)   L&L

Types of observation

There are two main kinds of observations to record.

Observational jottings (referred to as continuous observations in the example from Tachbrook Nursery School) are short, dated notes made by staff on a day-to-day basis to record significant aspects of children's development as they work with them. These may be jotted in a notebook or on self-stick notes notes which can be stuck neatly into the child's record. Staff need to record briefly what the child did and make one or two assessment statements and a note of the areas of learning the assessments relate to - using initials provides a quick coding system ie:

An example of a focused observation

Mark   alone
3. 11. 97, 2 - 2.10 p.m.   outside play area - on a tricycle.
4 yrs 6 mths.   M.E.

M. on tricycle stopped by hay-cart and carefully hooked handle of cart over saddle of trike - making a trailer. Ran across playground to get milk crate. Placed this in hay-cart - had to struggle to make it sit level because sides of cart slope. Went inside to water area and collected all the plastic bottles he could find - this took three journeys - and put these in the milk crate sections. He was three short of filling the crate. He then rode trike round a circuit of playground - as he went round corners he slowed down and looked round to make sure the cart handle had not caught against the tricycle. Half way round second circuit he stopped near an adult and said, "D'you want some milk?"

child's use of time by jotting down every 15 minutes during a session where the child is, with whom and what she or he is doing. Focused observations help staff to notice all children - many workers say that when they have focused on a child they notice him/her much more over the next few weeks and make more jottings.

Using these two main approaches to observation on a regular basis, teams can be confident that they are building up a detailed record of each child's experiences and achievements.

Managing observation

Here are a few ways in which teams can start to build observation into their practice:

❑ Help everyone see the importance of observation.

❑ Ensure that there is a clearly thought out manageable system which everyone understands.

❑ Ensure all staff know what is expected of them and have the tools for the job, for example a supply of self-stick notes notes, focused observation sheets, files for children's records.

❑ Make time each week for the team to share and discuss some of their observations and ideas for planning.

❑ Avoid interruptions during focused observations by:

- Planning to observe when there is another adult who knows you are observing and can deal with crises such as wet pants, and so on.

- Use a brightly coloured clip-board and tell children that when you are writing on this you do not want to be interrupted - they should go to the other adult.

- Make yourself as unobtrusive as possible - avoid direct eye contact with the child you are observing - concentrate on the task in hand and avoid being distracted.

❑ Monitor your records to ensure you have observed all aspects of a child learning. Remember that what works in one setting may not work in another. Some observation is better than none at all! It is important to be realistic about what can be achieved and not to give up if it seems difficult at first.

Margaret Edgington

Theory into practice:

How we manage observation at Tachbrook Nursery School

At our school there are 65 children between the ages of three to five years and five key workers (13 children each). The two classrooms and the garden are organised into curriculum areas. Most equipment is freely available to children. They get a mixture of self-chosen and adult initiated activities. Some play is planned in advance for each half-term; some is planned daily. All planning depends on our observations of what children are learning. This is to ensure that:

a) experiences are relevant to individual children's interests/needs

b) children progress in all areas of development

c) children have broad experiences.

We do this by having a programme of continuous and focused observations that feed into assessment and planning meetings as well as children's records.

A record folder for each child is kept in the classrooms. This has background information from parents/carers and sections for each area of the curriculum - social and emotional, knowledge and understanding of the world, moral and spiritual, physical, speaking and listening, writing, reading, 2-d and 3-d creative, music and dance, imaginative play, maths, science and technology. We also keep samples of work which can be drawings/paintings or photos of models.

Continuous observations of significant achievement/difficulty are done daily as we work with the children. We write them directly into the relevant page in the record or into notebooks we keep by us all the time. Each key worker has non-contact time in the week to transfer these observations from their notebooks to the records. We've made time for this by only having four key workers set up each morning and only having four story groups at the end of sessions. We aim to enter at least one continuous observation per curriculum area for each child per half term ie each key worker does a minimum of two observations per session (based on each key worker having 13 children covering 13 curricular areas). In practice, there is time to do lots more than that.

Each key worker has two 30-minute slots per week for focused observations. We track a target child for 15 minutes, recording everything she/he says and does (this can involve writing at great speed!) In the remaining 15 minutes we analyse the observation and make entries into the appropriate page of the record. Each child has one focused observation per half term. The absence of a key worker from teaching for this period is more than justified by the information focused observations give us about children's learning.

Once we have gathered this information, what do we do with it?

Staff meet at the end of each session for 15 minutes and share their observations with the rest of the team. Plans for the following session are then amended to take account of children's learning. In this way we can be responsive to children's immediate needs and interests.

In the last week of every half term each key worker has one day of non-contact time to review children's records. This enables us to check on development across all areas of the curriculum, see if there are any gaps in experience or special needs. We then decide on one learning aim for each child for the coming half-term. This will either be building on existing interests/strengths or to broaden experience. We will then think of four or five activities that the child will be encouraged to take part in which will support our learning intentions for the child. The progress, aims and activities are recorded on a separate sheet that goes into the record and is copied to parents/carers to keep them up-to-date with their children's progress.

Social and Emotional Development

(i) Relationships, Feelings and Needs. Observe and Comment on:

Any characteristic behaviour, self confidence, independence, assertiveness of the needs of others, self control, self esteem, ability to cope....

How the child makes choices, organises her/his own time , uses resources (people and equipment), plans their learning....

How she/he plays in a range of social contexts - alone, alongside, with other children and/or adults....

How she/he relates and responds to adults and children....

Whether she/he plays co-operatively/shares easily....

Date	Observation (note context)	Support to further this development
18/3/98	Adam upset again today as Mummy back in hospital because of pregnancy problems.	
20/3/98	Adam put all the dolls in the dustbin saying, "We don't ~~have~~ babies at school, do we?"	
23/3/98	From focussed observation- Adam organized his time well, looks after resources and asserts himself well if another child tries to snatch something from him.	

Because many children will have similar aims we can then choose themes or topics for the coming half-term that are relevant to the children's interests and learning needs. Topic plans, as well as outlining the range of activities and provision needed, also list

Half Term Review

Stage 1, Stage 2, Stage 3, Stage 4, Stage 5

Name   Adam

Date   25/3/98

learning intentions and target children.

Details of activities within topics are transferred to our weekly planning sheets so that we can carry them out with the children.

We then come full circle to the end of session meetings when staff report back their observations on children's responses to planned topic work as well as their self-chosen play.

This continuous cycle of planning, observation, record-keeping and assessment enables us to know the strengths and needs of each child, to plan for their development; to respond to their spontaneous interests, to make effective use of staff time and other resources; to communicate meaningfully with parents/carers. In other words, to provide truly child-centred education.

Dilwen Roberts and Denise Halvey

PREVIOUS AIM MET.
- Adam now plays co-operatively with groups of children, particularly in imaginative play.
- been very interested in books and story-telling.
- can now climb to top of large frame.
- has been anxious about expected baby and Mum's hospital stays.

To prepare Adam for arrival of his new baby.

- share books on new babies.
- incorporate babies into role play.
- survey all children on siblings.
- invite all recent new babies and their carers to nursery to play, have baths, be fed and changed.

Assessment goes hand in hand with observation and record-keeping. Pam Wybrant explains why assessment is so important and gives an insight into ways of planning observation and recording what children can do

Assessment and record **keeping**

What is assessment for?
- ❑ To find out what a child knows and identify his/her needs.
- ❑ To check on the rate of the child's progress.
- ❑ For diagnostic purposes, to identify successes and difficulties.
- ❑ To communicate information to others - teachers, parents,and outside agencies.
- ❑ To monitor and evaluate our provision and make changes if needed.
- ❑ To enable easy transfer to statutory education.

One of the most crucial factors in making early learning effective is the provision of a planned programme of experiences based on the observation of children. Every nursery or pre-school should maintain a continuous cycle of planning, observation, recording and assessment.

When planning for learning you need to build on the knowledge children have gained through previous experiences. This is something you should involve parents with. Planning should encompass the range of activities and materials you will provide and the areas of experience you want to develop.

Long-term planning should reflect an overview of the learning development which will take place during the period that each child is in the group. For example, that they will gain an appreciation of nature and an understanding of the changing seasons and of life-cycles.

Medium-term planning should consist of half-termly/termly topics which support the areas of experience and are relevant to the stage of the children involved. For example, a topic on 'Spring'.

Short-term planning will be weekly or daily. For example, going on a nature walk or a farm to see new born lambs. It should include how resources will be used, spontaneous activities can be added. These plans will rely heavily on information from observations which identify needs, such as language difficulties, cutting skills.

Purpose of assessment
There are four main purposes of assessment:
Diagnostic
This information is obtained by observing children over a short period of time, noting their behaviour. It provides an accurate picture of the child's current stage of development.

There are certain key elements for planning:

- ❑ You need to build on what each child knows so use information about what they can do which has been provided by a playgroup, private nursery or parents.

- ❑ Think about the learning outcomes and the skills, concepts and knowledge you want to develop through each activity.

- ❑ Think about how best to organise the learning activities. This includes: how you group the children, your teaching and learning approaches, resources and displays, the adult's role.

- ❑ What opportunities are there for responses from children? (This might include discussion but can also be painting, drawing or modelling.)

- ❑ What arrangements are there for observation, assessment and recording?

Formative

This enables you to draw a long-term picture of the child's rate of progress. Information is obtained by observing children and gathering evidence of their learning and development over a period of time. Formative assessment is significant for the individual child. It enables you to find out where to start planning work and identify strengths and weaknesses.

Summative

Information is gained from an overview of diagnostic and formative assessments made over a period of time. It gives accurate evidence of the child's current stage of development to communicate to others, parents and teachers.

Evaluative

This describes the assessment used for measuring the effectiveness of the learning programme. Baseline profile is one example. It gives a valuable indication of how much ground a child has covered. It also affects decisions made on curriculum provision, teaching styles and resources.

How to assess

The most useful way of assessing young children's learning and development is by watching them and noting what they say and do. Most of this information is useful to you because it helps you know what to do next - it is of no interest to anyone else. Observation and assessment are essential aspects of the planning cycle.

Observation is one of the most important skills that you can have and it is one that should be continually worked on so that you can improve your understanding of children and their learning. Often we rely on our gut reaction when further reflection might lead to other interpretations.

What is observation?

❑ Looking at the way children go about their work and not just what they produce.
❑ Listening to their reasoning. This means you have to stand back and try not to intervene.
❑ Discussing problems, responses and interpretation with children so that they reveal their ways of thinking to you.

One of the problems you will encounter when adopting observational procedures is what to note down and how to make it manageable. Observation should be planned as well as informal and should involve all adults working with children.

How can you plan observation?

1 Observation can be carried out by allocating time for each adult to focus either on an individual activity or on specific children. This information can then be shared with other adults to evaluate the development of individual children.
2 Observation can be carried out by using a family group or key worker system where an adult takes responsibility for the observation of a specific group of children under the leadership of the adult in charge.
3 Planning of observation depends on personal preferences. A systematic approach involves the observation of two to three children each week and recording information in a notebook or diary.
4 Devise a useful observation sheet.

Methods of assessment

❑ Observation, watching, listening and talking
❑ Discussion
❑ Pictorial and written work, drawings and painting
❑ Physical performance (gross and fine skills, set tasks and observation)
❑ Testing - eg graded puzzles
❑ Teaching Talking (published by NFER-Nelson, Darville House, 2 Oxford Road East, Windsor, Berks., SL4 1DF) - this is a screening and intervention programme which enables you to identify and work with children experiencing problems in understanding and using language.

Assessment may be written or verbal. It is important to record all significant developments if you are to keep track of all the children in your care. Assessment should include all aspects of a child's development and cover individuals, groups and activities.

First records

Assessment starts with parental input before the child starts nursery. Personal information can be recorded on a standard information/admission form and should provide information about the child's home and family, whether he/she has attended playgroup/day nursery/creche, as well as any medical and dietary details.

Methods of recording

❑ Initial record sheet
❑ Baseline profile
❑ Samples of work
❑ Early years profile (formative comments and assessed work)
❑ Diary for each key worker
❑ Observation sheets for six areas of learning
❑ Tape recordings
❑ Photographs of activities (individual and group)
❑ Teaching Talking sheets
❑ Reports to parents

You should also complete an initial record sheet with the parent to establish the child's current stage of development. The record may be a list of statements for parents to comment on or it can be in the parents' own words: 'Knows the name of some colours'; 'Can ride a bike'.

(A sample initial record sheet/parent's assessment sheet is provided on pages 163-164).

Children have vastly differing experiences before they start school and it is difficult matching appropriate teaching and learning activities to children. The first written assessment you make will be the baseline profile which should be completed during the first few weeks in nursery.

Observation for the baseline profile should focus on linguistic, social/emotional, and physical developments. This process is completed by observing children in a variety of contexts - indoors, outdoors, individual and group times - to provide a broad picture of each child's level of development at the time. (A sample of a baseline profile is supplied as a photocopiable page.)

The early years/foundation profile

A well-structured profile should include the following:

❏ Experiences of child before entering school
❏ Information about child's health and home background
❏ Details required for admission procedures
❏ A record of progress in acquiring skills and concepts, associated with the areas of learning and experiences
❏ Aspects of the child's physical, social, emotional and cultural development which are of significance
❏ Examples of work

These records should then be passed on to the Reception teacher of the school the child will attend. The various aspects of development will be recorded in the child's foundation profile which will provide Key Stage 1 teachers with a picture of the whole child. Keep parents informed of their child's progress throughout the year and encourage them to take activities home. Parents can be given a written report at the end of the nursery year.

Recording

Records should:

❏ Give information clearly and concisely
❏ Speak a common language
❏ Take into account diversity of backgrounds
❏ Be more than a check-list but not time consuming
❏ Be shared with parents
❏ Be constructive, accurate and truthful
❏ Be available for constant review
❏ Be formulated and agreed by staff and parents

Do keep detailed notes on child's development.
Don't duplicate record keeping.
Don't keep records for the sake of it.

Recording should be based on the observation and assessment of individuals across all areas of experience. These records should be shared with parents, and where possible parents should contribute to records.

Strategies may include:

❏ Collecting information from the parents and child.
❏ Writing up brief comments on observations of individual children in a range of learning activities.
❏ Collection of samples/photographs/tape recordings.

Information recorded should be positive, reflecting what a child can rather than cannot do.

Pam Wybrant

Baseline profile

Children's names

Social and emotional development

1. Separates confidently from carer

2. Plays alone

3. Plays in parallel

4. Plays co-operatively

5. Appears happy most of the time

Physical development

1. Physically confident, enjoys gross motor play

2. Can run, climb, balance

3. Can pedal a bike

4. Can handle small equipment, thread beads etc

5. Can handle pencil/paintbrush correctly

6. Can make a cut with scissors

Linguistic development

1. Responds to talk

2. Uses single words

3. Uses simple sentences

4. Follows simple instructions

5. Listens in small group

6. Interested in books

Drop the name and/or logo of your setting into this box.

Parent Assessment Check-list

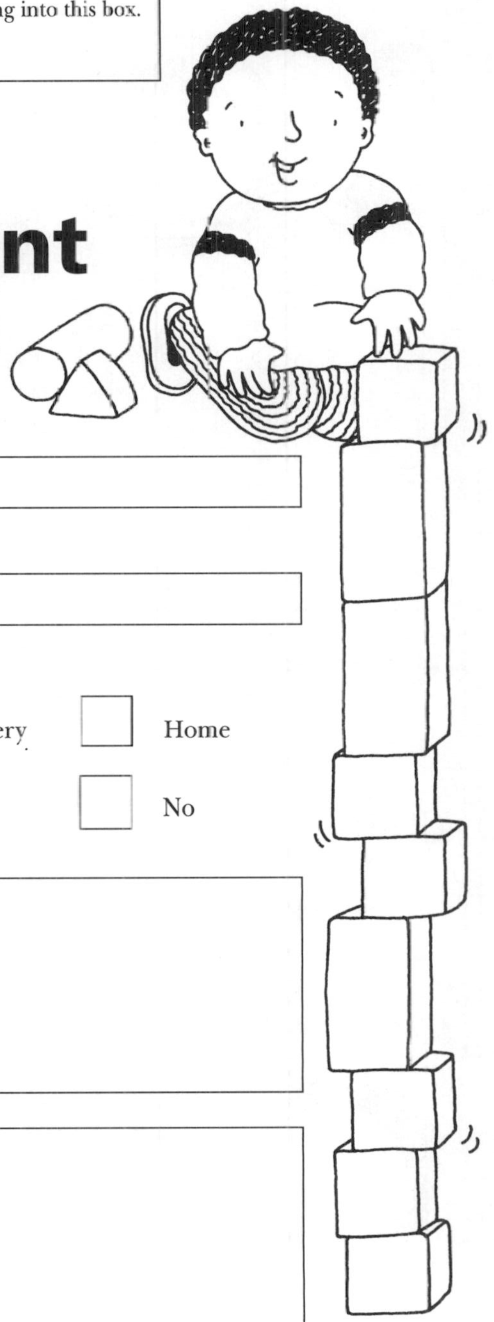

Name of child

Date of birth

Pre-school experience

| ☐ Playgroup | ☐ Nursery | ☐ Home |

Speech therapy　☐ Yes　☐ No

Any special needs?

Any other information?

--- Fold ---

Parent Assessment Check-list

Dear Parent,

Please don't look upon this form as a test which your child has to pass. There are no right or wrong answers.

This form is to give us some idea of what activities will benefit your child.

Try to answer the questions as honestly as you can. If you don't know all the answers, don't worry.

Please also use this form to let us know anything else, which you think is important, which might affect their learning.

2

Name (*as normally used*)

**Tick the statements
which apply to your child.**

Social and Emotional ❶

- ○ likes playing with other children
- ○ prefers to play alone
- ○ is shy
- ○ has an outgoing personality
- ○ will talk easily to adults
- ○ plays co-operatively

❷ Self Help

- ○ is able to do things for his/herself (go to the toilet, put on coat, without help).

❸ Language
(spoken and written)

- ○ knows simple songs and rhymes
- ○ is able to follow simple instructions
- ○ speaks clearly in sentences
- ○ is sometimes hard to understand
- ○ uses single words only

Use of Books ❹

- ○ likes to look at books
- ○ enjoys sitting quietly and listening to a story
- ○ will share a book with an adult telling them the story

---- Fold ----

- ○ likes to do jigsaws
- ○ can build a tower with blocks etc

Manual Skills ❺

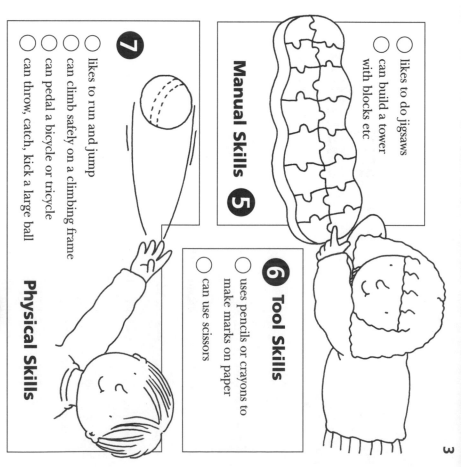

❻ Tool Skills

- ○ uses pencils or crayons to make marks on paper
- ○ can use scissors

❼

- ○ likes to run and jump
- ○ can climb safely on a climbing frame
- ○ can pedal a bicycle or tricycle
- ○ can throw, catch, kick a large ball

Physical Skills

❽ Colour and Shape

- ○ knows the colours
- ○ can count to 5 or 10
- ○ recognises these numbers 1 2 3 4 5 6 7 8 9 10
- ○ recognises a square, circle, triangle and rectangle

164

All pre-schools should 'have regard to' the Code of Practice on the identification and assessment of special educational needs. Sue Fisher explains what this means and how it should help you

Assessing special educational **needs**

It could be argued that all children have special needs at some time in their lives. However, some children's learning and development appears to be out of step with other children of the same age and is, in some ways, special or different.

What do we mean by 'special needs'?

The term 'special needs' can be used to cover a huge range in children's needs from severe disability to an exceptional level of ability. Although we shouldn't label children it is useful to distinguish between different types of special needs and how you might identify them.

It is out of the differences - in personality, background and need - that all children's unique identities are formed. Some disabilities may be present at birth or appear later as a consequence of disease, accident or circumstance. These special needs range from a severe disability to an exceptional level of ability - some children's disabilities are so slight their lives are hardly affected, whilst others may need special care.

Recent policy has been to integrate all those who might benefit into mainstream provision and this has resulted in a growth in the number of children with special needs in schools, nurseries and pre-schools.

Although there has been a move away from categorising children, some distinction between types of special needs is needed to ensure needs are met. Whilst there will be some overlap, the majority of special needs fit broadly under the following headings.

Language and communication

Staff may initially be alerted by a child who has difficulty following instructions and whose speech and vocabulary is limited and difficult to understand. On occasions, such children may be overlooked, especially if they appear happy and content and do not cause any management problems within the group.

Sensory difficulties

Most children with impairments of vision or hearing will already have been identified through parents' early concerns and contact with doctors and health visitors. Some children, however, learn to cope with such difficulties and adapt to enable them to appear to be achieving satisfactorily. Signs that staff should be alerted to include the child closing one eye regularly, an unusual head position or holding paper or books at odd angles or distances. Poor hand-eye co-

ordination, difficulty tracing or copying or 'immature' drawing may also be signs of a sensory difficulty, but it is important not to jump to conclusions. There can be many reasons for poor co-ordination and one indicator alone is rarely sufficient to trigger much concern. Signs which may indicate hearing difficulties are particularly difficult to isolate. However, a child who regularly gives inappropriate answers to questions, has immature speech sounds and poor skills in sound discrimination but has better skills in other, more practical areas should trigger further investigation.

Physical difficulties

These may be as a result of illness, injury or a congenital condition. A child may have difficulty with certain aspects of movement, gross or fine motor control or they may have severely restricted movement. It is likely that these will be identified before the pre-school

Learning difficulties

Signs that should alert staff to learning difficulties are similar to those with other areas of need but generally with a consistency that is not so apparent in other situations. The child is likely to make more progress when individual attention is given or when tasks are broken down into small steps.

Signs to look out for include difficulty following instructions, working slowly with poor output and open to distractions, and immature language and poor vocabulary.

Emotional and behavioural difficulties

There is a variety of underlying causes of such difficulties. Whilst they may be a result of abuse or neglect, such difficulties could also be the result of a medical condition such as Attention Deficit Hyperactivity Disorder (ADHD). Signs vary from withdrawn, preoccupied and depressed to aggressive, unco-operative and hyperactive. However, some of the effects of these difficulties remain the same whatever the cause and staff need to be constantly aware that children with emotional and behavioural difficulties invariably suffer from low self-esteem.

Able children

Although very able children are not always thought to have special needs, they do have needs to cater for and this requires additional planning and support. Very bright children may demand continued adult attention and can be insatiable, aggressive or indifferent if their needs are not properly addressed.

As childcare professionals, it is important we remember that all children should be given the opportunity to achieve their potential. Each child we encounter is unique and educational provision should respond to the wide diversities in needs and ensure that children with any special educational needs have access to high quality and appropriate provision.

The Code of Practice

The Code of Practice on the identification and assessment of special educational needs was written primarily for children in full-time schooling and since September 1994 schools have developed their provision for children with special educational needs in line with its guidance, particularly using the five staged model of assessment to provide appropriate support for children.

It is, however, a framework for good professional practice which is also applicable to the early years and the Nursery Education and Grant Maintained Schools Act of 1996 has now placed a duty on all pre-school settings to have regard to the code.

The code itself is quite lengthy but fairly user friendly. It is built around the notion that the sooner children's special needs are identified, the quicker extra help can be provided to overcome any learning or developmental difficulties.

A significant number of children at some time during their early development will have special educational needs and the code emphasises that the vast majority of these children will have their needs met through local nurseries or pre-schools, without the need for statutory assessment or a statement of special educational needs.

Your responsibilities

An important principle of the code is that everyone who works with young children should be knowledgeable about special needs and take some responsibility for supporting children and identifying any concerns as they arise.

In particular, each setting should appoint one member of staff who is familiar with the code and has a responsibility for special educational needs as part of their job description. This need not be a new member of staff and is as likely to be an existing staff member with an interest and enthusiasm for working with children with special needs.

This person should be responsible for managing and co-ordinating all work to do with special educational needs and is generally known as the special educational needs co-ordinator or SENCO.

They should act as a central point for information and support to other staff members and develop and maintain systems for recording and monitoring provision and monitoring and reviewing individual children's progress, as well as attending and providing relevant training.

The SENCO needs to ensure that children with special educational needs have access to a full and balanced curriculum. Early years settings working towards the Early Learning Goals will already be offering such a curriculum. It may be, however, that it needs to be broken down into smaller steps and adaptations made to resources or

environment. A requirement on all early years settings is the development of a SEN policy. There is no absolute standard or mould for this as policies reflect the distinctive nature of each group but the code does specify what kind of information should be included.

The five stage model

Few children's learning difficulties will be noticed for the first time in the pre-school setting and a number of three- and four-year-old children will already be known to have sensory impairments, global developmental delay, physical disabilities, problems with communication or social and emotional problems which may affect their learning.

Additionally, concerns about individual children may arise through staff observations. Behaviour that is difficult to manage and 'immature' communication skills are amongst those most readily noticed. Some needs can be overlooked for many weeks, especially if the child is cheerful and co-operative, and problems such as those associated with low self-esteem and difficulty in relating to others may initially be difficult to identify. It is vital that you have a system in place for identifying, assessing and planning for individual needs or many such needs may not be identified until the child is at school.

The Code of Practice provides a basis for this and sets out stages which match provision to individual need. Stage 1 reflects the least amount of individual support, Stage 5, the greatest amount.

Supporting children with special educational needs involves working in partnership with parents and other professionals involved with the child. Many of these children will already be known to health visitors, Portage workers, and so on, and their parents will have considerable information to pass on to you.

Stage 1

The trigger for this stage is often an expression of concern by a member of staff that a child is showing signs of experiencing learning difficulties. This should be discussed with the SENCO, who then places the child on the SEN register.

Parents should be informed of these concerns and the difficulties observed and discussed so that early action can be suggested and implemented in an attempt to resolve the child's difficulties within the pre-school environment.

As with all stages, at Stage 1 it is important to monitor, review and record each child's progress, but there is no set requirement to draw up an Individual Education Plan at this stage. You may, however, find it beneficial to do so right from the start so that targets can be set and achievements, or difficulties, identified more clearly.

Stage 2

Stage 2 is triggered when staff express a stronger level of concern and the SENCO should take the lead in assisting them to assess the child's learning difficulties. It is very important to talk to parents at this stage to see if they have any worries and find out more about how the child is at home. The best way forward for the child should then be discussed and a programme planned and implemented with targets for the child. This should take the form of an individual education plan (IEP) which should be monitored and reviewed regularly and should include information gathered from Stage 1, if appropriate - some children will have been placed at Stage 2 because they have made little or no progress despite actions taken at Stage 1, whilst others will be placed on Stage 2 straightaway.

At this stage, the co-ordinator may wish to consult with other support services and it is therefore important that they are aware of what is available and who to contact. This

differs from area to area. It is also worth considering seeking information from health visitors and others who already know the child to extend the information given by parents.

Stage 3

Stage 3 involves other agencies giving specialist support to help the child make progress, and should be considered when children continue to make little progress despite the support given at Stages 1 and 2. Again, some children may go straight to this stage, for example, when emotional or behavioural problems significantly interfere with the child's own educational programme or that of others on a regular basis, or those who require a regular visit from a specialist service.

After reviewing all information and talking with parents, a detailed intensive plan should be drawn up in conjunction with the appropriate specialist service.

Stage 4

At Stage 4 a multi-disciplinary assessment is carried out and reports are gathered from all agencies working with the child. This could include educational psychologists, speech therapists and doctors.

Statutory assessments must be completed within a time scale of 26 weeks from start to finish and may eventually result in the issuing of a statement of educational need.

Stage 5

If the child's needs have not been met through the support provided during the previous stages, the local education authority may consider the need for a statement.

A statement will only be considered when the local education authority is satisfied that the child's learning difficulties are 'significant' or complex, have not been met by measures taken by the early years setting and call for resources which cannot reasonably be provided within the budget of the setting.

A statement provides a precise description of the child's educational needs. It states what special provision is necessary and secures additional resources.

Parents receive a copy of the statement and the local education authority is now responsible for arranging, monitoring and reviewing the provision and providing funds for any extra staffing.

Planning and reviewing

Individual education plans need to be matched to each child's needs and the stage of the code they have been placed at. Each setting will decide upon their own format for these plans, incorporating short-term targets and long-term goals. These need to be positive and realistic and the criteria for success should be outlined. The plan should also include a time scale for review meetings.

Plans should be reviewed at regular intervals (approximately every four to six months) and these should focus on progress made, any new information and future plans, as well as evaluating the effectiveness of the plan.

Parents and support agencies working with the child should be involved in this process to ensure all relevant information and views are taken into account.

When reviewing at each stage, it is important to consider where more individual support or specialist input is required which would entail moving up a stage. Likewise, it may be most beneficial to remain at the same stage, or extra support may be decreased on occasions or the child be removed from the register.

The Government has made clear its intention to reduce the number of statements issued and to focus resources and intervention at lower stages, and with this in mind, it is important that needs are identified early and the necessary support provided to enable all children to benefit as fully as possible from the pre-school curriculum and the many enriching experiences settings provide.

Sue Fisher

An Individual Education Plan (IEP) helps you to monitor, review and record a child's progress. Caroline Jones highlights the important features of a good IEP and gives some examples

Writing an IEP

An Individual Education Plan (IEP) is a planning document for a child at Stage 2 or above of the Code of Practice. It is a working document to meet the needs of the child. It identifies and targets areas for action relating to the child's immediate learning needs and any arrangements which may need to be made to help the child make satisfactory progress. It also describes arrangements made to monitor and review progress and identifies any resources required.

What is the IEP for?
The purpose of the IEP is to benefit the children, in particular the following groups:

- ❑ Children whose levels of play or development are significantly/noticeably below those of children of similar age.

- ❑ Children about whom there has been an expression of concern from a parent or other professional, for example health visitor.

- ❑ Children requiring greater attention than most in the group because of their learning and/or behaviour difficulties.

- ❑ Children requiring special materials/equipment or alterations to the environment.

Who writes the IEP?
It can be written by the pre-school supervisor or the child's key worker/teacher. At Stage 3, this may be in consultation with outside agencies. Parents should be consulted at all stages. An IEP should be a straightforward, working document not simply another piece of bureaucracy. The IEP serves as a useful plan and record of what the setting is doing to meet the child's needs. The process of developing IEPs should be manageable and effective.

There is no 'correct' or standardised format for an IEP. Schools and LEAs will have developed their own formats for the various stages. It may be that a pre-school group can adopt the format used in the local area or school (some sample completed IEPs are given). It is important that an IEP is clear and easy to use, easy to read, and links with the established plans and routines of the pre-school. However, whatever the format, there are certain characteristics which make an IEP effective and should be included, under the guidance of the DfEE.

A good IEP will:
- ❑ be brief and action based
- ❑ indicate the child's strengths and current level of achievement
- ❑ identify the nature and extent of the child's learning needs
- ❑ include specific and relevant targets
- ❑ indicate how other adults/parents or carers may be involved
- ❑ note any additional resources or medical needs
- ❑ set dates for review

A useful starting point is to consider the following four questions:
- ❑ **Assessment:** What can Hannah do now?
- ❑ **Targets set:** What do we want Hannah to achieve next?
- ❑ **Strategy:** How shall we help her do this?
- ❑ **Review:** What has Hannah achieved?

Writing targets
It is important not to set too many targets, one or two is probably enough. Targets should be expressed positively and not set a child up for failure. It is important to focus on short-term goals and specific objectives rather than general aims. For example, whilst a general long-term aim may be 'improve language' the IEP should be more specific as to exactly what it is hoped the child will achieve at the end of a given period of time. This may be 'recognise and use words for body parts including eyes, mouth, ear, hair, nose'. Or, if the general aim is to 'improve social skills', the target

PLANNING CYCLE FOR IEPs

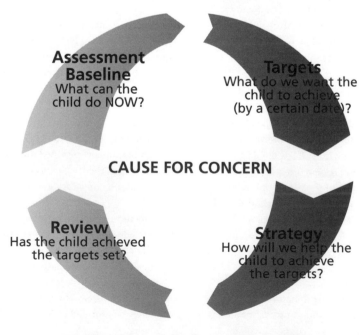

Assessment Baseline
What can the child do NOW?

Targets
What do we want the child to achieve (by a certain date)?

CAUSE FOR CONCERN

Review
Has the child achieved the targets set?

Strategy
How will we help the child to achieve the targets?

Individual Education Plan

Individual Education Plan (Pre-school)

Name: *George* **Period:** *Spring term*

Involved adults *Teacher: Jane Assistant: Liz*

Review date: *01.04.99*

Strengths	**Concerns Aim 2**
Eye-hand co-ordination. Physical skills.	Social skills. Listening/understanding.

Targets	**Targets**
1. To make verbal approaches to other children in play.	2. Points to big/little objects on request.

Materials and activities	**Materials and activities**
When George approaches another child, adult should interpret verbally, eg 'Can George build with you?' Discourage standing too close to other children or touching to communicate his wishes.	Size Lotto. Big/little cups/plates/spoons in home corner. Doll play - big/little dolls. Looking at mini beasts.

Range of possible activities

Group routines

Water play

Sand play

Puzzles

Posting blocks

Bricks

Painting

Large toys

Small toys

Picture books

Playdough

Dress up

Slide

Ride-astride toys

Imaginative play

Tactile/sensory

Others

Outcomes and future planning

1. George was observed to take a bat and ball to a child, offer them to her and say 'play tennis'.
2. Achieved.

Future plans
Continue target (1) and support when verbalising.
Introduce new concept, for example, hot/cold.

---

could be written as 'play co-operatively with one other child in the role play area'. Similarly, rather than write 'improve behaviour', the target could be 'sit for ten minutes without disrupting story time, keeping hands and feet to herself'. The SMART target is a commonly used successful approach:

- ❑ Specific - with parents, all staff and where appropriate the child
- ❑ Measurable - clear expected outcomes
- ❑ Achievable - given the level of support available
- ❑ Recorded - on the IEP
- ❑ Time defined - record the date by which you expect the child to achieve the target

A collaborative plan

The IEP provides a focus for those involved to work together towards a common goal for the child. A number of people may be involved. If a child is at Stage 3, the IEP includes details of which outside agencies are involved and their role in helping the child achieve the target. These could be one or more of the following: general practitioner, health visitor, speech and

| Name: *Joe* | Date of Birth *20.12.95* | Date: *06.01.99* |

| Pre-school supervisor: *Mrs A* | Stage: | 2 | ③ | 4 | 5 |

Strengths/Interests
Enjoys play with cars/trains/sand/water.
Pre-verbal communication skills: eye contact, attention getting, responding to others.

Nature of concerns or learning needs
Play remains isolated.
Uses one word and gesture to communicate.
Resists interaction with adults/children.

Evidence
Pre-school observations.
Reports from speech and language therapist.
Development profile.

Priority Targets
1. To play in parallel with other children.
2. To use two word phrases to communicate.

Assessment of progress:

Arrangements: (teaching, pastoral, medical, frequency of support staff involvement, external advice).

1.   Adult plays alongside Joe, imitating and extending play actions.
2. (i)   Adult models two-word phrase after Joe's attempt.
   (ii)   Use of simple picture books, eg Lift-the-flap books - 'Spot gone'.
   (iii)   Encourage to ask for 'more juice', 'more biscuit' at snack time.
   (iv)   Support expressive language with visual prompts.

Pupil involvement: N/A
Parent(s) involvement: Half-termly meetings

Proposed review and monitoring arrangements: Date of review: April 1999

Co-ordinated by: Pre-school supervisor   Date:

language therapists, paediatrician, dietician, physiotherapist, clinical psychologist, Portage services and local pre-school team. It is essential to involve parents and record the ways in which they may help the child at home.

What next? The review
The IEP must refer to the action to be taken at the review stage. At a Stage 2 review, for example, those involved will need to decide whether the child:
❑ Is still significantly behind other children - needs external advice and support -

moves on to Stage 3
❑ Is making good progress - remains at Stage 2 with revised/new targets
❑ Makes significantly good progress - moves back to Stage 1. Continue informal monitoring.

In summary, an IEP is a plan which outlines a child's individual teaching/learning activities and which is regularly reviewed and monitored so that identified targets can be re-assessed and

informed decisions made about future learning and teaching.

Caroline Jones

Acknowledgements:
Materials drawn from: Warwickshire Special Educational Needs Support Service - Central Area Manager, Dave Browne and Northern Area Pre-School Educational Psychologist, Marilyn Holden.
Reference: *The SENCO Guide* (DfEE).